Contracting Out Government Services

Contracting Out Government Services

Edited by
Paul Seidenstat

Privatizing Government: An Interdisciplinary Series
Simon Hakim and Gary Bowman, *Series Advisers*

Westport, Connecticut
London

Library of Congress Cataloging-in-Publication Data

Contracting out government services / edited by Paul Seidenstat.
    p. cm.—(Privatizing government, ISSN 1087–5603)
   Includes bibliographical references and index.
   ISBN 0–275–96542–2 (alk. paper)
   1. Municipal services—Contracting out United States. 2. Social
services—Contracting out—United States. 3. Public works—United
States. 4. Public contracts—United States. 5. Contracting out
—United States. 6. Privatization—United States. I. Seidenstat,
Paul. II. Series.
HD4605.C653 1999
352.5′38214′0973—dc21   98–44537

British Library Cataloguing in Publication Data is available.

Library of Congress Catalog Card Number: 98–44537
ISBN: 0–275–96542–2
ISSN: 1087–5603

First published in 1999

Praeger Publishers, 88 Post Road West, Westport, CT 06881
An imprint of Greenwood Publishing Group, Inc.
www.praeger.com

Printed in the United States of America

The paper used in this book complies with the
Permanent Paper Standard issued by the National
Information Standards Organization (Z39.48–1984).

10 9 8 7 6 5 4 3 2

Contents

Figures and Tables

FIGURES

TABLES

Part I

Overview

Chapter 1

Theory and Practice of Contracting Out in the United States

Paul Seidenstat

The role of government in the marketplace has been subject to the many crosswinds of change since World War II. The overriding movement that has occurred since the 1980s has been in the direction of less dependence on government and more reliance on the private sector of the economy. Worldwide, the abandonment of the communist system and its basic ideas of central planning and government dominance of the economy is the most dramatic example of this trend. In the noncommunist world, the trend has taken the form of modifying the welfare state and turning toward the private sector as the primary producer of goods and services.

The application of this trend in the United States has been less dramatic. Although government has become a powerful force in attempting to achieve greater equity through transfer payments, our country has relied upon government production to a relatively modest degree compared to many countries. The bulk of our effort here to reduce the role of government has been in the accelerated movement to privatize government operations at the state and local levels.

   Privatization, "any process aimed at shifting functions and responsibilities, in whole or in part, from the government to the private sector" (U.S. General Accounting Office, 1997: 46), is not a new concept in the U.S. Governments have long used the private sector. However, the use of private operators was very restricted. Their role was limited to providing a few in-house functions and a very limited number of direct services (Chi, 1993; Council of State Governments, 1993). The minor use by governments of private producers was evidenced by the fact that the word, "privatization," did not make the dictionary until the early 1980s.

   The acceleration of privatization efforts began in the mid-1980s as shown in Table 1.1. Using county data as representative of all state and local governments, the table shows that 34 percent of all counties contracted out services in 1992 compared to 24 percent of counties in 1987. In looking at specific service areas, we see a growth in privatization in every single area. Especially noticeable is that by 1992, almost all counties contracted out electric and gas utility services, and almost half of all counties contracted out hospital and transit operations.

   The forces behind this acceleration of privatization are discussed later. However, it should be noted that privatization can take various forms, even though, as we shall see, contracting out is the dominant form. A classification of those techniques provides some prospective for the examination of contracting out.

Table 1.1
Privatization in U.S. Counties

(Percentage of services contracted out)

Type of Service	1987	1992
Airports	30%	36%
Electric utility	74	96
Fire protection	22	37
Gas utility	78	89
Hospitals	34	48
Landfills	20	26
Libraries	14	23
Nursing homes	24	28
Public transit	37	48
Sewerage	18	30
Stadiums	21	29
Water supply	21	35
TOTAL	24%	34%

Source: U.S. Bureau of Census, *Census of Government*, 1987 and 1992.

CLASSIFICATION OF PRIVATIZATION OPTIONS

   Two functions are involved in rendering services to citizens: making provision for output and producing the service. Making provision basically involves the financing of the output. Road construction is an example of this distinction, as the government can pay to have a road built and maintained (make provision) but has a choice as to the construction and maintenance of the roadway (e.g., produce in-house or hire a private contractor)

Using these two variables, making provision and production, Table 1.2 shows a classification system for privatization processes. These nine processes are as follows:

Table 1.2
Classification System for Privatization Process

| | SECTOR MAKING PROVISION | |
	Private	Public
Private		Asset sales
		Contracting Out
		Service shedding
		Managed Competition
		Franchising
		Public-Private Partnership
SECTOR PRODUCING		Volunteerism
		Subsidies/Grants
		Vouchers
Public	Contracting In	No Privatization

Service Shedding

In the most complete form of privatization the government simply disassociates itself from providing the service and turns financing and production entirely over to the private sector; that is, service shedding (or simply allowing the service to disappear). Examples would be the government's eliminating existing recreation programs or not building a new sports stadium.

Even if the current government operation involves public ownership of buildings or equipment, those assets may be retained in the government inventory or converted to other uses. An example would be a trash collection service that is eliminated, but the trash trucks are kept in the government inventory, often to be held in reserve in case the privatization effort is aborted and public trash collection is resumed in the future.

Asset Sales

In many cases where there are existing assets owned by government, those assets may be sold to private buyers. The assets may be sold to a bidder, who would then use them to operate the previously publicly operated service such as trash collection or a golf course. In other cases, the government may just sell the assets to any buyer with no restrictions on their use. The assets may have other uses, in the case of an office-type building, or there may be no bidder who intends to continue the discontinued service. In the case where there may be a private provider, the private firm may use its own assets.

Franchising

A modified form of load shedding involves franchising; that is; a special privilege granted to a private operator. The service is turned over to the private sector, but the government chooses the private operator or operators. For example, a local government may decide to load shed trash collection but chooses to franchise the existing trash collection routes to one or more private collectors. The government also may exercise some operational control over the franchise such as setting quality standards for effluent discharges in the case of waste treatment plants.

Where infrastructure-type operations are involved, especially in the case of new (highway) or expanded (waste treatment) operations, there are at least two variants of franchising: build-transfer-operate (BTO) and build-operate-transfer (BOT). In the BTO case, the government agency can utilize a turnkey model in which the private operator designs, constructs, and transfers ownership upon completion to the government but operates the facility. This model has been used in wastewater treatment.

BOT is a more complete form of privatization since the private sector may continue to own the facility, often subject to government regulation, on a long-term basis. After a number of years, however, the private firm may transfer ownership to the public sector. This model has been used for toll roads, solid waste facilities, and water systems (Lick, 1995).

Vouchers, Grants, and Subsidies

The most market-oriented mode of privatization in which the public sector continues to make provision (i.e., pays) is the use of vouchers or grants/subsidies. In the voucher form, the government provides the user a check to pay the bill for the privately produced service. If there are competing suppliers, the user is afforded choice. Examples at the federal level include food stamps, Medicare, and housing vouchers and at the state and local level, Medicaid, mental health, job training, and other social services.

Instead of allowing the consumer to pay for the service from a producer of his or her choice with a government check, the government may directly provide a grant or subsidy to a private producer. In this case, the user may have less choice, as the subsidy or grant may go to one or only a handful of producers. Government subsidies have been given to universities, hospitals and other health-related facilities, art museums and other organizations that offer cultural services, and a wide variety of community service organizations

Public-Private Partnerships

A mixed technique of service provision/production is a public-private partnership. Under this relationship, the government fashions a contractual arrangement with its private-sector partners. Infrastructure projects illustrate this approach such as in the BTO model where each partner has carefully defined responsibilities. Also, a government agency may work with a private social service organization to address a particular social problem. An example is needle exchange or publicity efforts to reduce the incidence of HIV infection in which the government's role is to furnish the needles and provide educational materials, while the private organization operates the program.

Volunteer Activities

Under the umbrella of government provision and/or operation of some programs, citizen volunteers may be utilized. A service may be organized and funded by a government agency that enlists volunteers to provide all or a part of the services offered either directly under government supervision or through a nonprofit service group. Examples of programs utilizing volunteers include neighborhood crime watches, tutoring programs in schools, and delivery of food in a meals on wheels type of operation.

Contracting In

Although some of the preceding techniques are not widely used, contracting in is an even rarer option. In this case, the private sector is the provider but the government is the producer. For example, a private group or company may hire, at its own expense, public police personnel to secure a sporting event or patrol a shopping mall. In most cases, however, the public operation was established under public provision, and these additional services rendered to the private sector are incidental to the primary mission.

Contracting Out

Rather than employing some form of load shedding, most governments have preferred contracting as the method to shift operations to the private sector. In this model, the government entity retains ownership and overall control but employs the private vendor to actually render the service. Except for activities involving infrastructure or voucher/subsidy systems, contracting out is the way practically all privatization is now being implemented. Everything from in-house support services to direct taxpayer services falls under the contracting out umbrella. The rest of this chapter discusses contracting out.

Managed Competition/Competitive Contracting

One variant of contracting out is managed competition or competitive contracting. Government departments or agencies currently producing the service (or capable of producing the service) can bid on contracts. The entire service may be contracted out to private vendors or kept in-house if the agency bid is superior to the best bid of the private competitors. Where feasible, part of the service may be outsourced and the remainder of the service may be retained in-house. An example of the splitting technique is in trash collection or in bus transport where there is a geographical dimension to service or in solid waste operations where there are vertical processing steps such as collection and disposal.

DOMINANCE OF CONTRACTING OUT

Tables 1.3 and 1.4 show the dominance of contracting out as the preferred method of privatization at the state level. Overall, in 1993, 78 percent of state agencies used contracting out as the primary privatization device. The pattern at the local level also reflects this pattern.

As seen in Table 1.3, contracting out is used exclusively for some services. These services include administrative and general services and corrections. Excluding grants or vouchers, practically all privatization in education, health, mental health, social services, and transportation relies almost entirely on contracting out.

Table 1.4 also demonstrates the importance of contracting out in several key government services. There is extensive use of contract workers in waste collection, street repair, building maintenance, and data processing. Between 1987 and 1995, there was a doubling of use of contracted workers for many services.

If a government agency chooses to privatize, why would it most likely use the contracting out option? The answer appears to be that the choice of contracting out reflects a variety of practical and political considerations.

Practical Factors

Often, government officials wish to retain substantial control over service production while seeking the lower costs or improved performance promised by private sector producers. The major alternative to contracting out a service is to allow the private sector to have complete, or almost complete, control over the service. In the extreme case of load shedding, the public agency relinquishes provision as well as production. In the case of vouchers, subsidies, and even franchises the degree of public control is much less, as funding is the principal function of the government. By comparison, contracting out typically allows much greater involvement in the design and oversight of production by the public agency.

In the case of poor performance by the private producer, contracting out offers a degree of reversibility not available with other forms of privatization. Especially if the public agency retains some equipment and management expertise in the service area, it is not too difficult to resume public production if the private operation proves to be unsatisfactory or if the private operator goes out of business. This option to resume public operations is especially important if there are no other private producers on the horizon.

Table 1.3
Forms of Privatization and Frequency of Use

Forms of Privatization	Admin / Gen Services	Corrections	Education	Health	Mental Health	Social Services	Transport	Average
			Agencies frequency of use					
			(in percentage of total)					
Contracting Out	91.7	92.1	81.3	69.6	64.7	71.3	83.5	78.1
Grants	0.6	1.1	8.6	14.1	15.6	12.5	4.5	8.5
Vouchers	3.1	0.4	0.7	4.9	5.4	9.3	0.4	4.1
Volunteerism	1.4	3.6	1.4	3.3	3.6	3.0	5.4	3.3
Public-private partnership	1.7	2.4	5.0	5.4	3.9	2.2	2.6	3.0
Private donation	0.6	0.4	0.7	0.0	2.6	0.2	1.3	1.0
Franchise	0.3	0.0	1.4	1.1	1.7	0.4	1.5	0.9
Service shedding	0.3	0.0	0.7	1.1	0.9	0.7	0.4	0.6
Deregulation	0.0	0.0	0.0	0.5	1.5	0.4	0.2	0.5
Asset sales	0.6	0.0	0.0	0.2	0.2	0.0	0.2	0.2

Source: Council of State Governments (1993). *State Trends and Forecasts: Privatization.* Louisville, KY.

Table 1.4
Share of Public Services Handled by Contract Workers

| | (Percent of Total) | |
Activity	1995	1987
Waste collection	50	30
Building maintenance	42	32
Street repair	37	19
Data processing	31	16
Health/medical	27	15
Bill collection	20	10
Street cleaning	18	9

Source: *Wall Street Journal*, August 5, 1996, pp. A-5 and A-6.

Political Factors

The loss of control over the nature and level of service (or no service at all) with load shedding encourages public officials to rely upon contracting out to privatize services. Politically, a major loss of control opens elected officials to criticism by disgruntled citizen-consumers. The blame cannot easily be deflected, nor is it easy to make changes.

Moreover, the economic rent that often entices public provision, if not production, of services slips away with load shedding. Even with contracting out, favors for constituents are still possible to garner. Contract features may be designed to give substantial benefits to selected consumers. Even after the contract is let, public officials may be able to gain concessions for certain voters since contract renewal is on the horizon.

Contractors themselves may be encouraged to share some contract benefits with elected officials, even barring illegal forms of favors. Campaign contributions and the aforementioned favors for selected constituents may not be uncommon events.

A FORCE FIELD MODEL OF THE CONTRACTING OUT OPTION

Given the preference for contracting, what forces were at work to accelerate privatization by the mid-1980s? The answer to that question is best answered by developing an analytical model of privatization using a "force field" framework.

How a change in a fundamental government policy comes about requires an understanding of the forces for changes and their strength compared to the forces operating to maintain the status quo. For a change in policy to occur, the forces for change must grow in strength to the point where they can break through the resistance to change.

What happened in the United States by the late 1980s to propel the public sector to greatly accelerate the movement toward privatizing? The answer to this question lies in the weakening fiscal position of the public sector and changes in the political climate with regard to the size and role of government in the society. In the wake of the serious recession of the early 1980s, the growing concern about the federal government's budget deficit, and the continuing long-term fiscal crisis in the large cities, there was a serious effort to restrain the growth of government expenditures and make government operations more cost effective. At the same time, there was a stirring among the voters at the state level to quash proposed tax increases, to restrain the growth of tax revenue (e.g., Proposition 13 in California and Proposition 2.5 in Massachusetts), and to limit government spending.

Overall, the political environment was growing more hostile to the expansion of government budgets and increases in tax rates. The growing power of this message was reflected in the elections of Ronald Reagan in 1980 and 1984 and the slowing of the federal government's growth in both the Bush and Clinton administrations. The message was reinforced by the victory of anti-government-growth Republicans to the Congress in 1994 and 1996, accompanied by the decade long political success of many liked-minded candidates to governorships and state legislatures.

The coalition of stakeholders of government who were the chief beneficiaries and supporters of a growing government found their position to be weakened by the aforementioned fiscal pressures. The fact that monopolistic government can generate economic rents explains the strongly held position of the status quo coalition. Using these rents, elected officials and program administrators can offer benefits to stakeholders. For example, public school monopolies can provide benefits to input suppliers like school administrators, schoolteachers, and book publishers in the form of above-market average labor compensation and input prices. Parents of special student populations (e.g., mentally retarded, physically handicapped, etc.) could receive expanded (and very expensive) services. Particular firms could receive lucrative contracts to construct school buildings or make major repairs.

The growing pressure on elected officials to cut budget growth or even downsize government operations forced consideration of methods to restrain government spending without substantial reduction in services. Once the government agenda focused on this issue of restructuring or "rightsizing," then privatization became a major policy option as part of a restructuring program.

The political clout of the coalition supporting government operations then was challenged by the growing coalition that stressed lower taxes and privatization. The political weakening of the pro-government coalition was substantial in some areas, such as trash collection or street repairing, but was not as strong in others such as education and corrections. In those states and cities where the fiscal pressures were the greatest, and the weakening of the power of the major monopoly rent recipients was the most pronounced, major contracting out efforts were initiated.

An illustration of the force field model is the case of trash collection. Because of its inherent characteristics, trash collection is one of the public sector's services easiest to privatize. The collection activity is often performed by private companies in many suburban and small local urban government locations.

Typically, many possible suppliers can bid on a government contract. Given the largely unskilled nature of the work, a private labor force is easy to assemble. Contracts are easy to monitor and enforce, as the output is well defined.

Since many studies show that public trash collection is much more expensive than its privately operated counterpart, why have some cities been slow in contracting out this service? The answer may lie in the opposition of public unions, especially in large urban areas where they are strong. A study of the 1973-1988 period in municipalities with more than 10,000 people documents this union effect (Chandler and Feuille, 1991).

DETERMINANTS OF CONTRACTING OUT

The force field model of privatization suggests that certain factors would affect the relative strength of the pro-change and status quo forces. These factors include the relative cost of providing services, the policy influence of public employees and their unions, the strength of anti-taxation forces, competition among local governments, the scope of government services, and some non-quantifiable factors.

In developing a model of privatization, Kodrzycki (1994; 1998) theorized that several factors would influence the degree of privatization as follows.

Cost of Providing Services

The extent to which private contractors can reduce the cost of services, without diminishing quality, would push the public/private line in the private direction. Several factors would affect the potential cost differential:

1. the differential between public employee earnings and private employee compensation.
2. the extent of competition among potential private vendors; competition would be more likely in a metropolitan area rather than a non-metropolitan area.
3. the extent to which economies of scale are important; smaller governments are less likely to be able to take advantage of these economies.

Unionization of Public Employees and the Effect of Community Growth

Often the major opposition to contracting out is the public employee union. Consequently, the higher the percentage of unionized workers in a government agency, the stronger would be the resistance to change. However, in communities with faster growth rates and with larger populations and income, union opposition would be less aggressive since privatization can be accomplished without displacing existing public jobs.

Opposition to Higher Taxes

The attractiveness of cost savings that would be reflected in a stronger force field for privatization is directly related to the affluence of the average citizen. Lower than average income (using a national or regional benchmark) that usually is correlated with lower property values triggers greater support for government cost-saving measures.

Competition Among Local Governments

As local governments aggressively compete for businesses and affluent taxpayers, considerable effort may be exerted to minimize the cost of services in order to keep tax rates competitive. In more densely populated areas with more local governments, more inter-governmental competition can lead to greater use of the private sector in connection with the production of public services. In addition, the greater array of services offered, the greater the chance that some will be privatized.

Proportion of Government Services That Are Considered Core Services

If local governments provide only essential services (e.g., courts, police, and sewage treatment), then the opposition to minimizing the public labor force by contracting out would be weak. On the other hand, if a wide range of public sector services and income redistribution activities were provided, opposition to privatization would be stiffer.

Subjective Factors

Strong political leadership can enhance support or opposition to privatization, especially if driven by ideological preferences regarding the role of government. Strong political leadership can alter the position of the public/private line.

TESTING THE MODEL

Kodrzycki (1994) tested these hypotheses by performing a cross sectional multiple regression analysis of 655 municipalities and townships with at least a population of 25,000 based on 1987 U.S. Census data. The result of the regression analysis suggests that several of the objective factors suggested by Kodrzycki are statistically significant in explaining the extent of privatization.

Contracting out to the private sector is more likely if public sector wages are high relative to the private sector, if there is rapid population growth, if government services are highly concentrated on health and human services, and if a variety of functions or services is provided by local government. To a lesser extent, in communities where the local governments concentrate on providing core services, a more pronounced degree of privatization is found.

Other factors appear to have explanatory value. Possibly counted among these factors are strong political leaders who support or oppose contracting out, the reputation of local potential contractors, and differences in fringe benefits or productivity between the public and private sectors.

THE RECENT SLOWDOWN OF PRIVATIZATION EFFORTS: APPLICATION OF THE FIELD FORCE MODEL

The rapid movement toward privatization in the 1985-1992 period can be explained by the relative shift in the strength of the forces for change compared to the status-quo forces. In particular, the growing fiscal difficulties of state and local governments and the increasing opposition to tax increases pushed in the direction of contracting out services to allow the cutting of costs so as to avoid raising taxes or drastically cutting the level of services.

There is some evidence that a slowdown in the rate of privatization may have occurred starting in the early 1990s. One explanation of this slowing rate of new privatization efforts that included outsourcing or load shedding is that the state and local government economies began to recover from recession, thus easing the fiscal pressure to cut costs (Kodrzycki, 1998).

THE CONTRACTING OUT OPTION

As indicated earlier, in the vast majority of privatization cases, contracting the operation of the service to a private supplier (or suppliers) has been the preferred method. The government provider typically solicits bids from private suppliers and awards the contract or contracts based on price and/or quality of service to be supplied. Occasionally contract awards are made without bids, usually in the case of professional services such as engineers, lawyers, architects, and social service organizations. In most instances the contractor is a for profit enterprise but, in some cases, non-profit agencies are used, especially in the human or social service area.

Objectives of Contracting

Contracting out has been utilized as a management tool as well as a device to realign the public-private sector mix. The managerial objectives include cutting costs, improving the quality of services produced, or both. Most frequently, the primary aim has been to cut costs in order to relieve budgetary pressures rather than to improve services, especially since assessing the quality of output of many government services can be a complex and time-consuming activity. Privatizing was aimed also at increasing the flexibility of government operations such that expansion, contraction, or complete elimination of specific services could be accomplished with fewer obstacles and with greater speed.

Although the major thrust toward privatization in the United States seems to be motivated by practical managerial considerations, the movement toward the greater use of the private sector taps into the philosophical point of view of a reduced role for government in a market system.

Conditions Required for Success

In order to achieve the objectives set forth in a privatization initiative, certain environmental factors must be present. These factors include political support, managerial/political leadership, and a supportive private market structure.

Overcoming the bias toward the status quo protected by the stakeholders who receive monopoly rent is essential. A strong case must be made for change; the case must speak to the benefits to be received with a provision/production arrangement in comparison to the costs that may have to be incurred. Legislative and voter support offers the opportunity to move in the privatization direction and to allow the new structure a fair chance to demonstrate its advantages.

The full support of political leaders, especially in the executive branch, greatly enhances the chances of success. Not only is this support required for approval of change, but also enthusiastic and careful backing of the effort often is compelled to sustain it. Well-prepared and ardent political leaders often are needed to overcome the inertia of the status quo.

To achieve the required objectives requires more than political support and strong leadership. To achieve the maximum benefits of privatization, the private sector should be structured such that alternative suppliers exist to compete in providing the service in the case of load-shedding, can compete for contracts in the case of contracting out or franchising, or can supply services in the case of vouchers. Without competition, privatization might simply consist of a private monopoly substituting for a government monopoly.

Results: Cost Containment

The primary aim of contracting out was to reduce operating costs without sacrificing the quality of the service. In the vast majority of cases the results appear to be favorable. As one of the chief researchers of privatization has put it, "Savings from competitive contracting of public services-the most thoroughly studied form of privatization-average roughly 25 to 30 percent" (Savas, 1995: 16).

Results: Quality Enhancement

Although cost restraint or reduction (without compromising quality) is a major objective of contracting and the record suggests impressive results, achieving high quality is an important objective in producing some services. These services often are classified as "soft services" since they are involved with helping consumers (or "clients") directly. Such services include education, job training, drug rehabilitation, and prisoner services. Assessing the performance of these services is very difficult since defining and measuring "output" are an imprecise art.

The evidence of performance in the "soft services" is not clear-cut. In the few documented studies available, the quality of service was either improved or not significantly different than when publicly produced. For example, in the social service area where non-profit suppliers are relied upon to produce most of the contracted for services, the performance record appears to be slightly better or the same as the public sector's record (Straussner, 1988; Mulka, 1990).

Results: Public-Private Competition

Another purpose of outsourcing such services as solid waste collection, road maintenance, and park maintenance was to inject competition for the government agency producing the service. Where used, contracting out here usually takes the form of bidding for work previously the sole responsibility of a public agency producer.

The resultant competition typically results in lower costs and more efficient service. When spurred by outside competition, the public agency often reduces its costs and gains a share of the work. Indianapolis and Charlotte have made extensive use of managed competition.

Contracting out or its threat also can have the effect of weakening the power of public unions. Governor Whitman of New Jersey and Mayor Giuliani of New York City have used the threat of privatization in negotiating with turnpike workers, sanitation workers, school custodians, and school bus drivers, all of whom "agreed to major modifications in their work rules to stave off private competition" (Palley, 1995: 21).

Bases for Improved Performance

Why can private operators produce with lower costs, at a given level of service? Better performance flows from the role of competition in a market system and the existence of the profit motive. Most governments producing services are monopolies that may not be sensitive to user demand. The political process may insulate producers. Moreover, monopsony arrangements for input suppliers may be imposed with resultant inflexible union and/or civil service rules and elevated wage rates.

Managers can have the same insulation from user wants. Civil service protection may dull incentives for managers to innovate and improve the product in the public sector. On the other hand, managers for private producers can be induced to overcome the owner/agent tension by incorporating profit-based compensation arrangements.

It has been argued that public enterprises are inefficient because they are interested in high employment to placate their public union supporters rather than to maximize efficiency. By contrast, a private firm would seek the most profitable level of employment. Privatization is cost-effective because it controls political discretion that otherwise would work in the direction of lower efficiency (Boycko, Shleifer, and Vishny, 1996).

Privatization in a competitive market framework will drive unit cost to the minimum level. One way the private producer accomplishes cost minimization is by limiting labor costs in such ways as using more part-time and lower-skilled workers, paying for less time off (vacation time and paid absences), using less overtime, establishing clearer job definitions and greater worker accountability, and having more workers per supervisor. Other input costs can be reduced by holding first-line managers more responsible for equipment maintenance and giving them more authority to hire and fire, shifting toward a higher capital to labor ratio, and utilizing more effective purchasing methods.

Relating manager pay to profitability can lead to more emphasis on innovative ways to produce, incorporating new technology, dispensing with "red tape," and making timely decisions. On the other hand, changing managers in light of poor performance in a private organization typically can be accomplished with greater speed and with less disruption.

Contractual operation of airports demonstrates some of the advantages of multi-unit private operations. The U.S. government's General Accounting Office lists twenty airports, primarily general aviation, as under private management with several of the airports operated by one company (U.S. General Accounting Office, 1988).

Chains in highly complex businesses such as airports have several advantages over a single-unit operator. Economies of scale are important in the procurement and personnel areas. Chains have one purchasing system that specializes in the particular items required for airports. Personnel operations, not constrained by civil service, can promote from within to develop senior managers, can offer advancement by moving to another airport, and can use specialists to troubleshoot where necessary.

Cautions and Pitfalls

Several cautions must be exercised and pitfalls protected against when contracting out. Where there is little competition in the private sector prior to privatization, a viable bidding process may not take place such that the savings anticipated or the quality improvement desired may not take place; private monopoly may simply replace public monopoly. Even where there is competition and bidding is spirited, the contract must be carefully drafted and monitored. Especially in service categories where output is ill-defined, and relevant costs are hard to measure, vague contracts may lead to less than optimal results, and enforcement may not be effectively practiced.

Also, a reasonable contract period may be required for the vendor to demonstrate results, especially for social services where desirable outcomes may take years to achieve. During the length of this long contract, the government may not be able to rebid even if performance is marginal.

Undesirable outcomes could also occur during the contract period or at the time of rebidding. The private supplier may not perform according to the contract owing to strikes, other work stoppages, and business cessation or bankruptcy. The contracting government agency must be prepared to find an alternative supplier or to resume operations itself. Where large capital investments in plant and equipment are necessary for operations, the government must be wary of disinvesting itself of back up equipment in case it has to resume operations.

Maintaining operations is a particularly vital issue when infrastructure is involved; the public sector must have contingency plans to take over. Essential services such as waste water treatment, airport operations, and water treatment must not be interrupted.

In monitoring and at the rebidding phase there is also the danger that the provider and beneficiary coalition may subvert the public interest. The experience of contracting out social services in Michigan illustrates the problem. In quick order, the evaluation of services and the interpretation of the "needs" of client beneficiaries became heavily influenced by providers. "For their part, self-interested bureaucrats and legislators cannot fail to see the opportunities for developing mutually beneficial relationships with contractors" (DeHoog, 1984: 247).

Abuse of the public trust and favoritism in awarding contracts to political friends are always a possibility. Public officials who let contracts may wind up working for the contractor. A case in point was the recent Fairfax County, Virginia, episode where the Fairfax County Park Authority selected a company to build golf facilities at two parks. Shortly after the contract was let, a board member of the Authority quit and went to work for the contractor as a "$500 per day consultant" (Lipton, 1996). Large contracts may even be let without competitive bidding. For example, the Washington, D.C. school board hired a firm to handle a $21 million contract to operate school cafeterias without competitive bids (Vise, 1996).

Reliance on bidder competition and aggressive public watchdog activities are essential to avoid the undue influence of suppliers on the contracting process. "Sweetheart" contracts, guaranteed contract renewal, and collusion among bidders are always a threat to undermine the potential advantages of privatization.

Several critics of contracting out point to the history of widespread corruption when several large cities undertook contracting in the nineteenth century. Political favoritism, bribery, and the toleration of poor contractor performance were documented in New York City, Chicago, and Detroit. Adler traces the problem to the existence of personal incentives for the public servant who does the hiring. "The (private) entrepreneur is interested in performance and nothing else. The public servant may trade performance for a personal gain" (Adler, 1996: DF9).

LESSONS LEARNED

After a decade or more of the more intensive contracting out in the United States., some preliminary observations about what works and what does not work can be asserted. A consensus revolving around the following points seems to be present:

1. Strong public support and a political champion are essential for the move to a privatized operation and its successful implementation. To gain this support typically requires enthusiastic backing by the government's chief executive, his staff, and legislative leaders. Forceful promotion of the effort is especially important when the pro-status quo coalition of stakeholders is large and effective and/or when the privatization move represents a major departure from the past practice (e.g., privatization of secure

prisons, contracting out the management of public schools, or the building of a private toll road).

2. Politically, privatization efforts are most likely to proceed in an *ad hoc*, piecemeal, opportunistic fashion (Windsor, 1995). In the pragmatic American environment, rapid, comprehensive, wholesale efforts to privatize are not likely to be embraced by elected officials or by masses of voters. Where substantial benefits in the form of cost containment or improved services seem clear, where the pro-government stakeholders are not politically powerful or strongly entrenched, or where a major crisis erupts concerning uncontrolled costs or woeful service performance, opportunities will arise for privatization. The confluence of opportunity and a skilled political leadership eager for change can tilt the scale toward the new organizational arrangement.

3. To make better-informed judgments as to the feasibility of privatization, an accurate costing system should be developed. Besides whipping up political support, the government executive can establish some benchmarks. The major items to be benchmarked are the present cost of service and quality of output. Output must be clearly distinguished and measured. All costs, direct and indirect, then are identified and linked to output. This accounting technique usually is called "activity-based costing" (Eggers, 1994: 6-8). As a "before-and-after" measure of performance of privatization or as the basis for making a "buy-or-make" decision, accurate cost measurement allows for a more meaningful public/private comparison. In making the decision as to whether to contract out a government service or function, care must be taken if the primary objective is to reduce costs since most governments do not adequately cost their services, especially the appropriate allocation of supporting services and general government overhead. Attempting to compare the cost of in-house with contracted service delivery can be complex. A major national study suggests that the cost of in-house service delivery is frequently underestimated by as much as 30%. At the same time, the cost of buying services from a private vendor is often underestimated owing to a failure to account for such government costs as contract administration and contract monitoring (Martin, 1994).

4. Any privatization initiative is more likely to obtain its objectives if the maximum degree of competition possible is injected. As mentioned before, the existence of competition is an important environmental factor favoring a successful privatization effort. Very often there are choices as to how and how much competition to infuse. Choosing service sectors where multiple producers, competitive bidding, multi-vendor contracts, and generating public-private competition are all ways to ensure or enhance competition. For example, in contracting out refuse collection the local government could divide the city into several districts and award multiple contracts. The next time contracts were bid the city then would have a better feel for minimum average cost. Beyond the stage of utilizing multiple private contractors, the city could reserve a district for city operations and the city department could then bid for other districts in the rebidding process. Indianapolis, Phoenix, and Charlotte among other cities have made effective use of city-private competition.

5. In addition to competitive bidding, the structure of the contract and stringent contract administration are keys to successful privatization. After the operation of a service has been awarded to a private vendor, it is necessary to have a well-defined, performance-based contract. To be effective, the contract should have measurable standards of performance. For example, in trash collection, standards of frequency of collection and appearance of the collection area after pick-up can be incorporated into the contract. To ensure that the terms of the contract are adhered to, the contracting public

agency can require a performance bond. Also helpful is to have a relatively limited term of the contract, no more than a three to five year term at the maximum, so that rebidding is an expected occurrence. Procedures for the termination of the contract must be carefully specified to avoid transition problems, assure continuity of service, and avoid legal disputes when termination is initiated due to sub-par performance.

6. It is useful to incorporate evaluation procedures into the contract. If it is feasible, the evaluation will compare the costs and quality of programs and operations under the contract with those of similar public operations (in state or out of state if necessary). Alternatively or additionally, benchmarks can be established in the contract itself. In fairness to the private vendor, at least one year of full operation should be allowed before evaluation. To ensure objectivity, the evaluation might be conducted by an independent, impartial party such as a university, non-profit research group, or a firm with experience with evaluation techniques.

7. Privatization's impact on public employees can be mitigated. Treating potentially displaced workers with consideration and compassion can reduce opposition, especially from unions, to change. Indianapolis has had notable success in enlisting union support for its effort to constrain costs. A range of options is open to public officials to assist displaced public employees. Finding employment with the private contractor might be achieved by requiring or recommending the hiring of displaced workers or encouraging those workers to form their own company for the purposes of bidding for work. The government itself can attempt to find positions for the displaced by transfer to other jobs, including a possible freeze on new hiring until that is accomplished. At the least, a generous severance or early retirement package may be offered. To further garner worker support, bonuses might be paid to the public labor force out of the savings from privatization.

8. Certain functional areas of government operations lend themselves more readily to contracting out than other areas. Among the private-type, business-oriented services are state gaming, trash collection and disposal, lottery operations, airports, public transit, auditing, tax collection, toll roads, wastewater plants, water and gas utilities, ports, waste-to-energy plants, and college dormitories. These services fit into the business profile: potential profit making, financed by user charges, and devoid of significant external effects. These services also are the easiest to load shed.

CONCLUSION: THE FUTURE PATH OF PRIVATIZATION

The recent decade's spurt of privatization activities of non-federal governments either could represent a trend that will stretch well into the twenty-first century or could simply be a temporary acceleration in the use of a moderate application of a promising public management technique. The course that is followed will be a function of the relative strength of those forces pushing for rapid change compared to those elements moderating movement.

Since the mid-1980s the combination of fiscal constraints on governments and the growing popularity of the "smaller government" philosophy weakened opposition to privatization and encouraged the use of the privatizing option. Efficiency considerations moved to a position of greater prominence in the privatization debate, especially since the preponderance of evidence suggests that competently designed privatizing almost always leads to lower unit cost, improved product quality, or both. Also, the ability of private developers to raise funds and take risks more efficiently than the public sector in the case of infra-structure projects also seems clear.

In the face of the twin forces of budget pressure and the unpopularity of service cuts, public decision-makers became more sympathetic toward experi-menting with privatization initiatives. Once in place, the privatization efforts usually demonstrated their cost advantage, Success then generated momentum for more extensive privatization initiatives.

Another force for greater use of the private sector was the "anti-big govern-ment" point of view of some voting groups. This philosophical position may reflect an expected favorable distribution consequence of change or may be altruistic in its concern about the long-run effects on political/economic freedom of an encroaching government.

Countering the forces that push elected officials to move more rapidly toward privati-zation is the status quo coalition. Existing stakeholders attempt to hold onto their share of monopoly rents and attempt to erect obstacles to change. Change almost always threatens to cause redistribution of benefits and/or costs of government action.

Which set of forces is stronger will determine the particular course privatiza-tion will follow for state and local governments. Of course, in our highly decen-tralized federal system of government particular states or local government may deviate from the trend and can influence other governments and may even impact on the trend itself by engaging in innovative experimentation.

Contracting out production is a less threatening option and has a greater probability of being used than other, more drastic forms of privatization. The best chance of privatizing is when the number of public employees affected is small, specialized services are involved, output can be clearly defined and measured, several potential private suppliers exist or entry of others is easy, and the service beneficiaries are numerous.

However, where there is a large and entrenched pro-status quo group of stakeholders, where outcomes are not easily measured, and where significant externalities are believed to exist, breaking the mold will be very difficult. Examples would be in education and criminal justice functions.

Theoretically, government could transfer the production of all but a handful of services (some elements of law enforcement and a limited number of regulatory activities) to the private sector. The public sector could emerge primarily as the director rather than the producer of services. The interplay of many factors will determine the ultimate reach of the privatization movement. Although not a panacea for the fiscal problems facing our country, if properly managed, con-tracting out can be a strong force for delivering greater efficiency and effective-ness to the American economy.

A PREVIEW

The succeeding chapters cover the theory of contracting out, issues in imple-mentation-especially in the area of criminal justice, and some case studies of contracting out in practice.

Part I examines the theory and practice of contracting out. Ruth Hoogland DeHoog and Lana Stein investigated the extent to which municipalities actually were contracting out services in the 1980s; how the process of contracting out actually worked; and whether, on balance, the effort was beneficial. The results of a survey of large cities showed that most cities used the private sector to provide services in the 1980s.

The adoption or expansion of service contracting was both modest and incremental. The decision to contract out was typically an executive, rather than a legislative, decision. The major aim of the contract was cost savings and, most of the time, savings were achieved. Accountability and service quality were the items most identified as problem areas.

Applying modern organization theory to contracting out, Larkin S. Dudley provides the broad perspective as to how to contract out in an effective manner while maintaining the integrity of the government function. In examining the managing of contracting, Dudley pays special attention to the linkages among public and private participants and to the issue of the preservation of the character of government services when private contractors are used.

Frank W. Davis, Jr. describes the evolution in the theory and practice of procurement and how those principles apply to privatization efforts.

Privatization can involve a complex of contractors in the case of infrastructure. Jack W. Lillywhite discusses the use of contracting to affiliated companies of a concession consortium that has assumed the responsibility of handling a capital project. Often, the successful bidder for a major capital project includes a consortium of various firms such as engineering-construction, financial, and insurance providers. Very often the engineering-construction member will be given the contract for construction as a way of assuring result and reducing the risks to the consortium.

Part II looks at the application of contracting out. The initial chapters consider contracting out in the criminal justice area. William E. Botkin representing Rebound Colorado, a private supplier of juvenile justice services, argues that the private sector can play a positive role in the juvenile justice system by improving services and reducing costs. However, cooperation between private and public suppliers is necessary for the overall system to achieve optimum results.

Sheldon X. Zhang shows how Los Angeles County in California effectively employs the private sector to manage the efficient punishment technique of electronic monitoring. The benefits and problems of this experience are related.

Private management of jails as a method to control the ever rising costs of correctional services is examined by Sarah Armstrong and David Moulton. Given the special characteristics of jails with their transient population, the authors address the issues of accountability, legality, competition among vendors, and the possible use of non-profit suppliers.

Even in the area of complex services, contracting out to private producers can achieve positive results. Van R. Johnston examines the experience of Colorado in privatizing hospital and prison institutions.

Other interesting applications of contracting out also are included. The broadest of these cases is where a city had to consider every possible use of the private sector to survive. Ecorse, Michigan, was placed in receivership in the late 1980s. Using contracting out along with other policy changes, Robert T. Kleiman and Anandi P. Sahu found that Ecorse was able to achieve solvency and get on the road to fiscal recovery.

Solid waste collection particularly lends itself to privatization. Using Canadian data, Douglas K. Adie and James C. McDavid show that privatizing collection services improves efficiency and significantly reduces costs.

Raymond J. Keating examines the government operation of golf courses. He argues that a golf course is a private good and no persuasive case can be made for government operations. Short of selling public golf courses to private companies, the most politically feasible policy would be to contract out the operations to private contractors. Local governments that have contracted out have been able to cut costs and increase revenues from golf.

Part III investigates some major obstacles and techniques of contracting out. Successful contracting out requires a carefully thought out implementation process. Allan C. Rusten, an experienced management consultant to local governments, provides a blueprint for implementing a privatization initiative through contracting. Careful data collection and analysis, thoughtful handling of affected employees, and a well-designed public relations effort are keys to successful contracting.

A major obstacle to contracting out is the threat of a lawsuit to restrain the contracting act. Listing the four major bases for challenge to hiring private contractors, Nicholas Morgan offers the legal defenses for these challenges. With careful use of the notion of accountability, local governments can overcome these legal impediments.

The effects on employment due to privatization by local governments were investigated in a study done for the U.S. Department of Labor. Reporting on this study, Stephen Moore finds that over a five-year period few government workers lost their jobs, as most governments protected their workers. When the government failed to protect job security and wages of public employees, the privatization effort was less successful.

Jack Sterling relates the experience of Greeley, Colorado in using contracting out as an effective management method to improve the efficiency of government operations by challenging government departments to compete with private vendors. Although some complex issues have to be addressed, competitive contracting can be effective in reducing costs and improving the quality of service.

Finally, Paul Seidenstat examines the mechanics of contracting out. A detailed look at the steps involved in choosing a service to contract out to the monitoring of the contract is taken. The author also points out some of the dangers and pitfalls of contracting.

REFERENCES

Adler, M. (1996). "In City Services, Privatize and Beware." *New York Times* 145, April 7: p. DF9.

Boycko, M., A. Shleifer, and R. W. Vishny (1996). "A Theory of Privatization." *The Economic Journal* 106, March: pp. 309-319.

Chandler, T. and P. Feuille (1991). "Municipal Unions and Privatization." *Public Administration Review* 51, no. 1, January/February: pp. 15-21.

Chi, K. (1993). *Policy Options for Privatization in State and Local Government.* Unpublished manuscript.

Council of State Governments (1993). *State Trends and Forecasts: Privatization.* Louisville, KY.

DeHoog, R. H. (1984). "Theoretical Perspectives on Contracting Out for Services." In G.C. Edwards III, ed. *Public Policy Implementation.* Greenwich, CT: JAI Press: pp. 227-259.

Eggers, W. D. (1994). *Rightsizing Government: Lessons from America's Public Sector Innovators.* Los Angeles: Reason Foundation.

Goodman, J. C. (1990). Address at the Third National Conference, Privatization Council Washington, DC, June 11.

Kodrzycki, Y. (1998). "Fiscal Pressures and the Privatization of Local Services." *New England Economic Review,* January-February: pp. 39-50.

Kodrzycki, Y. (1994). "Privatization of Local Public Services: Lessons for New England." *New England Economic Review 010,* May-June: pp. 31-46.

Lick, D. M. (1995). "Public Franchising Renaissance." Paper presented at meeting of American Bar Association, Section of Public Contract Law. Miami, FL, February 10.

Lipton, E. (1996). "Fairfax Investigates Ex-Park Authority Official's Work for Bidder." *Washington Post,* July 26: p. B01.

Martin, L. (1994). "How to Compare Costs between In-House Contracted Services." *Public Private Cooperation.* Denver: Colorado Municipal League, pp. 24-37.

Mulka, S. (1990). "Contracting for Human Services: The Case of Pennsylvania's Subsidized Child Care Program: Policy Limitations and Prospects." *Administration in Social Work* 14: pp. 31-46.

Palley, B. (1995). "Threat of Privatization is Robbing Public Employees of Clout." *Wall Street Journal* 144, September 4: p. 21.

Reason Foundation (1994). *Eighth Annual Report on Privatization-Privatization 1994:* Los Angeles.

Savas, E. S. (1995). *Privatization in State and Local Government.* Unpublished manuscript.

Straussner, S.L.A. (1988). "Comparison of In-house and Contracted Out Employee Programs." *Social Work* 33, January/February: pp. 53-55.

U.S. General Accounting Office (1997). *Privatization Lessons Learned by State and Local Governments.* GAO/GGD-97-48 Washington, DC: U.S. Government Printing Office.

U.S. General Accounting Office (1988). *Federal Productivity: DOD Functions with Savings Potential from Private Sector Cost Comparisons.* Washington, DC: U.S. Government Printing Office.

Vise, D. (1996). "Dispute Over Food Service Bid Could Imperil Effort to Cut Jobs, Costs." *Washington Post,* July 25: p. A01.

Windsor, D. (1995). *Piecemeal Privatization: The U.S. Domestic Transportation Example*. Paper presented at Western Regional Science Association, San Diego, February 23.

Chapter 2

Municipal Contracting in the 1980s: Tinkering or Reinventing Government

Ruth Hoogland DeHoog and Lana Stein

In twenty years, we may look back on the 1980s as a decade of profound change in government at all levels and in virtually all policy areas. Through the process of privatization, decentralization, and cutbacks, the Reagan administration set out to alter fundamentally the way in which public agencies performed, paid for, and provided public services (President's Commission on Privatization, 1988). Even though some of the efforts were largely composed of rhetoric and not substance, the rhetoric itself changed the way in which the public viewed government. People believed more than ever that not only was government wasteful and interfering but government itself was the problem. The solution was to cut back government, to make it more efficient, and to bring in the private sector to help government provide or produce services.

Did a profound change actually occur in the frequency and type of private sector involvement? Did the federal efforts really trickle down to local governments? Did they really make a difference in how governments operate and how much it costs? Was it a fundamental change that occurred, or was it just more tinkering with government?

These questions are important to ask and answer, since the Clinton administration came into office with certain beliefs about the 1980s and how to "reinvent government" for the 1990s. The work of Osborne and Gaebler (1992) has been influential in offering ideas that were tried in many local governments during the 1980s and may have broader applications.

With emphasis on downsizing the federal government through Vice-President Al Gore's National Performance Review, the Clinton administration sought reform and reinvention in the areas of public procurement and contracting out for services (National Performance Review, 1993). Not only have federal officials embraced these notions, but many state and local governments have embarked on reinventing government, in which "entrepreneurial government" is a major motif (Kettl, 1993). Many questions remain. What can we learn from the experiences of local governments that have attempted to use some of the techniques offered by Osborne and Gaebler? Did government really change its methods and, consequently, its results? More systematic research must be conducted to begin to answer these questions and shed light on the feasibility of the "reinventing" mechanisms.

We set out here to examine these questions in one area, cities' public services. We examine, first, whether and to what extent the Reagan Revolution and the real world constraints faced by municipalities actually meant that cities increased their privatization and contracting. Therefore, our focus is on the decade of the 1980s, when this approach was so widely developed. This time frame will allow us to consider whether the most recent pro-contracting wave will actually lead to greater utilization of this technique.

Second, we analyze the process that cities used to privatize or contract for services. Who were involved in the decisions? How was the process designed to be open, fair, and effective? The process itself then may be seen as affecting the results of contracting, as well as producing political opposition to the alternative to public service production.

Third, we sought to determine if the cities had avoided the problems and realized the benefits that were frequently discussed during the late 1970s and early 1980s in the debates about privatization. What did city officials learn? What actually were the results, given a decade of experience? Which contracting issues that have been raised in the academic literature are actually salient to local officials?

Throughout our discussion we have a concern for the process of accountability that includes private contractors being held accountable for service production and public officials being held accountable by elected officials and the public for quality public services. While contracting out may have some benefits for cutting service costs (Savas, 1987), it has the potential for abuse and may result in poorer quality services if it is not carefully structured and reviewed by those outside the administrator-contractor relationship. In the view of some, such as James Q. Wilson (1989: 359), "Keeping market suppliers accountable to government buyers requires effort, but probably less effort than keeping government suppliers accountable."

Although our focus is on contracting for municipal public services with private firms, municipalities have used a variety of other techniques to cut costs and improve productivity (Valente and Manchester, 1984). What we learn in this area, however, may apply to other efforts to use the private sector for public service delivery.

LITERATURE REVIEW

During the decade of the 1980s, the topic of contracting out experienced a metamorphosis, perhaps a predictable one given the way many public innovations are often promoted, criticized, and then modified. Starting in the late 1970s, generally more ideologically conservative privatization proponents (primarily applied economists) were enamored with the use of private markets to improve government efficiency. They suggested that all types of government services would be improved, costs would be cut, and the size of government would shrink. Titles such as *Better Government at Half the Price* (Bennett and Johnson, 1981) and *Privatizing the Public Sector: How to Shrink Government* (Savas, 1982) suggest the perspectives and expectations of this group. Their primary evidence of the results of contracting was a series of research papers on solid waste and a smattering of empirical studies on other, primarily hard, municipal services. (See Savas, 1982 and 1987 for a review).

Public administrationists, sociologists, and political scientists then challenged these inflated claims. They raised many issues overlooked by the simple analyses of the economists. These included the effects of contracting on service quality, costs (Starr, 1987), service equity, individual constitutional rights (Sullivan, 1987), political corruption (Bailey, 1987), citizen input (Morgan and England, 1988), minority employment (Suggs, 1986), overall efficiency and savings to the municipality (Stein, 1990), and democratic values (Moe, 1987). Quite often the concern was not with the process or direct outcomes of contracting per se but with the ideology and values that contracting and privatization represented. Their empirical evidence was limited to a few municipal services and cases of federal and state contracting, more often than not in the human services (e.g., DeHoog, 1984).

What has come out of these debates is a modification of the claims, a clearer language with which to discuss these issues (Kolderie, 1983), a better understanding of the limitations of contracting, and a realization that changes in attitudes and behavior do not occur overnight (Hirsch, 1995). Those concerned about the blurred line between the public and private sectors suggest that certain core functions of government must be maintained and not privatized (Moe, 1987).

Several scholars have suggested that contracting should be approached on a case-by-case basis because it does not offer a panacea to the ills of government (Donahue, 1989). Others have suggested that certain types of contracting systems themselves must be accommodated to the types of services, the service market, and the degree of uncertainty involved (DeHoog, 1990). We are becoming more sophisticated in understanding the problems, process, and outcomes of this method of service delivery.

We expect that practitioners and elected officials who deal with contracting out have also become more experienced in its use and have learned some valuable, perhaps costly, lessons in the process of implementing this approach. Journalistic, anecdotal, and single-case evidence suggests that cities have used contracting successfully in a wide range of service areas after some failures (e.g., Katz, 1991). We need systematic and analytical evidence to determine how widespread the contracting is, what specific procedures are being used in the process, and what guidelines have been developed to deal with future efforts.

Our attention now turns to what municipalities actually experienced during the decade of the 1980s.

RESEARCH METHOD AND DATA

Our study focused on municipalities with populations of 50,000 or more. Convincing evidence exists (Florestano and Gordon, 1980; Stein, 1990) that smaller cities have some unique motives and procedures in contracting, for example they may have no choice but to contract out if they wish to offer a particular public service (see especially Stein, 1990). We were most concerned that municipalities offer a wide range of services, have a variety of alternative methods for service delivery, and employ a sizable professional personnel base.

Questionnaires were sent to 165 central, suburban, and independent cities of over 50,000 during the summer of 1991. Cost constraints limited sample size, but every effort was made to query a representative group of cities, according to geographic region, population, city type (e.g., central vs. suburban), and form of government. Responses were received from 104 cities, or 63 percent. Those cities responding were quite typical of those surveyed in the key variables used to draw the sample. The only difference was a slightly higher than average response from southern cities.

REGION	NUMBER OF CASES		
South	39	Midwest	26
Northeast	22	West	17

Of the l04 cities in the sample, 59 are council-manager cities, and 45 have a mayor-council form of government. Most cities in the sample have less than 250,000 people:

Population	Cases:	Population	Cases
50,000–99,999	31	250,000–499,999	24
100,000–249,999	37	500,000+	12

Eighteen of the l04 sample cities are suburban; the remainder are central cities or smaller, independent cities.

The questionnaire was extensive and allowed respondents to add comments at several points. Some respondents indicated that they would be willing to be interviewed by telephone at a later date. As is typical for these types of city-based surveys, a variety of municipal officials completed the survey, from the mayors and managers or their assistants, to budgeting, purchasing, and evaluation officials. No city or individual respondent is identified here by name; instead, we refer to city size and/or general location when relating comments from the written or telephone survey. We believed that some degree of confidentiality was needed to elicit more candid responses.

FINDINGS

Survey respondents were asked to focus on their contracting and privatization efforts during the 1980s. Most of the sample cities had had experience with contracting out, and some with privatization, and a few of the respondents mentioned that their cities had undergone a thorough review of their practices and services during the decade. (See, e.g., the Ad Hoc Task Force to Study Privatization, 1989.) It was clear that almost all of the cities not only were well aware of the option of contracting for services but also had considered or used it in their operations. A few respondents indicated that their cities had one or two contracts already in place (usually garbage collection) prior to the 1980s, and had not expanded their efforts.

Contracting out, rather than full privatization (or, as defined in the survey, service or load-shedding), is the most common route taken and 78.8 percent of the sample cities have done so in the past ten years. A little less than half, 43.4 percent, have privatized in that same time period. Form of government appears to have little effect on the decision to privatize or contract out. Of the mayor-council cities, 47.6 percent have privatized a service, and 77.8 percent have contracted out at least once. The figures for council-manager cities are very comparable: 44.6 percent have privatized, and 82.5 percent have contracted out. Findings also are similar across regions of the country, although there is somewhat less contracting in the Northeast, and the least privatization is in the Midwest.

Cities contract out or privatize many types of services. Table 2.1 enumerates the services most often contracted out or privatized. As the table shows, many cities tend to choose areas that require intermittent effort (such as legal or financial services) or that lack public visibility (e.g., vehicle maintenance). Some select services that impact most citizens but not in a daily or weekly manner: pest control, building inspections, parking enforcement, operation of a corrections facility. As expected, certain services such as those in the legal or financial areas have been in private hands for quite some time and may not have been used for efficiency improvements or cost reductions. This is especially the case when primarily overflow work is contracted out.

About a third of the sample cities chose to contract out or privatize a service that is very visible to residents and valued by most. Thirty-seven cities use private companies to handle residential garbage collection. Council-manager and mayor-council cities are equally as likely to contract out or privatize, although a smaller percentage of northeastern cities (where municipal unions are strong) embraces private garbage pickup. Twenty-six cities use private companies to collect commercial garbage. Again, there is no clear difference between council-manager and mayor-council cities, although privatization/contracting is less likely in the Northeast.

Several scholars (see, e.g., Wilson, 1989) have suggested that many units of government would find contracting better suited to areas where outputs are observable and measurable. Garbage collection fits that bill. The other areas cited earlier are less likely to fit but for various reasons may be more politically feasible choices, for example, internal legal or financial functions. They are less likely to affect government employment, and they do not touch the lives of every resident. Perhaps most interesting is the fact that contracting and/or privatization was not adopted extensively in any of the surveyed cities. Although several cities contracted out multiple services, they did not contract the majority of their functions.

Satisfaction with Contracting

In general, the level of satisfaction with municipal contracting was fairly high among survey respondents. However, many of these respondents had learned from the problems they had faced in introducing and implementing contracting arrangements in the last decade and could offer useful advice to other cities, in response to an open-ended question designed to draw from their experiences.

Cities have elected to contract out largely for budgetary reasons, as might be expected. Forty-one cities cite that as their chief reason, while fourteen others name efficiency. In the last ten years, fewer federal programs and a shrinking tax base in central cities combined to create conditions emblematic of fiscal stress. Increased economy is a very understandable objective. However, only five cities cite increased service quality as a reason for selecting private sector service deliverers.

Several respondents suggested that contracting out and privatization were not panaceas and must be entered into thoughtfully and carefully. When considering contracting for a particular service, one respondent declared, "Cost comparisons between public and private sector need to be complete, considering such aspects as avoidable indirect costs, insurance premiums, fixed assets disposition, etc." Other respondents suggested obtaining information from other cities that have contracted out for the same service or bringing in a consultant to perform a thorough cost analysis.

Most sample cities that have contracted out or privatized certain services expressed satisfaction with the economy they were able to achieve. Over 75 percent reported gains in this area. Similarly, 60 percent reported increases in efficiency. Two cities indicated that the contracting experience allowed them to reduce costs in-house. One mentioned that the city was able to negotiate reductions with municipal unions, so that services again could become municipal operations.

Few cities chose improved service quality as an important reason for electing to use the private sector. That is fortunate since only half the cities perceived a gain in this area. Forty-three cities reported improvement but forty-two cities found none after contracting out. Of the forty-two cities reporting no gain in service quality, thirty were less than 250,000 in population and thirteen were suburbs. Almost two-thirds of the suburbs in this sample reported that they experienced no improvement in service quality. Cities in this category had contracted out a variety of services including residential and commercial garbage collection, custodial work, pest control, and legal services.

In analyzing whether differences existed among the different types of cities, we found that mayor-council cities were more likely to experience no improvement (56 percent). Cities in the Midwest were least satisfied over the four regions, with 61 percent reporting no improvement in service quality.

The level of competition among potential suppliers appeared to be minimally acceptable, although, according to some respondents, the level of competition varies from the more technical (e.g., facilities management) to the less technical type of service (e.g., custodial services). Ninety-five percent of the cities chose from among two or more qualified bidders. Wide advertising of the contract availability was seen as very important to increasing competition, since "the greater the number of service competitors, the lower the price." Nonetheless, according to one respondent, "Do not automatically pick the lowest bidder for the contract."

Two cities strongly asserted that contracting was a method to increase competition in service delivery, thus enhancing efficiency. However, rather than turn over everything in a specific area to a private firm, these cities allowed their municipal departments to compete with private suppliers, as in the well-known case of Phoenix, with its many competitive services. The municipal departments seemed to do as well as private competition if prodded by this mechanism.

Problems in Contracting

A sizable number of cities expressed their dissatisfaction with contracting out or privatization, and half would not necessarily do it again in all areas. As one city official remarked, "Each situation should be judged on its merits. I've seen it good and bad."

An oft-mentioned problem with contracting for services was in obtaining approval for certain services to be supplied by private firms. Not only were councils sometimes skeptical, but several cities mentioned that their municipal unions provided strong opposition to contracting, as would be expected. Private employers selected to provide municipal services would not necessarily be organized nor would they have the same pay and benefit package as the public employer. In fact, a western city dispensed with its contracting because city council members objected to the lower wages paid to the private employees. In a similar vein, one midwestern city is now required to notify the appropriate municipal unions if it considers contracting out a service. It also requires contractors to use union employees, thereby limiting labor savings. However, the contractors still were viewed as having some advantages, in that they were able to use workers with less overhead expenses.

Once agreement among various officials has been reached to contract a service, problems may arise as cities advertise the contract. Widely circulating and advertising the bid were seen as a critical way to increase the competitive climate for contracts. In addition, a well-crafted bid or proposal request is key to insuring successful contracting. As a manager of a large city advised, "Make certain the needs and objectives to be achieved are absolutely clearly stated in the bid or request for proposal."

An administrator of a large southwestern city had several suggestions for other municipalities, once a request for proposals has been circulated, and the bids have been submitted: be sure the contractor can provide the services you are requesting; make sure to hold them to the terms of your arrangement; set liquidated damages for non-compliance; and require adequate reporting and monitor the contractor.

Many officials had similar advice about the importance of clearly specifying the contract terms, including quality standards, service delivery methods, monitoring procedures, and penalty provisions. One of these advised, "Make sure your contract is comprehensive and thoroughly understood by all parties involved."

Nonetheless, twenty-nine respondents indicated that contractors in their cities had failed to perform services as their contracts specified. Some cities mentioned the following problems pertaining to contractors: illegal behavior, criminal indictments, bankruptcy, and conflicts of interest. Work not up to city standards was mentioned most frequently by those dissatisfied with private providers. Few wrote of major debacles, but a fiscal officer in a midwestern city did mention an animal control contractor who absconded with public funds and was subsequently indicted.

An experienced manager cautioned, "Always be prepared to terminate the contract and resume service with city forces if goals are not being met," a position clearly not practiced in many other surveyed cities. Interestingly, only 34 percent of the respondents said they would be able to resume municipal delivery of the contracted service. If an inadequate supply of contractors exists, the city's ability to hold the contractor accountable is negated. Of the thirty-three cities that had terminated at least one contract, only four resumed the service themselves; most sought another contractor.

While 63.5 percent of cities said that, in retrospect, they would contract or privatize again, 36.5 percent or thirty-one cities said that it would depend on the service. This may not, however, be an indicator of discontent with private sector arrangements. After all, a majority of these cities reported that service quality had improved. It could signify an increased understanding of the advantages and disadvantages of contracting in various service areas. Even more interesting is the fact that, while forty cities said that they planned on additional contracting, thirty-nine did not. Further, seventeen of the sample cities not only said that they planned no further contracting but in retrospect said they would not contract out all service areas again. Puzzling is the fact that desiring no additional contracting had an inverse relation to service quality, albeit a mild one. This seems to again indicate that some cities view contracting as limited to certain specific functions and not as an across the board approach to management.

Accountability Issues

One of the most common criticisms of contracting out for public services is the potential for the unscrupulous to make a profit at government expense, often through illegal means such as bid-rigging, bribery, kickbacks, conflict-of-interest violations, and so on. The more common problems in contracting, however, are non performance of services or poor quality services. In any case, encouraging appropriate oversight and monitoring is essential to efficient and effective service delivery.

In this survey, we included several questions to determine the contracting procedures that are designed to ensure that contractors were held accountable to contracting officers, elected officials, interested groups, and the client/citizens. We examined who were involved in the process of contract awards, how citizen complaints were handled, and which oversight or monitoring methods were employed during contract implementation.

Executive staff most often had made the decision to contract out or privatize, yet council members played a role in slightly over two-thirds of the cities that engaged private business. Business leaders played a role in just twelve cities, while neighborhood groups had input in only five. One respondent said, "Neighborhood groups don't care. Citizens just want the service; they don't care who delivers it."

In involving elected officials in the process, one respondent advised, "Make certain you have necessary political support. Do not lay anyone off from their jobs as a result of privatization." In the same vein, a respondent warned, "Be aware of the politics that may be involved. Unions will surely react. If unions are strong, it won't be easy." Another experienced official suggested that planning had to involve all those affected by the decision: employees, council, citizens, and the city staff that would organize the process.

Although citizens were not often involved directly in contracting arrangements, respondents in eleven cities noted that citizens had complained about some facet of using private agents for service delivery. In addition, council members raised questions or objections in eleven cities as well. Their concerns related to liability issues, union employment, service continuity, and long-term cost savings.

While time constraints or unfamiliarity with the contracting process caused difficulties in a few cases, cities generally monitored citizen complaints and received contractor progress reports. Most carried out visual inspections of contractor work and performed regular financial reviews, while some cities periodically mailed surveys to citizens for their service evaluations. Several respondents noted that their annual and semiannual renewal of contracts encouraged regular performance reviews. Ultimately, contractors may be replaced if they do not perform to the city's satisfaction, although some respondents noted that this option was limited in some specialized services where virtually no other private contractors were available.

In providing advice to other cities, city officials emphasized the importance of traditional managerial controls, not outside oversight by citizens and elected officials.

Survey respondents recommended having a clearly specified contract, qualified staff, and careful reviews by more than simply the line departments. One manager suggested, "Don't expect a contractor to be any better than the contract administration process demands." Another official also noted, "A highly trained auditing staff is essential." Still others noted the importance of the service departments as well as purchasing officers understanding the contracting process and how to negotiate and enforce tight contracts. This expertise may be costly, however. As Osborne and Gaebler (1992: 87) note, cities often can spend "20 percent of the cost of service on contract management."

CONCLUSION

Overall, most cities have used the private sector in the 1980s to supply services of one kind or another. We would categorize these widespread efforts as "tinkering" rather than "reinventing" local government. Despite the encouragement of the Reagan administration, professional conferences, and the growing literature on privatization benefits, it did not appear that cities had adopted a fundamental alteration in either the privatization/contracting process or the types of services for which service delivery alternatives were considered. More important perhaps, most city operations were not touched by a transfer from public to private management.

The adoption or expansion of service contracting especially was both modest and incremental, often involving a trial-and-error process. Many times the contracted services are intermittent or less visible to the citizenry, with one clear exception. Many cities now contract for residential and/or commercial garbage collection, a visible service that operates in a competitive environment and has measurable outputs.

The decision to contract was generally an executive decision, though over half the cities involved council members. The cities mainly sought cost savings, and they were frequently successful in their quest. However, service quality was not enhanced in half the cities. Further, a number of cities indicated they would not go to the private sector to the extent they had before, and half the sample contemplated no further contracting or privatization. Accountability was a problem in a few cities; service quality was problematic in more.

Although contracting out and privatization became the "buzzwords" of the 1980s, major American cities have not embraced these strategies unequivocally, nor have they found them to be problem-free solutions in difficult economic times. Contracting out and privatization present alternatives that save money but do not necessarily guarantee service quality. Special effort is required to ensure that providers live up to the terms of their contracts. This effort is often greater for executives than keeping track of city agencies. Osborne and Gaebler (1992: 87) note that "contracting is one of the most difficult methods a public organization can choose, because writing and monitoring require so much skill."

For example, the same level of information about contracted services may not be available or in the desired form. Mayors, city managers, and council members cannot assume that their own departments will be accountable to them. Contracting and privatization transfer this problem to a new realm, and one type of vigilance must replace another.

Although contracting out and privatization will be utilized for a long time to come, it is apparent from this examination that all cities are not equally happy with the employment of the private sector. Most cities find the arrangement better in certain activities than others. Perhaps some readers would find it surprising, given the level of public discussion of contracting, that no cities in this survey use this approach in any comprehensive way.

REFERENCES

Ad Hoc Task Force to Study Privatization (1989). *Report of Privatization Task Force.*

Bailey, Robert W. (1987). "Uses and Misuses of Privatization." In Steve H. Hanke, ed., *Prospects for Privatization.* New York: Academy for Political Science.

Bennett, James T., and Manuel H. Johnson (1981). *Better Government at Half the Price.* Ottawa, IL: Caroline House.

DeHoog, Ruth H. (1990). "Competition, Negotiation, or Cooperation?" *Administration and Society* 22, November: pp. 317-340.

DeHoog, Ruth H. (1984). *Contracting Out for Human Serices: Political, Economic, and Organizational Perspectives.* Albany: SUNY Press.

Donahue, John D. (1989). *The Privatization Decision: Public Ends, Private Means.* New York: Basic Books.

Ferris, James M. (1986). "The Decision to Contract Out." *Urban Affairs Quarterly* 22: pp. 289-311.

Ferris, James M., and Elizabeth Graddy (1986). "Contracting Out: For What? With Whom?" *Public Administration Review* 46: pp. 332-344.

Florestano, Patricia S., and Stephen Gordon (1980). "Public vs. Private: Small Government Contracting with the Private Sector." *Public Administration Review* 40: pp. 29-34.

Hirsch, Werner Z. (1995). "Contracting Out by Urban Governments: A Review." *Urban Affairs Review* 30: January: pp. 458-472.

Johnson, Gerald W., and Douglas J. Watson (1991). "Privatization: Provision or Production of Services? Two Case Studies." *State and Local Government Review* 23, Spring: pp. 82–89.

Katz, Jeffrey L. (1991). "Privatizing Without Tears." *Governing* 4, June: pp. 38-42.

Kettl, Donald F. (1993). *Sharing Power: Public Governance and Private Markets.* Washington, DC: Brookings Institution.

Kolderie, Theodore (1983). "The Two Different Concepts of Privatization." *Public Administration Review* 43: pp. 285-291.

Lowery, David (1982). "The Political Incentives of Government Contracting." *Social Science Quarterly* 54: pp. 517–529.

Lyons, William, and Michael R. Fitzgerald (1986). "The City as Purchasing Agent: Privatization and the Urban Polity in America." In Terry Nichols Clark, ed., *Research in Urban Policy: Managing Cities*, vol. 2. Greenwich, CT: JAI Press.

Miller, Gary (1981). *Cities by Contract*. Cambridge: MIT Press.

Moe, Ronald (1987). "Exploring the Limits of Privatization." *Public Administration Review* 47: pp. 453-460.

Morgan, David R., and Robert E. England (1988). "The Two Faces of Privatization." *Public Administration Review* 48, November./December: pp. 979-987

National Performance Review. (1993). *Reinventing Federal Procurement*. Washington, DC: U.S. Government Printing Office.

Osborne, David, and Ted Gaebler (1992*). Reinventing Government*. Reading, MA: Addison-Wesley.

President's Commission on Privatization. (1988). *Privatization: Toward More Effective Government*. Washington, DC: U.S. Government Printing Office.

Savas, E. S. (1982). *Privatizing the Public Sector: How to Shrink Government*. Chatham, NJ: Chatham House.

Savas, E. S. (1987). *Privatization: The Key to Better Government*. Chatham, NJ: Chatham House.

Starr, Paul (1987). "The Limits of Privatization." In Steve H. Hanke, ed., *Prospects for Privatization*. New York: Academy of Political Science.

Stein, Robert M. (1990). *Urban Alternatives: Public and Private Markets in the Provision of Local Services*. Pittsburgh: University of Pittsburgh Press.

Straussman, Jeffrey (1981). "More Bang for Fewer Bucks? Or How Local Governments Can Rediscover the Potentials and Pitfalls of the Market." *Public Administration Review* 41: pp. 140-157.

Suggs, Robert E. (1986). "Minorities and Privatization: Issues of Equity." *Public Management*, December: pp. 14–15.

Sullivan, Harold J. (1987). "Privatization of Public Services: A Growing Threat to Constitutional Rights." *Public Administration Review* 47: pp. 461-468.

Valente, Carl F., and Lydia D. Manchester (1984). *Rethinking Local Services: Examining Alternative Delivery Approaches*. Washington, DC: Department of Housing and Urban Development.

Wilson, James Q. (1989). *Bureaucracy*. New York: Basic Books.

Chapter 3

Public and Private: Learning, Linking, and Legitimating

Larkin S. Dudley

"The rules they are a changin" is a paraphrase one of Bob Dylan's famous refrains. Government, business, nonprofits, and volunteers find themselves intermingled in service co-production, competition, and cooperation. The sectors blur in an era in which as much as a half of government services may be co-produced. The literature's focus has been on whether to involve the private sector and on the end results in terms of costs. However, managers at all levels of government must make decisions of how to blend private services with those provided by government personnel and how to work to make both more effective within public organizations.

The burgeoning literature on privatization, particularly on contracting, reveals the attempt by many to solidify the lessons learned in contracting and to give guidance to those at all levels of government. Most of the advice deals with the immediate problems of contracting: cost comparison methodology, selection of contractors, protection against individual abuse, and insurance of good solicitation. Addressed also, but not as well, is the management of contracting.

Although the management of monitoring and quality assurance and the costs of administration have been discussed, less attention has been paid to reviewing thelinkages among public and private and to the preservation of the character of government services. This paper contends that the neglect of these areas can be remedied through drawing upon our knowledge of organizational theory.

In the attempts to design and structure service provision, managers, of course, turn to their own experience, the advice and experience of others, and the research reported in professional publications. One element permeates all these sources: the theory of how organizations work that is implicit in how managers conceptualize the situation, alternative courses of action, and possible solutions. Since the decision to privatize or to provide in-house; the management of contracts; and the success or failure of service provision occur within public organizations, reflections on what seems to work in government contracting out efforts and in current theories of public organizations should serve to assist us to design management processes better in the future. This chapter will add to the literature through a demonstration of why the current conception of public organizations needs revision, a review of some of the recent organizational theories that could aid in that revision, and, finally, the implications for those managing contracts at any level of government.

PROBLEMS WITH THEORIES OF PRACTICE

No matter which of the end results seem more convincing, much of agency thinking and practice still reflect the "classical organization theory" of public administration. Traditional public administration draws sharp lines between the public and private sectors and among levels of government and emphasizes hierarchical patterns of authority (Salamon, 1989). Classical orthodox theory is preoccupied with the anatomy of government organizations and is concerned primarily with arrangements to ensure that 1) each function is assigned an appropriate niche; 2) component parts of the executive branch are properly related; and 3) authorities and responsibilities are clearly assigned (Seidman and Gilmour, 1986: 6). Settlement of disputes usually lies in reliance on hierarchy and a clear chain of command.

In contrast, the current tools of government action, including procurement contracting, involve a blurring of sector lines and a sharing of authority. The public management problems include not only running an agency, but attempting to coordinate goals among a complex network of players and institutions over which the public manager has only imperfect control, yet on which he or she must depend to operate an agency's program (Salamon, 1989). Thus, third party government creates serious problems of management and accountability for which standard public administration theory fails to prepare us.

Several studies of efforts to implement contracts reveal misguided ssumptions, many of them based in classical theory. The results of research by Ruth DeHoog, Kate Asher, and Susan Bernstein below indicate some of the problems that a more thorough examination of assumptions about contracting might have prevented.

Ruth Hoogland DeHoog, in her studies of contracting in the Michigan Department of Social Services and the Michigan Department of Labor, notes lack of competition in a sequential search process (the incremental approach); decision makers retained previous services and contractors routinely; new alternatives were sought only when additional funds were allocated. Lack of coordination was also a characteristic of the process with organizational divisions between program staff where each did not take advantage of the other's expertise. Further, monitoring and evaluation of contracts were not sufficient. Lack of choice was also evident. Officials felt they had few real choices— previous contractors got renewals and new contracts were awarded to the only available reputable agencies. Finally, DeHoog observed that significant cost reductions were probably not realized due to high administrative costs.

A later study by Susan R. Bernstein (1991) gives us the mirror image of managing contracting agencies from a nonprofit agency viewpoint in her ethnograph with 18 managers of nonprofit social services agencies in the New York metropolitan area. Bernstein reports the nonprofit managers' opinions that managing services is paradoxical; agency contracts conflict with the reality of providing good service; monitoring is uneven; and, that her results confirm Lester Salamon's (1989) observation that neither government officials nor nonprofits have developed a meaningful and coherent set of standards to guide their interactions.

Both DeHoog and Bernstein examined state and local delivery of social services, "soft" services that are difficult to measure, and, thus, difficult to monitor. In-depth studies of contracting out at the national level for more easily measurable services, e.g., cleaning, laundry, catering in Great Britain (Asher, 1987) and for transportation and supply services under Circular A-76 in the U. S. (Dudley, 1990) also reveal difficulties in implementation. These latter programs are ones which are replacement of former governmental provision, bringing out strong union opposition, and often pitting individual agencies against the instructions of a centralized mandate. Nevertheless, lack of clarity in standards in transition from government to contractor provision was characteristic of these programs. Furthermore, contradictions of an adversarial orientation to contractors while forming a solicitation and a lack of methods to ease into co-production after contract award were characteristic of the Circular A-76 programs.

Many of the problems mentioned above are those of organizational design. Some areas neglected by the contracting literature can be informed by theories of complex organizations. These are theories aimed at 1) a focus on learning our own organizations; 2) linking public and private organizations–choosing designs with emphasis on integration and networks; and 3) considering the public interest in privatization.

LEARNING: CULTURE AND PRIVATIZATION

Learning is a focus of several recent theoretical thrusts in organizations—how do we design organizations that can adjust to changes in the environment or perceptual apparatuses that can perceive the need for changes (Weick, 1979). The need for "smart" organizations has paralleled the development of "smart" roads and technologies. As Chris Argyris (1993) has succinctly summarized our aspirations for organizational design,

> Two types of learning are necessary in all organizations. The first is single-loop learning: learning that corrects errors by changing routine behavior.The second is double-loop learning: learning that corrects errors by examining the underlying values and policies of the organization. Picture, if you will, an "intelligent" thermostat that can evaluate whether or not 68 degrees is the right temperature for optimum efficiency.

The need for the thermostat that can see if and when the room needs to be 68 degrees requires an image of organizational processes that feedback information on both the internal and external environment. Third party government intensifies that need because the "smart" organization does not simply gather information, but instead information is interpreted by organizational members and the organizational processes they design. More attention to how we interpret both the internal and external environment becomes crucial and focuses our attention on organizational "cultures."

Popularized in the last decade, the organizational culture school reminds us to consider organizations as systems of shared meanings (e.g., Schein, 1985). According to this perspective, culture is the pattern of basic assumptions that is considered valid and, therefore, is taught to new members as the correct way to perceive, think, and feel in relation to recurring problems (Schein, 1985). The organization of any group, then, depends upon the existence of common modes of interpretation and shared understanding of experience (Smircich, 1983). What the leader stands for and communicates to others is considered important—his or her ability to give others a sense of understanding about the meanings of their behavior. From this perspective, contracting and partnerships represent in some cases, not only a disruption of everyday routines, but a possible disruption to the "meaning" of work within an agency and to the "meaning" of one's role in the public sector.

Questions that arise in many contracting and public/private partnerships include those concerning how work fits into the public sector if it can be contracted out; the transition necessary to move from a supervisor of action to one who monitors and evaluates; and how the public and private sector personnel understand the routines, limits, and mandates of each other's organizations. These questions arise in many contracting situations and, in general, public sector management has not prepared the organization for contracting, either in terms of managing the meaning of contracting out for a public organization, in explicating well to contracting agencies what working within the public sector means, or in training for surveillance and evaluation (DeHoog, 1985; Bernstein, 1991; Kettl, 1991).

Sense making of somewhat random events is aided by organizational culture. At the individual level, sense making is an activity in which individuals use their cognitive structures to perceive situations. Even though individuals may be the "carriers" of cultures within organizations, organizational members come to share common interpretations of events and actions and thus, collective interpretations do arise.

These interpretations are passed on through rituals, socialization of new members, and are reflected in processes, procedures, and regulations. The combinations of these sources "interpret" inside and outside activities and tell participants whether others are friends or foes, whether actions are productive or destructive. More specifically describing the components of culture, Sonja Sackman (1992) has recently delineated four different kinds of cultural knowledge: dictionary (commonly held descriptions, including labels and definitions used in a particular organization); directory (commonly held practices, knowledge about chains of events); recipes (prescriptions for repair and improvement); and axiomatic (reasons and explanations of the causes perceived to underlie a particular event).

Directory and dictionary knowledge have to be passed to co-producers in a systematic fashion if work is to progress. Training needs to be part of the move for government supervisors from roles of monitoring, not managing. Part of that monitoring role is an educator one of transferring organizational culture to coproducers, e.g., educating them in dictionary, directory, recipe, and axiomatic knowledge.

Sackman's concept of recipes is also thought provoking in terms of transferring work to contract, to partnership, or to disinvestment. Part of any governmental recipe for improvement includes a notion that "Government is a model employer, concerned with reflecting the diversity of the workforce and of protecting employees' benefits." In line with this cultural norm are procedures requiring that shifting work to other sectors does not unduly destroy diversity. Further, organizational members need to be prepared for transition through honest explanations of the process from the beginning and constant updates to quell rumors. A clear case must be made for the options for employees, both those directly and indirectly affected, to gain employment with the private sector involved and for the training or educational opportunities for those displaced. Since employee displacement is becoming more of a problem generally in our culture, government should take leadership in this realm.

Another effect of including the cultural variable should be the consideration of an organization's axiomatic reasoning—a consideration of how much contracting is too much before an organization loses the self-correcting ability of shared consensus and knowledge about what are appropriate responses. The tendency of classical theory to conceptualize work into units and subunits, rather than think in terms of the whole, does not address the protection of the holistic culture of an organization or organizational memory and learning. Not explicit in decisions of contracting, lack of consideration of the whole is often only lamented after the fact. The case of the Challenger incident for NASA where contracting employees outnumber government employees and probably added to the difficulties of decision making, may be a case in point.

Understanding each other's routines could help transitions go faster but also should assist in learning new techniques and management innovations from each other. In addition to the usual organizational aids of standard operating procedures, periodic assessments of how well the understanding of government personnel and private producers' concepts of the four kinds of cultural knowledge may prove valuable. For private-public relationships based closer to the discrete contract model, techniques, such as negotiation skills, conflict management, and control management should be part of any government agency's skill bank. For arrangements closer to relational contracting, techniques emphasizing a deeper shared understanding are more appropriate. Frank Blackler (1992) reports the work of those, including Y. Engestrom, who have pioneered a process of having coworkers examine their mirror images of recipes and axiomatic knowledge to work toward a consensus of expectations. However, a caution is in order here in that recipes and axiomatic knowledge are formed from a different base for the public sector and are more difficult to reconcile with the private sector than dictionary and directory knowledge.

LINKING
Because of its emphasis on hierarchy, much of classical theory does not

consider linkages, both the necessity for horizontal linkages among subunits of work within organizations and thick linkages among organizations. Images of work organizations still focus primarily on the internal arrangements of work and on control, rather than integration.

One focus of the theory in public organizations in the last decade has been an underlying systems orientation. An open systems perspective, popularized in the organizational literature and practitioner thinking in the 1970s, became dominant over the machine image of classical theory in the 1980s and is one of the pillars upon which current management philosophies, such as Total Quality Management, is built. The systems' perspective, characterized by a dominant metaphor of the organization as a biological organism, requires close attention to a holistic view of the organization; the input, processing, and output of energy; interdependencies with the environment; and the reduction of uncertainty to achieve control over or adapt to the environment.

NEED FOR INTERNAL LINKAGES

Involving the private sector in coproduction necessitates more attention to internal linkages within the flow of work among subunits of an organization. The tendency from classical theory is to think statically, to think in terms of specific units or subunits as boundaries for work. Quite often added to this tendency for public organizations is the necessity of keeping contracts small enough to allow small businesses to be competitive, adding to the necessity for dividing work into small units, boundaries that may be artificial. The reality of the work world, according to the insights of systems theory, however, is that work flows from one unit to another and that cooperation among units is necessary for completion.

Considering the workflow dictated by work technology should be useful. James D. Thompson's (1967) notion of serial interdependence, a description of workflow where B's production depends upon A's completion of a task as in an assembly line, is illustrative of the caution that must be taken when work is considered for contracting. Agencies who have attempted contracting out serial work, where agency tasks depended upon contractors producing work in the midst of an agency flow, have often found difficulties in completing work production. For example, contracting out the supply receiving dock in a federal agency, but retaining the receipt control in-house resulted in numerous squabbles. Goods were received by the contractor, but paperwork was processed by government personnel and then returned to the contractor before he could deliver goods. Timing and flow were constant sources of irritation.

One other advantage of considering workflow is the warning a look at work processes gives to the need for connections between private and private sectors either in terms of contracting or partnerships. If an agency contracts out two work functions, for example, supply and transportation, to two different contractors, the need to serve as mediator between them becomes an additional administrative role. In the case of partnerships, more than one contractor or subcontractor involvement may become a concern either directly or indirectly for the government demanding services. Thus, attention to workflow, not simply an assumption that the usual boundaries of a subunit represents the whole of the work, is important.

EXTERNAL LINKAGES

The focus on organizational survival and adaptability to the environment coalesced notions that no one organizational structure is suited for all situations. To this idea has been added a focus from political economy on the incentives that guide behavior in organizations and the incentives to link organizations. Building from the notion that the two means for organizing work were market mechanisms, incentives of price, and hierarchies, structures of authority (Williamson, 1985), recent literature in organizational theory posits a growing number of governing arrangements, forms that reside between markets and hierarchies. These may take the form of formal contracting relationships, quasi-public enterprises, and/or informal relationships of trust used to manage interorganizational dependencies and gain access to know-how unavailable in-house (Bradach and Eccles, 1989).

Price (market control), authority (hierarchical control), and trust (characteristic of "networks") all play a part in successful interorganizational relationships and ventures. To maintain these interorganizational networks, a new focus is needed on linkages, both formal and informal, and on the relationships among public-public, public-private, and private-private (Heilman and Johnson, 1992). A recent case study by John G. Heilman and Gerald W. Johnson (1992) on the public-private arrangements in wastewater treatment in the city of Auburn, Alabama is illustrative.

Heilman and Johnson note that because there were no national expectations and routines for proceeding with the wastewater partnership, public-public mechanisms had to be established through a change in state law. Formal power required a change in authority, a shift from the state to the local government and the building of a network of trust through agreements among the city, the legislature, and interest groups. In addition, private-private mechanisms were necessary. The private provider in the Auburn case reorganized authority vertically to better coordinate design and operations, as well as worked informally with contractors, subcontractors, and supplier to accomplish tasks more quickly, a combination of price mechanisms and building of a network of trust. Public to private mechanisms included also a guarantee to existing public employees to relocate within the public sector or remain with the wastewater treatment facility, price and authority combined. According to Heilman and Johnson (1992), these complex and varied interorganizational linkages provide a model form of comprehensive privatization. From the viewpoint of organizational theory, the case illustrates how the mechanisms of authority, price, and trust are all necessary in today's complex governing interactions.

Contracting represents somewhat of a different situation with recent literature positing that contracts often are not as well managed as they should be. Attention to linkages could help. In fact, recent literature in contracting (Kettner and Martin, 1986; DeHoog, 1985) has begun to explore different types of contracting. Building primarily upon the work of Ian MacNeil (1980) contracts can be seen on a continuum between the discrete contract, a performance contract of limited scope, and the relational contract, a longer term implied contract as seen in the relations among trusting partners (MacNeil, 1980). For new contracts or contracts of limited scope and defined tasks, more attention needs to be paid to control management (e.g., Anthony, 1988, and Swiss, 1991) with specified linking of public and private through quality control techniques and surveillance, a focus that combines price and authority (Kettl, 1992).

On the other hand, for situations involving long term contracts with proven suppliers, the possibility exists for forging more informal relationships based partially on trust and emphasizing flexibility. Although relational contracting is susceptible to opportunism and "cozy contracting," protection lies in the nonprofit or for-profit concern for reputation and desire to continue the relationship, a focus of the "network" approach.

LEGITIMATING: A NORMATIVE APPROACH

Some insight into organizations' axiomatic knowledge has come under a different name in public administration, that of the "normative approach." Whereas the study of cultural knowledge, directory, dictionary, axiomatic and recipe, focus more on the means of organizing, the patterns existing within and among organizations, the normative approach focusses on the why of public organizations. The normative approach includes an understanding of axiomatic reasoning in public organizations, but also reminds us that public organizations symbolically and realistically should have other important goals to accomplish along with efficient service delivery.

Although the normative approach has often focused on the responsibility and character of the administrator (e.g., see Harmon, 1989), the approach more consistent with much of current organizational theory reflects a concern for how public administration practices and agencies, as well as practitioners, are legitimate in a democratic government. In fact, the current controversy over privatization helped bring many of these concerns to the forefront.

Literature in the 1980s raised a concern that privatization as a movement was illegitimate in a disregard for the protection of the public interest (Carroll, 1987; Kolderie, 1986; Moe, 1986). The question of privatization as a threat to a needed strong public sector or the concern about the appropriateness of privatization techniques has not been resolved yet (e.g., see Savas, 1982, President's Council, 1983). Thus, the first lesson from the normative position is continually to engage whether, when, and what services should be considered for privatization. For that dialogue, some normative guidance is needed on the role of public administration within government, what authority agencies legitimately possess, and what authority can be delegated to other sectors.

One prescription is posited by John Rohr (1990) in a recent book on refounding public administration (Wamsley et al. 1990). Rohr recommends that the practice of public administration, including the running of public organizations, be conceptualized as a balance wheel, a balance wheel which must use its discretionary power to maintain the constitutional balance of powers in support of individual rights. Rohr reminds us that part of the socialization for those that take an oath to uphold the Constitution should be the development of both an appreciation of Constitutional principles and the attitudes necessary to think of themselves as men and women who "run a Constitution" (Rohr, 1990). In doing so, administrators must act like "statesmen," who avoid collapsing their judgment into managerial utilitarianism. Instead, like "statesmen," they must appreciate, understand, and think like judges, legislators, and executives. Because they are all three of these things in a regime of separation of powers, administrators are called upon to sometimes choose among competing powers, sometimes facilitate existing agreements (Rohr, 1990), but above all else learn what axioms and recipes are consistent with their constitutional parts in protecting individual rights.

The guidance of others writing in the normative tradition in *Refounding Public Administration* (Wamsley et al. 1990) both attends to the way in which we design and lead our public institutions and to the methods government uses to reach out to the community. Prescriptions include returning to a much needed revitalized concept of the public interest; assisting public administrators to become active catalysts for purposive, systemic direction in governance (Wamsley, 1990); linking practically and concretely professional competence, individual efforts and goals, and public purpose; reasserting a moral dialectical dialogue around the public interest, including engaging counter themes of political marketing, competitive spirit, anti-authoritarianism, and the building of conglomerates; and joining citizens with public administrators in interactive administrative governance.

These prescriptions are ones requiring not only powerful medicine, but time, effort, and learning to administer. Although reviews of the efforts to link public, private, and nonprofits have engaged the concept of the public interest in a limited fashion, more emphasis needs to be placed on all levels of government undergoing privatization to define and redefine their positions in governing. Only through an articulation of government's role vis a vis the other sectors can government legitimate the means through which services are produced and provided.

A systematic review of efforts made at socialization of both agency and contract employees is one place to begin: what are the messages, or lack thereof, that we give to those entering our organizations temporarily and permanently? Part of the socialization would include that of assisting members of an organization to accept that some work should be performed by the private sector and to prepare personnel for new roles regarding coproducers from different sectors.

A wise second course may be an attempt to surface our most important axiomatic knowledge and review how well dictionary, directory, and recipe knowledge fit with the axiomatic. This can be accomplished both by a researching of assumptions behind policies and by gaining an understanding of how practices are implemented. For example, examining the rules about confidentiality and corresponding openness to citizen requests for a task to be performed by another sector is crucial. Ingrained also into nearly every government task to a larger degree than the nonprofit or market is concern about due process, consensus of those affected, and safety. Since public agencies generally serve many constituents, a review should surface points of tensions, acknowledge them, and suggest guidance on how to resolve them situation by situation. Representatives of an individual government agency which has some clarity in its own policies and procedures can more successfully link with representatives of other sectors.

Finally, as one reviews the literature on contracting and third party governance one emphasis is missing—that of citizen involvement—the missed opportunity. Because privatization has been seen as merely another management decision, the privatization debate has been confined to either the arguments of academia or the palaver of practitioners. The few exceptions of community involvement have centered around acrimonious debate between unions and government. Both voices are certainly important, but the creation of a different way of governing–through third parties–should have involved more citizen participation. Does the entrance of other sectors, whether volunteer, nonprofit, or business, allow more opportunity for citizen involvement–more of a chance for government to create "local communities"—or does it offer simply more "game-playing" with government seen as the one to outsmart? (Bernstein, 1992).

SUMMARY AND IMPLICATIONS

Managers will need to work at combining service delivery systems in ways that take advantage of each and that increase the likelihood of co-production among them, whether that be channeling competition or building trust. Lessons from the current theories of organizational structure alert those entering arrangements to understand and rethink their own "cultures" in terms of dictionary, directory, recipe, and axiomatic knowledge.

Second, a "systems" approach admonishes designers of delivery systems to focus on both internal and external linkages and to assess possibilities in terms of the number and types of incentives available to them. Blending the inducements of price, authority, and trust in proportions appropriate to the privatization situation must be considered. The simultaneous use of both an in-house authority structure and contracting may allow for retention of organizational memory, expertise, and opportunities to ensure that a broader concept of the public interest is preserved. In cases where unions are involved or employees displaced, negotiation, mediation, and, finally, representing government interests in administrative hearings may be skills needed. Where interorganizational trust is the main linking mechanisms, learning new methods of resolving conflicts and promoting consensus may be necessary.

Finally, an improved conception of public service and the place of public administration in a constitutional order seems mandated. The case built here is that the organizational theory heretofore implicit in our designs of organizations and the metaphors of insiders and outsiders seriously impede the realities with which managers must deal in the 1990s world of governing.

The lessons, then, from these different strands of current organizational theory, remind us of the opportunities and cautions involved with bringing together organizations from different sectoral bases. Since privatization takes places within and among public and private organizations, public managers and other voices—academics, politicians, the press, unions—have an obligation to review how the means of government reflect the ends government should promote. It is important for those in the public sector to review the best ways to mix the incentives of price, authority, and trust and to find ways to articulate the meaning of provision of services to the public. Service provision must take place within an ethos of articulated ethics based on a sense of the public organization's mission, culture, and constitutional mandates. The way in which services are delivered, as much as what services are delivered, says much to citizens about the concept of community and public regard.

REFERENCES

Anthony, R. N. (1988). *The Management Control Function*. Boston: Harvard Business School Press.

Argyris, C. (1993). "Education for Leading-Learning." *Organizational Dynamics*. 21, no. 3: Winter: 5-18.

Asher, K. (1987). *The Politics of Privatization: Contracting Out Public Services*. New York: St. Martin's Press.

Bernstein, S. R. (1991). *Managing Contracted Services in the Non-Profit Agency: Administrative, Ethical and, Political Issues*. Philadelphia: Temple University Press.

Blackler, F. (1992). "Formative Contexts and Activity Systems: Postmodern Approaches to the Management of Change." In M. Reed and M. Hughes, eds., *Rethinking Organizations: New Directions in Organization Theory and Analysis*: pp. 273-294.

Bradach, J. L., and R. G. Eccles (1991). "Price, Authority, and Trust: From Ideal Types to Plural Forms." In G. Thompson, J. Frances, R. Levacic, and J. Mitchell, eds., *Markets, Hierarchies, and Networks: The Coordination of Social Life*. London: Sage.

Carroll, J. D. (1987) "Public Administration in the Third Century of the Constitution: Supply-Side Management, Privatization, or Public Investment?" *Public Administration Review,* January/February: pp. 107-112.

DeHoog, R. H. (1985). "Human Services Contracting: Environmental, Behavioral, and Organizational Conditions." *Administration and Society* 164, February: pp. 427-454.

DeHoog, R. H. (1984). *Contracting Out for Human Services: Economic, Political, and Organizational Perspectives*. Albany: SUNY Press.

Dudley, L. S. (1990). "Contractual Governance: Theory and Practice in Circular A-76." Unpublished dissertation. Blacksburg, Virginia: Center for Public Administration and Policy, Virginia Tech.

Harmon, M. M., and R. T. Mayer (1989). *Organization Theory for Public Administration*. Boston: Little, Brown.

Heilman, J. G., and G. W. Johnson (1992). *The Politics and Economics of Privatization: The Case of Wastewater Treatment*. Tuscaloosa: The University of Alabama Press.

Kettl, D. F. (1991). "Privatization: Implications for the Public Work Force." In O. C. Ban, and N. M. Riccucci, *Public Personnel Management: Current Concerns—Future Challenges*. White Plains, NY: Longman.

Kettner, P. M. and L. L. Martin (1986). "Making Decisions About Purchase of Service Contracting." *Public Welfare*. 44, No. 4, Fall: pp. 30-37.

Kolderie, T. (1986). "The Two Different Concepts of Privatization." *Public Administration Review*. July/August: pp. 285–344.

MacNeil, I. (1980). *The New Social Contract: An Inquiry into Modern Contractual Relations*. New Haven: Yale University.

Moe, D. C. (1986). "Privatization: An Overview from the Perspective of Public Administration." Report No. 86-134 Gov HD 3840, June 30. Washington, DC: Congressional Research Service, The Library of Congress.

President's Private Sector Survey on Cost Control (1983). *Report of Privatization*. Washington, DC:. U.S. Government Printing Office.

Sackman, S. (1992). *Administrative Science Quarterly* no.2, July-August: pp. 194-221.

Salamon, L. M. (1989). *Beyond Privatization: The Tools of Government Action*. Washington, D. C.: The Urban Institute.

Savas, E. S. (1982). *Privatizing the Public Sector: How To Shrink Government*. Chatham, NJ: Chatham House.

Schein, E. H. (1985). *Organizational Culture and Leadership*. San Francisco: Jossey-Bass.

Seidman, H. (1997). *Politics, Position, and Power: The Dynamics of Federal Organization*. New York: Oxford University Press.

Smircich, L. (1983). "Organizations as Shared Meanings." In L. R. Pondy and others, eds., *Organizational Symbolism*. Greenwich, CT: JAI Press: pp. 55-65.

Swiss, J. E. (1991). *Public Management Systems: Monitoring and Managing Government Performance*. Englewood Cliffs, NJ: Prentice-Hall.

Thompson, J. (1967). *Organizations In Action*. New York: McGraw-Hill.

Wamsley, G. L., et al. (1990). *Refounding Public Administration*. Newbury Park: Sage Publications.

Weick, K. (1979). *The Social Psychology of Organizing*. 2nd Edition. Reading, MA: Addison-Wesley.

Williamson, O. (1975). *Markets and Hierarchy: Analysis and Antitrust Implications*. New York: Free Press.

Chapter 4

Developing a Privatization Strategy Using Competitive Bidding, Cooperative Partnerships, and Networks

Frank W. Davis, Jr.

The Nobel laureate James Buchanan initiated much of the interest in privatization by emphasizing that government financing of an activity is not the same as government production of a service—they are two distinct and separate functions. He said, "Governmental financing of goods and services must be divorced from direct governmental provision or production of these goods and services" (Buchanan, 1977).

Although complete privatization would have government turn both financing and operations over to the private sector, many have tried to equate privatization with "contracting out" all public service under the assumption that the private sector is uncategorically a more cost-effective provider of services than is government. This is a very simplistic view that is based on a very simplistic view of procurement.

It is too easy for procurement departments to view their jobs too narrowly. It is sometimes too easy for procurement groups to state authoritatively that their role is to make sure that all of the legal requirements specified in the Federal Acquisition Regulations (FAR) are followed. This very narrow view of procurement misses the primary concept behind privatization and the very flexible FAR.

From a broader perspective, privatization has five basic objectives. The first is to improve delivery effectiveness to the user. There are often two users whose needs must be met: the public agency and the beneficiary. In the case of public transportation, the agency may be the transportation authority. The beneficiary may be not only the riders but also the drivers who support transit to reduce congestion. For the service to be effective, it must meet the needs of riders sufficiently for them to use the service. If the service is not effective in meeting individual riders' needs, they will not ride. If they do not ride, the service is not effective in accomplishing the drivers' goal of reducing congestion. Unless both of these users' needs are met, the service is not effective in meeting the authority's goals, which may be as diverse as reducing congestion, improving air quality, increasing employment opportunities for residents of public housing projects, or reducing the high school dropout rate.

Privatization's second objective is to increase flexibility for both the agency and the beneficiaries. Every organization wants to be flexible so it can be responsive. It wants to be responsive to changing customer needs, changing environmental conditions, changing competition, and changing government goals. Privatization should not simply replace an institutionalized public service with an institutionalized private service. The source or reasons for the inflexibilities are immaterial. Inflexibilities for whatever reason limit the organization from adapting to changing user needs, changing environments, and changing goals.

Privatization's third objective is to become more self-administering. Services become self-administering when provider selection is based on delivery effectiveness, not political maneuvering. The strength of the free market is that it is largely self-administering. Users select the provider that best meets their needs.

The fourth objective of privatization is to help reduce the economic cost of providing services. This can be done in several ways. The traditional approach was to let competition rather than the political process establish prices. Another equally important method is to increase utilization ratios. Hotels, consultants, and truck lines use measures of utilization to show the percent of capacity used to generate revenue. The terms include occupancy rates, percent billable hours, percent deadheading, and load factors.

Finally, privatization's fifth objective should minimize the noneconomic cost ("hassle") of obtaining service—issuing requests for proposals (RFPs), selecting and evaluating proposals, waiting for potential providers responses, resolving conflicts, preparing contracts, changing contracts to address new needs, and all the administrative overhead of obtaining the needed services. Hassle is especially evident when needs change, since all groups seem to resist change.

The overall objective of privatization is to provide a more flexible, responsive service that better fits the needs of the agency and the beneficiary at lower cost and with less hassle. In other words, the objective of privatization is to make the service more cost-effective. Whether these concepts go by the term reinventing government, reengineering, (Hammer and Champy, 1993) (Stewart, 1993) service response logistics (Davis and Manrodt, 1991) (Davis and Manrodt, 1992) or privatization, the objective is all the same—how to make organizations and the services they provide more flexible so they can be more responsive and more cost-effective.

The purpose of this chapter is to describe the evolution that is occurring in management and economic thought as they relate to procurement and show how these principles apply to government privatization efforts. Although these concepts have developed primarily in the private sector, the same principles also form the foundation for evolving public sector privatization concepts.

EVOLVING MANAGEMENT THOUGHT

Business management has evolved through three stages. The first two stages are familiar–the traditional production stage and the total quality management (TQM) stage. The third stage, the flexible response model, is now evolving. Because each of these approaches to management is based on very different economic assumptions, it is only natural that the purchasing efforts necessary to support these activities be based on very different economic assumptions (Davis, et al., 1989). The focus of this chapter is explanation of the following points:

1. Competitive purchasing methods were based on the economic assumptions implicit in traditional production.
2. Industrial partnershipping methods are based on the assumptions implicit in the TQM approach to management.
3. Networking methods evolve as firms seek more flexible access to resources so they in turn can be more responsive to changing needs.

Furthermore, the FAR provides for each of these concepts. Competitive procurement relies on invitations for bids. The partnership models are implemented primarily through requests for proposals. Networking can be implemented using creative supply schedules or requirements contracts.

THE TRADITIONAL PURCHASING MODEL

The traditional approach to production is based on microeconomics theory developed by Adam Smith in 1776 (Smith, 1952) and later refined by Alfred Marshall (Marshall, 1989). The original economic model saw the firm as an organization that obtained raw materials that it used to produce a product. In this model, developed during the 1700s and 1800s, resources were considered to be commodities, whether cotton, beef, or iron. Even labor was considered to be unskilled, as it truly was at that time.

This belief was so pervasive that labor was not defined by skill but by the generic term "hands." Even when organizations recognized that different jobs needed different skills, jobs applicants were not evaluated on skill levels but rather whether they met minimum requirements for the specific job. When inputs were basic, undifferentiated commodities, the only basis for selecting a provider was price and availability.

Under this model there were two ways to change costs. First, the firm could obtain resources at a lower purchase price and second, the resources could be blended in different ways in the production process. Just as the firm could substitute capital for labor, so could it blend any other resources to minimize costs. Microeconomics texts would combine these two concepts and say that the firm would operate where the ratio of marginal physical products (MPP) to prices (P) was the same for all inputs.

Purchasing was responsible for reducing acquisition costs (P), and production was responsible for blending resources. Thus, traditional production economics provided purchasing with two methods for controlling resource costs:

Increase the Size of Purchase

This approach assumes that the larger the purchase, the lower the unit cost. This belief was so strong that the Robinson-Patman Act of 1936, focused on protecting local merchants from the new chain stores, recognized that price differences based on purchase size were justified even if unpopular.

Control the Market Structure

Market structure theory, developed in the early 1930s, (Robinson, 1933) (Chamberlin, 1933) became the heart of purchasing thought. Although Robinson recognized that pure competition seldom existed, procurement thought stated that prices are lowest in purely competitive markets and highest in monopolistic markets. Therefore, purchasing had to make sure there were multiple providers and that quotes were competitive.

With time, additional costs, which traditionally had been ignored in the basic economics models, began to be considered as part of the purchase price. By the late 1800s, transportation cost became important as the railroads evolved to the point where firms actually had the option of multiple sourcing from vendors located in different geographic areas. The transportation rate structure provided very large differences between car load (CL) and less than carload (LCL) rates. The timing of the purchase became important, and purchasing agents became even more concerned about the cost of carrying inventory. Firms also began recognizing the cost of placing an order. From these factors, firms began developing models for calculating the optimum economic order quantity (EOQ). The tradeoffs between the cost of carrying inventory and the cost of placing an order were considered in these models.

Purchasing agents, familiar with traditional microeconomics assumptions, realized that their job was to define needs (or collect them from operating departments), consolidate requirements (economies of scale), "go out for competitive bid," select the most responsive provider, and develop backup providers to handle unforeseen contingencies.

In the traditional model the emphasis on competition created an adversarial relationship between buyer and seller. Everyone "knew" that when competitors share information (collaborate) on pricing, the market was no longer competitive. In fact, this information sharing leads to pricefixing charges. Sellers are also aware of the power of the buyer to gain information about innovations from various sellers to blend the best of each offering to his or her advantage.

Therefore, relationships tend to be "arm's length," with limited information sharing between buyer and seller. This may lead to the assumption that the process of buying and selling is a "zero-sum" game; that is, the gains of one party are necessarily the loss of the other. This stimulates an antagonistic relationship between buyers and sellers, with each side taking elaborate steps to minimize the other party's bargaining power. Bargaining power can be limited by controlling the flow of competitive information about both the product and its price. This approach to purchasing with its many variations is well understood. In fact, it is so well understood that too many in procurement feel it is the only way to make public purchases. When that is done, mistakes are made that prevent the accomplishment of privatization goals.

In spite of the widespread acceptance of the competitive model in both business and government, it is rapidly being questioned and changed. The change is because of a fundamental rethinking of the economics of the firm initiated by the TQM movement.

TOTAL QUALITY MOVEMENT IDENTIFIES NEW SOURCES OF COSTS

With the TQM movement came recognition of additional costs of using resources. Once these costs were recognized, they could be managed. Juran (Juran and Gryna, 1980) developed a cost of quality accounting system. In his system he identified the following components:

1. Appraisal costs required to inspect and examine material to determine that it is not defective. Because the cost of usage is more important than purchase price, the cost of inspecting purchases must be added.
2. Internal failure costs caused by scrapping and/or reworking defective parts. The cost of using defective parts and then having to scrap or repair the final assembly also has to be added to purchase cost.
3. External failure costs incurred when defects are not discovered until the product reaches the field. Premature failure of parts is very expensive in terms of field repair, unhappy customers, and the scrapping of high-value assemblies of which the defective part is only one component. External failure cost also must be added to the cost of a purchased item.
4. Prevention costs incurred by the purchaser to monitor and control the quality of the purchased resources. Prevention cost also must be added to purchase price, ideally, by increasing prevention costs the firm can reduce other costs.

Crosby (1979) emphasized that "quality is free" if you organize to avoid defects. If the procurement process is controlled tightly so no defective parts are received, then many of these four costs can be reduced. According to his estimate, defects accounted for between 15 and 20 percent of total production costs. As long as you pay less than 20 percent more for zero defects, "quality is free."

Deming (1982) used statistical process control, developed by Walter Shewart at Bell Labs in the 1930s, to show that 85 percent of all errors were not caused by the workers but by the processes designed by management. He emphasized the need for consistency in processes and continual improvement. Consistency in process requires consistency in inputs. This led Deming to the realization that a key to maintaining continual improvement is the relationship between the customer and supplier. He advocated the development of a cooperative relationship between customer and supplier rather than the traditional arms-length one.

Deming has suggested that the provider must know and understand what the customers want and how they want to use it. This will reduce the costs of failures because of inappropriate inputs to the production process. He has recommended that firms should select suppliers based not on low purchase price alone but on the total cost of using the supplies. He has encouraged the cultivation of long-term relationships with fewer suppliers so that the suppliers can be trained to meet the needs of the customer more exactly. Because there is greater variation in the parts provided by multiple providers than in parts obtained from a single supplier, Deming has advised firms to limit the number of suppliers. Thus, the total quality movement changed procurement practice in two ways:

Cost is determined by total cost of usage rather than just purchase price.
The relationship between buyer and seller shifted from adversarial to cooperative. The Japanese call this process Kaizen.

"Kaizen means ongoing improvement involving everyone-top management, managers, and workers" (Imai, 1986). Everyone is not limited to just employees but also includes suppliers. Purchasers began seeing the role of the provider as being more than the supplier of a single component. The supplier also has the know-how and technology that can be tapped. Why not use this know-how to help design the product? Why not inform the supplier of the firm's needs and have the supplier develop the most cost-effective method of meeting that need? Why not take advantage of the supplier's know-how at the earliest stage of the design process? Why not define what the product should look like; set the price, lead time, and performance goals; and ask the supplier to become part of the design team? After all, who should know more about brakes than brake manufacturers? Who should know more about tires than tire manufacturers? That is the supplier's core competence. Why expect the suppliers to be limited to designing and producing the component? Why not provide the suppliers with the firm's production schedule and let them develop the most cost-effective method of getting the component to the production line? Why pay only for components? Why not pay for contributions to the firm's finished product?

Before the firm can take advantage of the supplier's know-how, the firm must establish a different type of relationship with the supplier. This relationship must be based on two-way communication, mutual gain, and trust. The better each party understands the needs and operational constraints of the other, the more options become evident. As these additional options become evident, the firm realizes that its ability to serve customers is no longer limited to its own resources. It now has access to the know-how and technology of its suppliers to help design its offering to its customers. As this happens, the relationship shifts from adversarial to cooperative. In an adversarial relationship, both parties contest each point of the current transaction so they can win as much as possible. In the cooperative model, both parties see the long-term value of future business being so much greater than the value of any current transaction that they both have a strong incentive to work it out and preserve the relationship. They also recognize the importance of understanding the purchaser's needs so that they can make suggestions to improve the relationship. This requires the free flow of information across all members of the channel and the mutual objective of meeting the needs of the final customer. This requires that the relationship between supplier and purchaser must be based on mutual trust.

As suppliers and purchasers work together, both parties obtain value from the relationship: the suppliers by obtaining steady, reliable customers and thus cash source, and the customers by decreased quality costs and thus increased total profits and satisfaction to their customers. There is a continuous incentive to reduce and resolve conflicts for both parties because the value of the relationship is based on its long-term nature and is much more important than "winning" an argument over a single transaction. This continual relationship and continuous incentive is the basis for continuous improvement in responding to the customers. The value of a relationship is determined by the ability of both partners to make collective innovations that increase market share by serving final customers better.

COOPERATIVE (COLLABORATIVE) PARTNERSHIP (MODELS)

The competitive model works well when the needs are totally defined, there are many suppliers, and there is virtually no difference in the ability of various providers to make deliveries. Competition can be very effective for construction projects or the purchase of products where the need is totally defined before the invitation for bid (IFB) is released. The more changes that must be made during the life of the contract, the more important the cooperative nature of the relationship. Likewise, the more important the technical know-how, service, variation in delivery methods, variation in needs, and varying requirement rates, the more important it is to develop cooperative relationships. The key is to know when to use each approach.

Cooperative partnership implementation is much different from the traditional procurement model. Instead of vendor selection being based on the vendor's response to a single request, selection is based on expectations that the supplier can be the most effective contributor to the cooperative effort. Emphasis is on evaluating the providers' know-how and ability to interact with the agency in making changes as the project evolves. The selected supplier is expected to work with the agency to evaluate and modify both the provider's and the agency's delivery processes and operating procedures so that goals are accomplished. As firms begin to work more closely with suppliers, they discover that it takes effort to create an effective relationship. Because of this effort (and experience that variation between suppliers is greater than within suppliers), industrial purchasers have begun to reduce the number of suppliers. As the number of relationships are reduced, both supplier and purchaser become more dependent on each other, so the selection process must be made carefully. No longer is the purchasing department simply buying a single item; instead, they are entering into a long-term cooperative effort to accomplish agency and client goals.

Supplier evaluation efforts may be based on a system of tiered certification where current and potential suppliers are categorized into various tiers based on a wide variety of factors. Examples of this type of tiered system are the James River Corporation's approved, qualified, preferred, and certified (Cayer and Morgan, 1991); Carrier Corporation's unacceptable, normal, long-term contract, alliance and partner (Cayer and Morgan, 1992); and Tenant Corporation's non-qualified, qualified, preferred and select.

Typically, the top-tier is assured of a continual relationship with the purchaser as long as it continues to be so classified. The second-tier can expect to receive contracts with the provider as well as assistance and training to become a top-tier provider. The third-tier organizations know what is required to obtain first or second-tier classification but cannot expect extensive purchaser assistance in reaching it. Such a tiered system encourages suppliers to make changes in order to be moved into a higher tier.

A tiered system is not sufficient to shift relationships from adversarial to cooperative. The shift is determined by the criteria used to classify suppliers into the categories. If the selection criteria are still cost, technical, and management, the relationship remains adversarial. If the criteria are expanded to include factors such as a common strategic purpose of providing and continually improving the delivery of customer value, organizational compatibility (e.g., culture, information), vision, stability, and innovativeness, then it is becoming cooperative.

Once a supplier has been selected, efforts are made to integrate that supplier into the organization's operations. Don Bechtel has described the WalMart-P&G partnership as bringing the provider's and the customer's technical equivalents together to work on common issues, whether they be information, accounting, financial, marketing, or logistics. Each group identifies pressure points, identifies opportunities for improving cost-effectiveness, and develops joint strategies for implementation. "The mission of the joint WalMart-Procter & Gamble business industries to better serve our mutual customer--the consumer." The operating principles are trust, confidentiality, adherence to both firm's policies, an understanding that encourages disagreement, and the open sharing of data common to both groups. Emphasis is on issues, not positions.

Another example of placing supplier employees on the customer's site is Bose Corporation's JIT-II system. These employees work on everything from cooperative design to paperless ordering where the in-plant employee does the ordering rather than the buying firm.

Cooperative partnerships with a limited number of providers are appropriate where the customer has a long-term, fairly predictable requirement for supplies or services. Government contracts for many partnerships. For example, contracts are negotiated to operate toll roads, manage airports, operate transit systems, and provide janitorial service for buildings. It is not unusual for these projects to have a life of 5 to 10 years. Neither partner can define clearly what is needed when a request for proposal (RFP) is issued. Therefore, the primary consideration for selecting a provider is not just price but the ability of the firm to respond to the dynamics of the relationship and user needs. Once the relationship becomes adversarial, the relationship is over, and delivery is not effective for the agency, the client, or the provider.

Many organizations do not conform to the preceding model. What about organizations that are expected to respond to widely differing client needs? How are these needs met best? Cooperative networks are applicable for firms that take a customer-responsive rather than an offering or operational approach to doing business. The offering approach to doing business is shown in Figure 4.1.

According to the offering approach model of the organization, the firm decides what product or service it wants to offer its customers. It then sets up an organization to produce the offering (product) to inventory, which it distributes to the market place where it is sold to the customer, who consumes it to derive the desired benefits.

Responsive organizations operate in a very different manner. Such organizations are based on the concept of developing the resources (capability and capacity) to respond to a range of needs and creating a process for coordinating delivery. Instead of the customers going to the marketplace to select from what is offered, the individual customer approaches an organization in which that individual has confidence. The customer is met with the greeting, "How can I help you?" The customer and organization interact to diagnose the customer's individual needs, and the organization puts together a customized

Figure 4.1
Traditional Offering or Operating Model

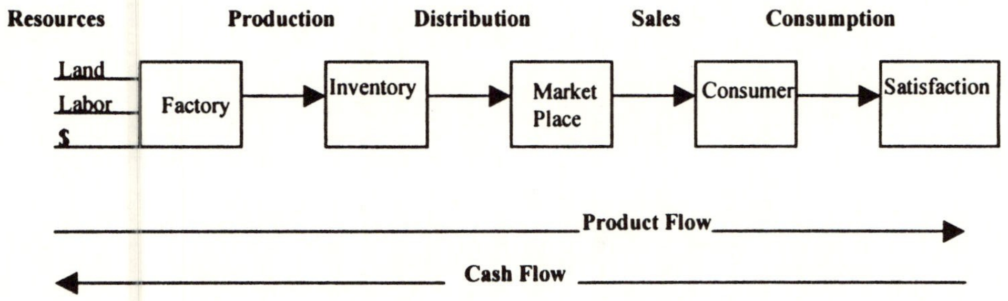

| Resources | Production | Distribution | Sales | Consumption |

Land
Labor
$

Factory → Inventory → Market Place → Consumer → Satisfaction

Product Flow

Cash Flow

delivery that meets the individual customer's needs. Instead of trying to sell the person what the firm wants to produce, the responsive organization attempts to organize resources dynamically to meet the individual customer's needs. The responsive model is shown in Figure 4.2.

Responsive organizations such as hospitals, consultants, travel agencies, systems integrators, contract logistics firms, value-added resellers, and brokers continually look for a greater range of resources that can be used to respond to customer needs. Hospitals may use their own laboratories for routine tests but send other specimens out to a network of specialty labs for other tests. The larger the network, the greater the hospital's ability to respond to customers. Primary emphasis is on effectively meeting the customer's need, not keeping in-house delivery units busy.

In some cases the firm will network with a large number of providers, and in other cases the firm will develop a partnership with a networking firm. For example, many firms use temporary employment firms to meet fluctuating needs for staff. The temporary personnel firm maintains a large network of individuals with varying skills; that pool may have a range from physicians and engineers, to clerical workers and manual laborers. In like manner, some firms will network with a large number of transportation and warehousing firms, whereas other companies will contract with a single, third-party logistics firm that specializes in coordinating a distribution network.

Response-based organizations cannot predict their future requirements accurately for two basic reasons. First, responsive organizations typically must have a greater diversity of capabilities, as they respond to a wide variety of individual customer needs. Because of the potential diversity of responses, they need access to a great diversity of competences. For example, it is not unusual for a large hospital to have 600 to 1,000 different physicians, each with very different skills, on its staff. Staff physicians are not employees of the hospital but rather independent physicians in private practice who have been granted the medical privileges of using hospital facilities. The hospital does not need the specialists full-time, but it does need instant access when the specific skill is needed.

A second reason for building a large network is that responsive units must be able to respond to demand levels that vary dramatically over time. For example, security companies need a large workforce during surge periods such as sporting events and rock concerts but may have very limited requirements at other times.

The ability of a response-based organization to meet its customers' needs is limited by the firm's capability (what it can do) and capacity (how much it can do).

Figure 4.2
Responsive Model of Organization

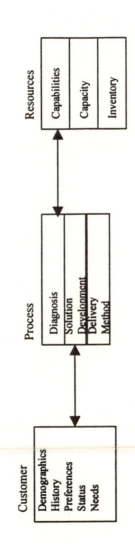

The economic basis of profitability for response-based firms is significantly different from that for firms that produce a product to inventory. Without inventory, unused capacity is wasted. Typically, there are three categories of costs for these organizations:

Fixed capacity costs (FCC), those long-term costs incurred in order to be in business (e.g., airport facilities, airplanes);
Scheduled capacity costs (SCC), those costs incurred when the capacity is scheduled and whether or not it is used (e.g., flight crews, fuel, maintenance);
Service delivery costs (SDC), those costs incurred when the service actually is delivered (e.g., in-flight meals, travel agents' commissions).

Typically, the service delivery costs constitute less than 10 percent of the total cost of delivering the service to the ultimate consumer. The remaining 90 percent is incurred whether or not a service is delivered. Therefore, profitability of the firm depends on reducing the fixed and scheduled capacity costs and increasing the percent utilization. Consultants track billable hours; hotels monitor bookings; trucking companies track load factors and balance. By any name, percent utilization is the portion of available capacity actually delivered to a firm's customers. In contrast, school districts may buy large fleets of buses that operate one hour each morning and evening for only 180 school days. Even when the buses are in use, approximately half of the mileage may be empty as they go from garage to the beginning of the route. Actual cost that must be paid by the school board may be reduced by developing a network of individual bus owners who can provide services to other groups during the day.

In order to respond to diverse customer needs, the organization must have access to a wide range of capabilities. To control costs, the firm must maintain a high percent utilization. To accomplish both of these objectives, the firm must establish a network of suppliers who are always on call and who can be utilized at a moment's notice. From a capacity cost perspective, it may be more efficient on a per-hour basis to have the resource in house, but on a per-use basis, it is more efficient to network. Thus, the network approach to cooperation allows the accomplishment of two basic goals: greater ability to respond to customers' needs (effectiveness) and reduction in the cost of the response (efficiency).

When establishing relationships with suppliers, a firm must decide whether there is sufficient ongoing requirements to merit establishment of a cooperative partnership with each supplier. Where requirements are variable in type and amount, cooperative networks can be established. The more diverse the potential resource needs, the broader the network necessary to provide access to more core competencies (capability). The greater the variation in capacity needs, the great the depth of the network, thus providing the capacity required for each core competency. The criteria for selecting network members are similar to those for cooperative partnerships.

The challenge to cooperative networks is to establish procedures that facilitate the interaction between the response-based firm and its suppliers. Examples of such procedures include the following:

1. Searching procedures—When its customer has a special need, the response-based firm must have networked with a supplier that has the appropriate capabilities and capacity to respond. Most response-based firms will have a data base of potential providers showing their capabilities, capacity, responsiveness, effectiveness, and costs.
2. Start-up procedures—Any time a new relationship is established, many details must be worked out and understandings reached. This takes time and effort but must be recognized as an investment in establishing capability and capacity just as there is investment in plant and equipment for an inventory-based firm. Typically, lawyers work on retainers, consultants establish letters of agreement, and carriers maintain tariffs. Once these are in place, getting delivery of services can be as simple as a phone call.
3. Transaction procedures—A responsive organization cannot be any more responsive than its suppliers. Thus response-based organizations typically use dispatching methods rather than scheduling methods. Toyota uses Kanbans to let its suppliers know what is wanted and when. Wal-Mart uses scanned data to transmit requests to distribution centers each morning. These procedures not only make interaction more responsive but also lower the cost of each transaction.
4. Coordination procedures—In cooperative partnerships, there is a limited number of organizations involved. In cooperative networks, many organizations may be working on a single project. It is very important to establish procedures for assuring that functional groups from each organization are working together. The necessary infrastructure often is information based.
5. Communication procedures—There must be a point person. Someone must take responsibility for processing all communication in a cooperative network. Consultants establish project managers, vendors have an on-site person, and hospitals use an admitting physician to coordinate communications.

There are many examples of cooperative networks. FTD, for example, has developed a network of florists who sell and deliver floral arrangements over widely scattered geographical locations. Hospitals typically develop a network of labs, physicians, pharmaceutical distributors, therapists, and other suppliers to provide a wide range of services to patients when needed. In each case, the purpose of the network is to make service easy to obtain when needed to serve a customer without incurring the cost of idle capacity when it is not needed.

SELECTING THE BEST APPROACH FOR GOVERNMENT PROCUREMENT

There is no one best approach for all purchasing. The best approach for a given purchase must be based on the economic assumptions about the item or service being procured. These can be summarized as follows:

If the need is defined totally in advance and no changes are expected over the life of the contract, traditional competitive bidding is preferred.

If the agency is looking for a long-term relationship where the contractor supplies extensive know-how to perform a generally understood mission, then the RFP approach works well. It allows the agency to understand the provider's know-how and capability. Special attention should be given to cooperativeness in responding to changing conditions.

If the needs are expected to vary widely, then networks should be developed and cultivated. Creative supply schedules and requirements contracts can be used for the process.

Procurement works well when the purchasing department understands the need and can develop delivery strategies consistent with the economics of the situation. When the wrong procurement strategies are used, problems can make a mockery out of the procurement process.

EFFECT OF INAPPROPRIATE PROCUREMENT STRATEGIES

Perhaps the most effective method of illustrating the results of poorly thought out procurement strategy is to give examples. These can be considered within several broad categories.

Use of Competitive Bidding for Undefined Need

Imagine an individual working for a transportation agency that serves elderly and handicapped clients. This individual attends a meeting in which organizations are admonished to make better use of private providers. The individual enthusiastically requests bids for private operators to provide service to elderly and handicapped clients for the next year. Imagine the following dialogue between the agency and a potential provider:

Q. "How long is the contract period?"
A. "One year."
Q. "How many people will be transported?"
A. "It depends on how many people need rides and qualify for the program."
Q. "Where will the trips originate?"
A. "That depends upon where the people live."

Q. "Where are the trips to?"

A. "It depends on the purpose of the trip. Some people go to meal sites, others to health care facilities, and some will go to stores or recreational facilities."

Q. "When will they need transportation?"

A. "It depends on when they schedule their appointments. You know how difficult it is to schedule appointments with doctors."

Q. "How long will the trips be?"

A. "It depends on where the clients live and where they need to go."

Q. "What kind of bid do you want?"

A. "Preferably a fixed amount for the year because this will make it easier for us to budget for the service. An alternative will be a fixed price for each trip with a guarantee that no one will have to wait more than 30 minutes and that the prices will not change during the year."

The bidder, attempting to understand how these needs will integrate with his or her existing business, may be at a total loss about how to bid. Can the service be provided with existing vehicles and drivers? Can fixed routes be established, or will each vehicle only be able to transport a single rider on each trip? Because the needs are not explicit, the bidder may perceive only two alternatives. The bidder can pad the bid to cover the uncertainties or else refuse to bid. In either case, the agency funding the service may believe that the bids are too high or that no one is interested in providing the service. A perceptive agency may recognize that bidders do not have enough information upon which to bid. The less perceptive agencies may simply purchase vehicles and provide the service themselves (assuming no potential providers are available) and use the high bid price to show how a long-wait, advance-reservation, in-house system is less expensive than a privatized service based on quick-response individualized service.

The more perceptive agency, recognizing the need to be more definitive in the bidding process, may structure a bid that includes a definition of what it needs. As the agency develops specifications, the agency staff realize it is impossible to know details of individual trips in advance. Frequently, the agency does not have adequate records to do an effective job of forecasting trips by origin, destination, and schedule. If the agency makes a forecasting error, the contractor may attempt to renegotiate the contract or reduce service levels. Thus, to avoid the hassle of coping with uncertainty, the next step is for agency personnel or a consultant to follow traditional planning methodology. However it is accomplished, the output typically will be an organizational plan. This plan then can be used as the basis for the procurement process. The bid specification might be as follows:

"The agency is accepting bids to provide 6 vans each with seating capacity for at least 6 adults and 2 wheelchairs. Vehicles will have wheelchair ramps and tie-downs equivalent to Apex model 2000 or equivalent. The contractor will have at least 12 fully qualified drivers who have been trained in CPR, passenger assistance techniques, and defensive driving. The contractor will have a radio dispatch system with radios in each vehicle and at least 3 incoming telephone lines to the dispatch center. The dispatch center will be staffed from 7 a.m. to 8 p.m. every day except Christmas, New Year's Day, Thanksgiving and Easter."

This example has been used to illustrate that the agency is not able to predefine client needs any better than the private providers. The only way it can predefine what is needed is to specify an organization, not a service. Contracting for an organization rather than a service creates additional problems.

Instead of taking advantage of the private sector's experience, the agency has specified the same organization that the agency would use if it provided the service in-house. Instead of privatization, the contractor is actually bidding to operate a public-agency-designed system. Under this system, the private operator has no market incentive to improve service. The only obligation is to operate the prescribed system as defined. If this obligation is met, then the government is obligated to pay the promised amount.

Because the contract is typically for an extended period of time, there is no competition or bench mark against which to compare costs of the service provided. Not only is the bidder shielded from competition and the responsibility to satisfy customers, but the contract protects the contractor from the administrative and legislative review that controls public agencies. Thus the contractor is controlled neither by the market system nor by administrative controls of the public system. This process in essence "publicizes the private sector." The private contractor has neither a market incentive to keep delivery effective nor a competitive incentive to economize.

Instead of improving delivery effectiveness, this form of contracting tends to bureaucratize the entire service delivery process. When activity becomes bureaucratic, the service loses its ability to respond to diverse needs. Because the agency specified not only the equipment but also the operating procedures, the operator may handle conflicts with customers by suggesting that any service changes must be approved by the funding agency. If there are clients with special needs, they may be told that the agency does not allow the contractor to provide that type of service. It is not a cost-effective solution.

A much more logical approach would be to develop a network of private providers including taxi cabs, jitneys, limousine services, quasi-volunteers, other agencies and rescue squads which are willing to accept calls on an as needed basis at agreed rates. The agency can then collect calls and dispatch trips to the most-cost effective providers for each trip.

Use of All-or-Nothing Bidding to Create a Monopoly

When agencies opt for an all-or-nothing bid for service in a large geographic area, they may be creating a monopoly by putting competing organizations out of business. In one city, over 105 independent school bus operators provide service on over 520 routes each morning and evening. If the county decided to award all of the business to a single contractor based on the lowest bid each year, it could destroy all local competition. None of the local operators would be large enough to operate 520 vehicles, so bidding would be limited to a few large school bus management firms in the county, such as ATE or Ryder. Without the revenue from the school bus runs, the local school bus operators who were not awarded the contract would go out of business and no longer be able to provide charter service to local churches, civic groups, scout troops, and other community groups. The school bus management firm probably would not provide this service because the buses might be owned publicly and could not be used for such entrepreneurial activity. The local operators would not be in business to run shuttles to university football games, which would aggravate traffic congestion.

When the contract comes up for renewal the following year, there frequently is no real competition but simply an almost automatic renegotiation of a contract extension. This lack of competition occurs for two reasons. First, the local providers not selected would be put out of business. Second, there are many start-up costs when a new company receives a contract. Consequently, large management firms are not anxious to start bidding wars or upset their competitors' relationships with the client. Therefore, competitors are reluctant to submit bids unless they know the community is dissatisfied with the existing contract and is definitely looking for a change. Further, it is easier for local administrators simply to extend an existing contract than to go through rebidding and establishing rapport with a new provider.

Use of Inappropriate Contract Scope

All-or-nothing contracts should be avoided, even though they initially appear to reduce contracting effort. Consider the case of a state faced with the need to provide meals for congregate meal sites in that State for the fiscal year. Not wanting to go through the bidding or RFP process for each individual meal, the state might lump the needs into one large purchase. By doing this, the state would limit competition and flexibility severely. In addition, it would exclude any opportunity for small or minority businesses to participate in the award. The state would pay top dollar for the meals received.

To meet the requirements of this solicitation, the provider would have to develop a statewide system to mass-produce meals and deliver them. Only a few large organizations have the financial resources or organizational skills to bid on such a large undertaking. Although the solicitation might include all of the familiar boilerplate requirements about encouraging small and minority business, the scope of the project would make participation by small businesses virtually impossible. The scope of the award would assure that one of the world's largest service organizations would receive the contract to prepare and transport standardized, mass-produced meals hundreds of miles to meal sites throughout the state.

Ironically, in every community served, there would be numerous restaurants, cafeterias, and caterers offering a wide variety of meals ranging from home-cooked meals to fast foods to ethnic specialties within a short distance of each congregate meal site. Many of these institutions would have been willing to serve the meals either at the meal sites or on their own premises. This is an ideal situation for supply schedules and requirements contracts.

By aggregating needs and using a bidding (competitive) or RFP (partnership) approach rather than multiple supply schedules (network) for obtaining the meals, the state virtually would ensure several outcomes:

Each person would be served a standard institutional-style meal each time he or she ate at a congregate meal site.

The meal would be centrally prepared and transported great distances across the state.

Individuals with special needs (e.g., vegetarian, kosher, high-fiber, or low-carbohydrate diets) would have more limited options than if they could order from the menu at local food service locations.

The local food services would not have an opportunity to participate in the procurement process. Local food services would be affected adversely.

The number of people served by local businesses would decrease because some senior citizens might elect to eat at the meal center rather than the local food services in order to get companionship. If the decrease in business was sufficient, this could put some restaurants out of business, especially those that cater to senior citizens, because they would no longer have enough business to support their overhead.

This approach would restrain the meal centers' creative flexibility unduly. All meals in the state for the entire year would be planned and satisfied by contract. The agency and the local center would have neither the funding nor the flexibility to adapt to diverse needs or different conditions if they evolve during the year. The state would have no option for switching to more responsive providers. If a change were desired, the only option would be to negotiate a contract modification. Because there would be no competition in negotiating the modification, the cost of the change would be expected to be at a higher-than-competitive price.

Also, the environment would have been set to eliminate competition on future contracts. Because there are only a limited number of large firms able to bid on such contracts, they develop an unwritten protocol: "compete keenly only on the first contract." This principle is based on recognition that a new contract will not be extremely profitable because there are many start-up costs. Profits are to be made on contract renewals, where start-up costs are eliminated, and few competitive options exist because competitors are reluctant to start a "bidding war" unless the agency is actively seeking a change in providers. In essence, the process of aggregating needs to minimize the contracting effort is, in reality, a misapplication of the solicitation method and not in harmony with the promotion of competition. Also, because the relationship is already established, it is easier for the agency simply to extend the contract rather than to rebid the contract.

An alternative would be to solicit menus and quotes from local food services as well as from the national food services. Those providers that give acceptable discounts and terms would be added to the food service supply schedule. The local agencies and their clients could select from a variety of menus based on price and personal preferences. If the quality of food from one provider slipped, then alternative providers could be used. This also would give local agencies greater flexibility in making trade-offs between food selection and other budget needs. If individuals had strong preferences for Oriental, soul, kosher, or other specialty foods, they perhaps could pay the differences between the budgeted amount and the supply schedule price. It would strengthen the local network of food providers rather than make the community more dependent on outside, publicly supported sources of food. It even might increase local employment opportunities.

In essence, the supply schedule gives control over meals back to the agency and local site. It also keeps the employment at home rather than at the central preparation site. Although this list is not exhaustive, it illustrates the idea that correct procurement methods but unwise procurement strategies can destroy the intent of privatization.

OVEREMPHASIS ON CONTRACTING

Where markets work effectively in the private sector, contracts typically are implied, not written–especially when relationships are long-term. The bread producer usually delivers bread to a grocery store on an implied contract. The customer buys bread on an implied contract. Under the implied contracts, the buyer agrees to pay an agreed-upon amount and the seller promises there is no hidden defect, fraud, or misrepresentation. If the product or service is unsatisfactory, it will be corrected. "Satisfaction guaranteed" is not enforced by contract but by keeping the value of regular, repeat future business more than the value of any current transaction. Under this arrangement, the bread manufacturer does whatever is necessary to keep the merchant happy and the manufacturer's brand on the shelf. The merchant's self-interest requires keeping the customer happy so the customer will return to buy more bread. Thus, in the market allocation world of day-to-day business, there are few, if any, written contracts for most people.

Written contracts have an entirely different objective than does privatization. The principle of written contracts began in 1677 when the English Parliament prohibited bringing any fraud case to court over a year after the agreement unless the agreement was written (Calamcli and Periollo, 1977). Thus written contracts were a method of spelling out all conditions of long-term agreements as understood by both parties at consummation. This was done to prevent the courtroom confusion when the testimony of each party, polarized by the emotions of conflict and time, provided no objective method of determining intent at the time the agreement was made.

Written contracts now are required by law under the following conditions (Emanuel and Knowles, 1984):

The agreement cannot be fully carried out in less than one year.
The agreement is made upon consideration of marriage.
The agreement is for the sale of land.
The agreement is to serve as an executor or administrator of an estate.
The agreement is for suretyship to be responsible for the debt of another person.

In practical terms, however, written contracts typically are used only where:

1. The desired benefit is understood clearly by both parties to the extent that all details can be stated explicitly. If the need is still so general that it can be stated only in abstract terms such as "high quality," "satisfactory service," "fair prices," and "to be provided when needed," it is difficult to write a contract.
2. The agreement is for an extended time period, such as a conditional sales contract or a lease.
3. It is a large purchase where there may be extreme risk to either or both parties, as with the purchase of a home or business.
4. Delivery is to occur in the future, as in the case of constructing a home or payment of insurance.

Attorneys who write contracts are trained to write comprehensive, consolidated contracts. Contracts are considered to be comprehensive when they cover all possible future eventualities. Contracts are considered to be consolidated when all possible aspects of the agreement are covered. A consolidated contract covers not only the price but also such items as payment method, conflict resolution, performance criteria, all possible conditions for nonperformance, and contract changes.

The purpose of contracts is to create legal certainty and stability. Contracts are to be explicit (all relevant duties and conditions totally defined) and for a stated period of time. This provides certainty and stability for both sides for the life of the contract.

The objective of privatization, on the other hand, is to increase cost-effective delivery. Privatization encourages flexibility, multiple suppliers, competition, improved fit, and reduced hassle, whereas contracting typically tends to reduce flexibility, reduce variation in service provided, and eliminate competition. A marriage contract, for example, does not encourage the husband or wife to seek new options but rather to make a long-term commitment that excludes competition regardless of future situations.

When the Corrections Corporation of America offered to pay the State of Tennessee $250 million for a ninety-nine-year lease on the entire Tennessee prison system, it was to promote contracting out, not cost-effective delivery of service. Like a marriage contract, this offer was designed to establish a long-term operating agreement with the state for a period of ninety-nine years without fear of competition. Consider the situation if the state sought a "divorce" within the 99-year period. A massive "property" suit could follow before Tennessee would be able to operate its prisons again. If the state became dissatisfied with the operating arrangement, the court might require extensive "alimony payment" to finalize the "divorce."

Open-ended contracts, such as supply schedules and requirements contracts, are a method for adding a supplier to the network of providers while maintaining the flexibility to select the providers that are most responsive in meeting agency needs. Hotels, for example, provide government rates and can be used on an as-needed basis.

DEVELOPING A PRIVATIZATION STRATEGY

Procurement is more than contracting out. In fact, most of the criticism about procurement has occurred because many agencies simply equate privatization with contracting out and do "whatever they need to do" to get the contracts approved without developing procurement strategies. If the problems are to be avoided, the agencies need to understand the economics of procurement and to develop a long-term procurement strategy that allows hassle-free delivery of cost-effective service. A flow chart that can be used to select a procurement strategy designed to avoid many potential conflicts is presented in Figure 4.3.

General Procurement Questions

Question 1: Is the product or service available from another agency? If the other agency has surplus units or already has the capacity to provide the service, it should be used.

Question 2: Is the product or service available from one of the protected sources? If one of the protected sources such as prisons or sheltered workshops is able to meet the need, then that source should be used.

Question 3: Are multiple sources able to provide the product or service? If the answer is no, then procurement must be limited to one provider, and the only questions to be resolved through negotiations would be price, quantity, and delivery. Although this option may simplify the solicitation and evaluation stage of procurement, it severely limits the agency's leverage in case of changing needs. The agency frequently is placed in the position of accepting what is available in the way the provider wants to provide it and at the price the provider wants to charge.

Question 4: Is the need for a product or for a service? Products are bundles of benefits that can be "consumed" by the agency to create the benefits desired. Services are benefits that are delivered directly without existing first as products. Each of these categories must be approached differently. If a product is desired, then the product procurement process should be used. If a service is desired, then the services procurement process should be used.

Question 5: Is the procurement for a single, well-understood need? A single service is one that can be identified before procurement. A school bus run can be defined. The route is defined, the time is defined, and the time period is defined. However, the need for broad categories of services (e.g., elderly and handicapped transportation services) is not defined to the extent that the provider knows exactly what is wanted. See Figure 4.4. When the procurement is for vaguely defined, multiple services, agencies tend to enter into "marriage contracts" for organizations rather than fee-for-service contracts. If a well-understood, single-service is desired, then the single service procurement process may be followed.

Question 6: If the contract is for multiple service needs (Figure 4.5) is there adequate lead time between the definition of individual needs and required service delivery to allow the normal procurement process to work for each individual need? If not, then the multiservice procurement process may be used.

Question 7: If the lead time is adequate to allow separate procurement for each individual need, is the purchase large enough to justify individual procurement? If not, then the supply schedule should be used, as is typically done for the purchase

Figure 4.3
Public Procurement Process

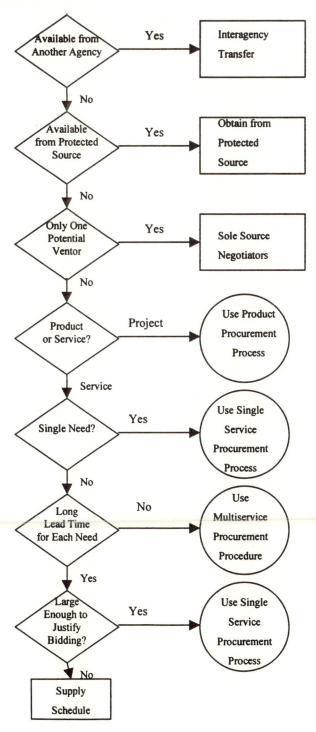

of small items such as supplies of various types. If the purchase is large, and there is adequate lead time, then the single-service procurement process may be used to purchase each service as the need arises.

Product Procurement Questions

If the product procurement process is indicated, (Figure 4.4) then the following questions should be asked:

Question 1: Is the purchase for a single need? If procurement is being made for many, often small items, cost-effective procurement should involve negotiations by government of acceptable government rate. The items then should be placed on a supply schedule so that they can be purchased by any agency needing the items at any time.

Question 2: Is the need totally defined? If so, the products can be specified totally, and the bid let. If all firms have the ability to deliver, then a straight IFB should be issued. If there is concern about the ability of the bidder to deliver the desired product effectively, then only qualified bidders should be allowed to bid.

Question 3: Is the need defined totally except for delivery date and exact quantity? If so, then an IFB should be extended for a requirements contract. Again, if there is concern about the ability of all firms to deliver, only bidders who meet specified qualifications should be allowed to bid. If the desired product has not been defined, as is often the case with new weapons or hardware, then an RFP should be extended so that the proposers can define the products that they would suggest. The selection should be made on the basis of the effectiveness and flexibility of the proposed solution as much as on the cost of the proposed product. The more vague the definition, the more important the supplier's flexibility and cooperativeness in making contract changes.

Single-Service Procurement Questions

If the need is for a single service (See Figure 4.5), slightly different questions need to be asked:

Question 1: Is the need for the service defined fully? If the need is defined totally (e.g., "moving 5,000 yards of dirt from Point A to Point B between Day X and Day Y"), then an IFB should be issued. If there is concern about the ability of various firms to meet the need, then an IFB with qualifications should be issued.

Question 2: If the need is not defined fully, is it defined fully except for delivery date and number of deliveries? If so, then an IFB should be issued for a requirements contract. If there is concern about qualifications, then bids can be accepted only from bidders who meet stated qualifications. An example might be snow removal along a specific section of highway. This need is defined totally except for the dates the service will be needed and the number of times it will be needed during the season. If the need is not defined fully, then an RFP can be issued.

Figure 4.4
Product Procurement Process

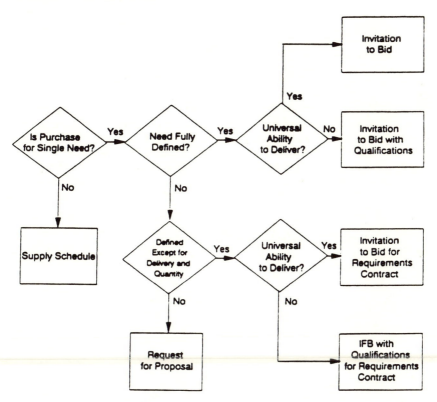

Figure 4.5
Single Service Procurement Process

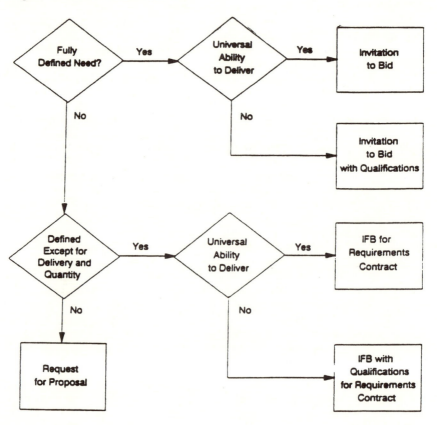

Most research projects are done this way. There is a general research question, but the detailed approach that will be used to address the research question is not defined. The proposals in which various approaches are presented allow the agency to select the approach predicted to be most cost-effective.

Multiservice Procurement Questions

If the service is for multiple needs, (See Figure 4.6) a different set of questions must be answered:

Question 1: Is the need for a commonly used existing service? Commonly used existing services include hotel rooms, freight transportation, physical therapy, and other services purchased by private as well as public funds. If the services are already available, a second question needs to be asked. Will bidding lessen market competition? In the case of multiple airlines serving city pairs, the General Services Administration (GSA) determined that the bidding process would not lessen market competition. Therefore, an IFB for a requirements contract was issued. If government's share of the market is so large that a shift of government business to one vendor would jeopardize the viability of the other providers, then a supply schedule should be used. If government is a small share of the market, then an IFB for a requirements contract may be issued. If the needed service does not exist, then the agency must decide whether to seek a single provider or a network approach to providing the service.

Question 2: Should a network or single service system approach be used? The answer to this question will depend on a thorough understanding of the user needs. If the needs are homogeneous and the demand for service capacity is constant, then a single provider can be very effective. The greater the diversity of needs and the variation in utilization rates, the more critical it is to use a network approach. For example, food stamps allow individuals to use the existing network of food distributors rather than developing a specialized system for distributing food to their clients. If a system is already in place, the agency needs only to add the service to the existing public supply schedule and use the existing service whenever it is needed. For example, schoolchildren can be given transit passes to use the existing transit system rather than developing a dedicated school bus system. If no system is in place, the agency should specify the systems that it wants designed and extend an RFP for a firm to develop a dedicated system.

Question 3: If diversity of needs and variation in capacity demand are great enough to justify a network, the agency must determine if a network of potential providers already exists. If so, then existing providers should be listed in the supply schedule. If a network does not exist, then a public supply schedule can be developed schedule. If a network does not exist, then a public supply schedule can be developed with incentives to induce the development of a network of providers. School bus contracts, for example, can be used to attract private providers into the transportation business. If the providers have flexibility in

Figure 4.6
Multiservice Procurement Process

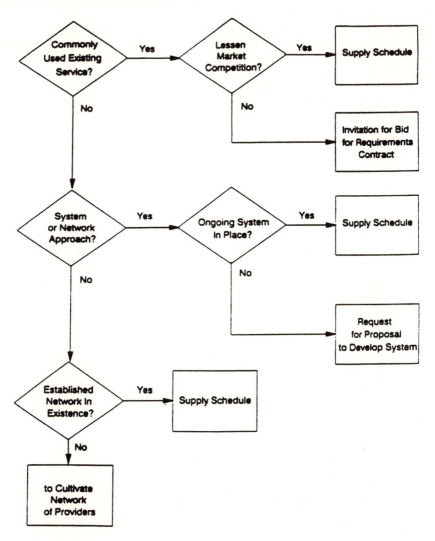

the selection of vehicles and equipment, they may be able to use the equipment to provide service to other groups.

CONCLUSION

Privatization has as many meanings as there are individuals using the word. Privatization is not a procedure. It is a process for obtaining service that effectively meets agency and client goals in the most cost-effective manner and with a minimum of hassle. It needs to be a flexible, responsive process. Public agencies need to develop a procurement strategy for each purchase. The FAR not only allows flexibility but encourages supply schedules and requirements contracts in preference to the stereotypic competitive IFBs. Procurement is more than a clerical function of making sure rules are followed: It is a strategic function that can change the impact of privatization efforts dramatically. The key is to know which rules to apply and when to apply them.

REFERENCES

Buchanan, J. (1977). "Why Does Government Grow?" In T. Borcherding, ed., *Bureaucrats: The Source of Government Growth* Durham: Duke University Press.

Calamcli, J., and J. Periollo (1977). *Contracts*. St. Paul: West Publishing.

Cayer, S., and J. P. Morgan (1991). "What It Takes to Make World Class Suppliers." *Purchasing,* August 15: p. 61.

Cayer, S., and J. P. Morgan (1992). "True Believers." *Purchasing,* August 13: p. 61.

Chamberlin, E. H. (1933). *The Theory of Monopolistic Competition.* Cambridge: Harvard University Press.

Cole. A. and A. Kamauff. (1993). *A New Agenda for the Purchasing Professional.* Unpublished manuscript, Knoxville, TN: University of Tennessee Development Center.

Crosby, P. B. (1979). *Quality Is Free.* New York: McGraw-Hill.

Davis, F. W., Jr., et al. (1989). *Development of a Public Service Providing Strategy: Agency Provided vs. Privatization; Single Provider vs. Strategic Network.* Washington, DC: UMTA TN-11-0008, September.

Davis, F. W., Jr., and K. Manrodt. (1991). "Service Logistics: An Introduction" In P. K. Bagchi, ed. Special Edition, *Information Systems and Quantitative Techniques in Logistics Management, Special Issue, International Journal of Physical Distribution and Logistics Management,* 21, no. 7: pp. 2-13.

Davis, F. W., Jr., and K. Manrodt (1992). "Teaching Service Response Logistics." *Journal of Business Logistics* 13, no. 2: pp. 199-229.

Deming, W. E. (1982). *Quality, Productivity, and Competitive Position.* Cambridge: Massachusetts Institute of Technology, Center for Advanced Engineering Study.

Ellram, L. M. (1990). "The Supplier Selection Decision in Strategic Partnerships." *Journal of Purchasing and Materials Management,* Fall: pp. 8-14.

Emanuel, S., and S. Knowles (1984). *Contracts*, 2d ed. New Rochelle, NY: Emanuel Law Outlines.

Hammer, M., J. and Champy (1993). *Reengineering the Corporation*. New York: Harper Business.

Imai, M. (1986). *Kaizen*. New York: McGraw-Hill.

Juran, J. J., and F. Gryna, Jr. (1980). *Quality Planning and Analysis*. New York: McGraw-Hill.

Marshall, A. (1989). *Principles of Economics*. London: Macmillan.

N A P M Guide to Purchasing. New York: NAPM.

Robinson, J. (1933). *The Economics of Imperfect Competition*. London: Macmillan.

Smith, A. (1952). *An Inquiry Into the Nature and Causes of the Wealth of Nations* Vol. 39, *Great Books of the Western World*. Chicago: Encyclopedia Britannica.

Stewart, T. (1993). "Reengineering: The Hot Managing Tool." *Fortune*, August 23: pp. 41-48.

Chapter 5

Contracting to Affiliated Companies under Concessions: The Economic Approach

Jack W. Lillywhite

A routine feature of major privatized infrastructure concessions is the practice of contracting major portions of the capital programs to affiliated or parent companies of the concession consortium. Usually, under these arrangements there is a need for additional facility or systems and/or the requirement for extensive rehabilitation, modernization, or expansion of existing assets. In addition, the consortium may elect to handle its assignment of other operational and administrative business functions by contract to affiliates of the consortium's member companies. All in all, this is an issue that receives a certain amount of discussion early on in the design of concession programs and for a number of reasons (usually political, socio-economic, and localized) is often misinterpretedby regulators, the user community, and responsible government officials.

It is, however, understood well by the external community of financial houses, contractors, operators, investors, legal and insurance professionals, and othersactively involved in the implementation and risk undertaking associated with the transfer of obligations from government to the private sector. The following offers the most common (but not inclusive) reasons for this approach tocontracting. Dependence on contracting to affiliated or parent companies is often the motivation to accept the risks and opportunities associated with development of private infrastructure.

CERTAINTY OF PROJECT FINANCE

In almost all cases of private project finance, where project cash flow is the only recourse for debt service and return on equity (ROE), the lenders and investors insist on a high degree of certainty. This certainty is required, not just for the project cash flow and ROE, which lenders and investors evaluate based on overall risk, but rather to also add confidence and credibility to the risk undertaking. As such, lenders and investors insist that others assume the risk associated with capital construction costs, design defects, facility and system technology, capital project execution schedule (time of delivery) and quality of design, construction, and system or facility performance.

Since project cash flow is required to secure the great majority of overall project funding, it is important to the operational concessionaire that it obtain from the engineering, materials and technology, and construction marketplace the most reliable guarantees of cost, schedule, and performance before it receives the project's financing. This fact of private infrastructure development and financing has resulted in the natural draw of large engineering-construction companies to the concession programs being initiated around the world.

In almost all cases (with only very minor exceptions) of major infrastructure concession or BOT programs, the engineering-construction member of the concession consortium receives the preference of executing the needed works, usually on a turnkey, fixed price, guaranteed basis.

If the concessions construction work was competitively and selectively contracted, the consortium would have to be prepared to accept the risk of construction completion prior to financing the engineering design in order to obtain fixed price, guaranteed construction contracts, which would be required as documentation of risk allocation for the lenders and investors. The same would be required of a design to prepare definitive specifications for the technology equipment and materials, which would also require detailed and precise costs and guarantees.

This level of precision in the procurement process would also require more time to plan, evaluate, negotiate, and award the work, thus adding significant time to the schedule. It would not benefit the operating period of the system and/or facility to have a myriad of contracts, purchase orders, and warranties to maintain for a sustained period. This added burden of operational administration is therefore eliminated by including the placement of guarantees and warranties under one, credible contractor (i.e., engineering-construction member company turnkey contract).

The affiliated company engineering-construction contractor should have the experience, capability, and credibility to design, estimate, and execute guaranteed performance contracts. The concession consortium would involve the affiliated company contractors in much of the capital program planning, feasibility, and technology selection. The contractor would then undertake to do conceptual designs and engineering in order to generate' a fixed price turnkey estimate using an "open book" method.

In the "open book" method of estimating and fixing costs, the contractor works directly with the concessionaire (i.e., owner) and establishes quantities, unit costs, contingencies, degree of risk, and fees in a cooperative, negotiated manner. Both the "owner" and the contractor work in a good-faith manner to establish the most complete and accurate estimate of project costs, risks, schedule, and performance requirements without complete designs, lengthy formal procurement process, and protracted approvals. The degree of engineering completion is recognized in the project contingencies and is usually based on both the contractor's and owner's experience and knowledge of system and facility details. In addition, the owner can place most of the technology and material guarantee requirements with the turnkey contractor since the contractor is experienced in bidding and executing under this type of risk arrangement and is prepared to develop a "wrap" of the project warranties and guarantees. Later in the chapter we will discuss the limitation of competitively bid contracts (in which low bid or local presence is overriding) in providing the necessary level of credibility, certainty, and confidence to obtain adequate project financing.

RISK CONTROL

There are many risks confronted by the private infrastructure operator or entrepreneur, none of which is more contentious and serious than "construction completion risk." Not only is this a risk traditionally avoided by long-term debt lenders, but also it is often mismanaged and misapplied in the early stages of a concession or build, operate, transfer (BOT) contract.

As government organizations struggle to deal with the emerging procurement acquisition process known as privatization, they believe that they must continue to exercise control over not only the contracting process but also the execution process, while passing on very high levels of performance and completion risk. This is normally contrary to the objective of the privatization, which is to inject private concepts of management, technology, efficiency, and finance into the process.

Therefore, it is important to provide an equitable balance of risk and control for both the executing concession contractor and the government. One of the issues to deal with early on in the design of the concession is the execution of the concession's capital programs.

By allowing the affiliated companies to negotiate and execute, they are able to couple the need for "control" with the requirements of the "risk" undertaking passed on by the owner and/or the government. When owners or governments restrict the level of "control" or pass on "risk" without the attendant control, then competition is severely limited to contractors that will be either shallow capital organizations or ones with a fine-tuned claims and change order program. An affiliated company contractor will invariably approach the project with a "no claims" attitude since it recognizes the need to protect the "owner's" interest as being in their best interest also.

ACCELERATED PROJECT EXECUTION

Under a negotiated, "open book," turnkey engineering-construction contract, the concessionaire is able to take advantage of a "fast-track" approach to project capital programs. Allowing the project to proceed under the fastest scenario possible without affecting quality or level of service is one of the added-values of private infrastructure concessions. Service and quality are synonymous with private enterprise involvement with infrastructure.

Affiliated company contractor's involvement in the planning, design, and construction contributes to that added-value by providing the most immediate and accessible execution plan possible. Disputes, conflicts, and communications are all handled more expeditiously and cooperatively for the overall good and objective of the concession. Users, whose requirements are also time and quality-sensitive, get more prompt, effective delivery of the end product, whether it is water, waste disposal, or environmental protection.

In "fast-track" construction the contractor controls both the engineering and construction process, thus giving him the ability to begin construction with less than 100 percent design complete or the protracted procurement process. Construction works closely with engineering to effect the most concise and accurate plan for the new or modernized work based on actual site conditions, constructions planning assessment, and its knowledge of the process productivity and material requirements.

LIMITATION OF LOCAL FIRMS

With few exceptions, most small local design and construction companies are unable to accept the stringent conditions imposed by either the concession contractual agreement or the project finance documents. The project finance document, in particular, will require that all projects be guaranteed in terms of cost, schedule, and performance by the concessionaire, who, in turn, will pass on most, if not all, of these risks to the consortium's execution contractor.

As stated before the concessionaire will accept the stringent construction completion risk and cost confinement requirements of the lenders and investors. The concessionaire can do this because it has commitments from its engineering-construction equity partners to assume this risk under contract to the concession owner group.

Local firms remain important, however, as a valuable source of subcontracting. In fact, it is highly irregular and unusual to see major infrastructure work done without substantial subcontracting to regional or local contractors. It is also usually the most cost effective and expeditious process to utilize local sources of equipment, materials and construction services than export from in-country or offshore. However, due to the lack of ability of these smaller local firms to accept high levels of risk, the affiliated company contractor takes on the risk of guaranteeing performance and quality of the local purchases and subcontracts.

PROCUREMENT PROCESS CONTROL

Of concern to the owner or government authority entering into the concession is the process control to be exercised in the contracting (procurement) program to deal with the perceived conflict of interest. Under the engineering-construction turnkey contract, the contractor will normally be held to a higher standard of performance than usual for public contracts. To effect compliance with this higher standard, liquidated damages will be set and capped to encourage compliance and performance.

In addition, the contract's terms, conditions, price, and guarantees will all be transparent and documented to the government authorities for their information. Although the contracts have been negotiated, they have been done so in a very visible, open fashion with the owner group with great care to accurately reflect the cost, risk, schedule, and delivery requirements of the project.

CONSOLIDATED MANAGEMENT

Finally, one must consider the importance to continuity, timing and program management to be able to access a single source of authority and control of the construction process. Of all the most visible benefits during execution of important construction works, none are more pronounced to an owner than the ability to deal with one authorized entity on all questions and concerns.

CONCLUSION

It is important to the success of any private development, project financing or infrastructure concession, or BOT project that a full understanding of the capital program execution be reached early and with consensus among all interested parties. The process of contracting, on a reserved, exclusive basis, to affiliated companies of concession members is a historically effective means of executing capital programs with major risk demands and undertakings. It utilizes the open book method of estimating in which owner participation is welcome and encouraged. For engineer-constructors it provides the best possible reason to accept the ownership risk and equity investment requirement that the project needs. In short, it is a win-win-win situation for the project, the owners, and the contractors.

Part II

The Practice of Contracting Out

Chapter 6

Role of Public/Private Juvenile Programs

William E. Botkin

In 1988, when Rebound! Colorado, (Rebound) a Colorado-based juvenile training organization, opened its first facility on the high plains of Colorado, privately operated, secure juvenile facilities were new and few. Today, there are at least a dozen organizations operating one or more privately managed, secure juvenile programs in the United States. As the problem of violent juvenile delinquency spirals worldwide, international interest in privately managed U.S. programs is also growing.

From the growth numbers alone it is obvious that privately operated juvenile detention and treatment programs have made major inroads into an area historically reserved for public sector providers. Not surprisingly, this rapid growth has not improved the relationship between public and private sectors, which remains tenuous at best. The times and the future success or failure of tens of thousands of young men and women in our society demand that the public/private political debate be resolved. We are in a struggle calling for the best and brightest from both the public and private sectors to join together and address the frustrating growth of violent juvenile crime that is threatening to decay our society not only in the United States but throughout the world.

Nothing makes this more evident than the fact that, despite all the differences and growth, the public sector remains the largest provider of private juvenile corrections services. Nevertheless, there is a concern by public employees that private providers jeopardize the viability of their employment and programs. According to an American Correctional Association (ACA) report, "Contracting out a service that has been traditionally provided by government means that public employees will be impacted in some, often threatening, way. Resistance to privatization, not surprisingly, generally comes from public employees and their representatives" (American Correctional Association, 1992).

While that apprehension has some validity, there is also an understanding that the public juvenile system does not have enough trained people or space to serve the overwhelming numbers of juveniles entering the corrections system today. State-operated juvenile facilities are often outdated, severely overcrowded, underfunded, and yet pressured by legislatures to get the job done. Despite an aversion to private juvenile facility operators, many in the public sector confidentially acknowledge there are few other options.

This delicate public/private relationship is following closely the path of the privatization movement sweeping the adult corrections industry. Colorado, for instance, is facing a crunch all too common these days: stronger sentencing laws require more prison space, but limited funding prevents construction of prisons. The Colorado constitution specifically prevents privatization of adult corrections facilities if it replaces public employee positions, and the Colorado Association of Public Employees has successfully defended that limitation in court and challenges every effort to privatize existing adult institutions.

The juvenile corrections sector has more leeway. The privatization of some programs has been forced by dramatic rises in juvenile incarceration and has been mandated by legislatures. Some in the public sector, while remaining strongly opposed to privatization efforts, realize that the demand for specialized juvenile programs will undoubtedly exceed the public supply for years to come, somewhat reducing the threat to public jobs and programs.

It is also understood that no one entity, public or private, has all the answers to today's juvenile crime problems. Further, it is understood that a concerted effort will be required to effectively redirect the huge volume of youths who will be entering juvenile programs over the next decade.

The mix of private and public entities that makes up today's juvenile treatment providers was created out of necessity in the early 1990s when state and county governments, responding to a public outcry over soaring juvenile crime rates, started seeking answers in the private sector. Constituents clamoring for protection from increasingly violent juvenile crimes pressured state legislatures across the country to find an answer. Enter privatized juvenile programs.

The motivation behind the move to privatization is improved efficiency, reduction in bureaucracy (gridlock), and equal or better services at lower costs. In theory, private enterprise could build new juvenile facilities faster and cheaper, get programs up and running sooner, provide increased flexibility in personnel and procurement practices, offer new and innovative treatment approaches and overall operate more cost-effectively. The concept from the point of view of a government strapped for funds and facing an overtaxed constituency appears to be an excellent choice. However, after nearly a decade of privately operated juvenile treatment and detention programs, some questions still remain in the minds of many observers:

Are the needs of the youths in the public/private programs being appropriately served?
Can it be demonstrated that privately operated programs are, indeed, more cost-effective?
Are efficiencies gained with private providers lost through the public oversight process?
Have the public and the private sectors–two very different cultures–established an effective operational interface process that maximizes the strengths of each?

Finally,

What steps can be taken to ensure that public/private programs operate most effectively, providing governments and their supporting taxpayers with maximum return on their tax dollars?

PRIVATIZATION: A DEFINITION

To begin, it's important to understand the term "privatization." Webster's describes it as an action taken "to transfer from public or government control or ownership to private enterprise." A key word is "control." If control is not transferred, privatization has not taken place. What is formed instead is a private/public partnership. This distinction is very important. Frequently, what is referred to as a move to privatize is actually a public/private partnership. While some efficiencies can be gained through such partnerships, comparing these organizations with truly privatized programs where all or most operational control has been relinquished to the private operator is inappropriate.

When examined by these criteria, some of the early, so-called privatization efforts of state-owned juvenile programs were actually public/private partnerships. The contractor–either states or counties–not only maintained control over the length of stay and the number and type of juveniles entering the programs but also held the purse strings, often limiting the expenditure of funds needed for capital improvements when private operators are expected to operate programs in public facilities. The only changes in these cases were the people running the day-to-day program. While this offered some benefits, the entire juvenile system was not examined with a view toward changes and improvements, and some early, so-called privatization attempts failed.

Early privatization efforts held other unexpected pitfalls for unaware private operators. States often are not held to the same local health and safety standards as private sector operators, and many, older, state-run facilities are frequently grandfathered in, effectively bypassing state standards. Once a "privatization" contract is signed, the private operator often was immediately responsible for upgrading decades-old facilities to meet modern building codes. That meant white-glove code inspections followed by highly critical reports, all done under the watchful eye of skeptical print and broadcast media and detractors of privatization.

The privatized facilities frequently required major construction commitments, funding for which was usually controlled by the same public-sector system that was being replaced on the operational side. State systems that have developed over decades do not die gracefully. Often they are dedicated to maintaining the status quo and self-preservation.

Despite the best intentions of those involved in early privatization efforts, many projects failed because control of too many key issues was not transferred along with the responsibilities. Regardless, legislatures, under pressure from an increasingly demanding constituency, saw privatization as an immediate relief valve. Force-feeding privatized programs into an entrenched public bureaucracy is, in effect, stuffing a modern, high-powered engine into a rusty Model-T Ford. It might look OK from the outside, but before you can get up to full speed, the wheels come off.

Creating one effective program from two divergent cultures requires an unusually high level of cooperation, trust, teamwork, and an unwavering focus on the ultimate objective. This level of relationship cannot be forced or rushed; it gradually develops and evolves. Both public and private sectors have to realize that if we are truly going to respond to the needs of today's juveniles and reduce the recidivism rate of those in our programs, we must change the way that private enterprise and the public sector work together. We must focus on solutions and develop creative public/private partnerships that solve problems without regard for ownership. We must begin to learn to understand each other and cultivate working relationships that generate positive results.

To that end I offer the following guidelines for both the private sector companies venturing into public sector work and governmental and public entities considering private/public partnerships:

For the private sector providers:

1. Develop, with the public sector contractor, a comprehensive definition of the job proposed, including responsibilities, expected results for each phase, timelines, and overall goals. These should be stated clearly in the original request for proposal, the private provider's response, and the final contract. Private providers should expect and require that clear and measurable standards be established by the public sector. Standards, to the extent possible, should be based on ACA standards for juvenile facilities and monitored on some predetermined basis. Ideally, facilities operated by the public sector should be monitored by the same standards. Audit teams that are composed of both private and public sector employees would provide some level of neutrality to the process.
2. Assume nothing. People in private and public business operate in different cultures and speak different languages. As a private business owner, it is very important to understand the government process and how it can affect planned operations.
3. It is critical that both the private provider and the governmental agency contracting for the service are clear about responsibilities and expectations. Clarity at the outset will avoid difficulties once the program is operational. Review all documentation carefully. Compare your interpretation and understanding of contract language with your public sector counterpart to make sure you concur. Beware of any areas that require subjective interpretation or personal assurances. Negotiate necessary changes prior to making any agreement and get all changes and interpretations included in the proposal or contract. Put it in writing. Philosophies, attitudes, and personnel within an agency are affected by the political climate and can change quickly and without notice. Often key administrative positions are appointed posts that can change with changes in the governor's office.
4. Inflexibility in state personnel practices is a factor in the increase in privatization. If, in privatizing or forming a public/private partnership, you inherit former public employees, consider increasing the transition period. You should allow enough time to carefully screen each employee to determine qualifications, skills, attitude, goals, and so on. This is particularly true for takeovers involving cultural or work changes. Change is difficult in any case, especially when transitioning staff from the public to the private sector.

5. During the due diligence phase, evaluate not only the project to be privatized but also all of the related systems that affect the operation of the project. A revision of the entire system may be required to develop the support and commitment necessary for success.

6. Understand that a government agency does not and cannot operate like a business. It is frequently more dependent on the whim of the voter and the political winds than the bottom line. It is important to determine political and public attitude regarding your privatization project. A solid community relations/public affairs program is essential. Change often is resisted out of fear of the unknown. Open and honest communication allows divergent stakeholder groups to take ownership in the changes and to help work toward the common objective of helping juveniles. Failure to address community stakeholder concerns can be fatal and can be traced to the root cause for unsuccessful public/private partnerships. The ACA says, "The neighborhood may have developed considerable confidence in the ability of the publicly operated program to assure safety in the community. The (current) program administration may be very responsive to community involvement. Contracting such a program to a private provider unknown to the community may cause anxiety and opposition" (American Corrrectional Association, 1992). Specific stakeholder groups, including civic and business organizations, neighborhood groups, individual opinion leaders, and local and state political representatives, should be identified early in the process through formal or informal research. Relationships with these groups should be cultivated and maintained.

7. Establish a relationship with all senior managers within the public sector and be especially attentive to those whose opinions you trust. They can provide insight, direction, and contacts within the system. Once you have established your contacts, listen to them carefully. They are your customers, and you need to understand and be responsive to their needs and expectations.

Experience also offers many lessons for public agencies considering privatization or public/private partnerships. I recommend that agencies considering privatization carefully and honestly evaluate the following:

1. What is the impetus to privatize? To save operations costs? To reduce the need for capital appropriations to fund new construction? To provide innovation in programming? It is critical to be clear about the reason for privatization so that these factors can be described in the RFP document.

2. Is it a clearly defined contract? Is there consensus with all affected departments, agencies, management, and employee groups for the project?

3. Does the contractor thoroughly understand the scope of the job?

4. Does the surrounding system support the area to be privatized? Are system changes needed? Are these suggested/recommended changes spelled out in the contract? If changes are needed in the overall system, how committed is the state agency to ensuring that necessary changes are implemented?

5. Is staff committed to the success of the privatization effort? Does the staff understand the changes that privatization will bring, and it is willing to make those changes? Is staff adequately trained or trainable to work effectively with the new program?
6. Are there political forces that could negatively impact the initiative? Is the political culture supportive of the privatization efforts? Who are the key stakeholders in the privatization and what are their motives?
7. Is the privatization effort part of your agency's long-range planning? Privatization, done well, can deliver many services of better or equal quality at lower costs. It can mean new business and increased profits for the private sector, savings for taxpayers, and more efficient government programs. Opportunities for privatization and public sector contracting are expanding in many areas as government is more and more frequently seeking assistance from private enterprise. As taxpayers and private business owners, we should do all we can to encourage that trend, so we must be able to demonstrate that privatization does provide a better return on investment.

PRIVATE VERSUS PUBLIC: THE ISSUE OF COST SAVINGS

Over the past several years, a number of studies have been conducted to determine whether privatization actually does reduce operational costs. Strong cases can be made for both sides.

A report in *Corrections Journal* (1996: 3) stated that the General Accounting Office (GAO) found no clear evidence that "in general" private corrections facilities were better operated or less expensive than public sector operations. The GAO report concluded that the "few studies it reviewed do not permit drawing generalized conclusions about the comparative operational costs and/or quality of service of private and public prisons."

The report was sharply criticized by Dr. Charles W. Thomas, a professor of criminology and director of the Private Corrections Project at the University of Florida in Gainesville. Dr. Thomas said that private firms provide correctional services at least equal to those of programs provided by public agencies and at less cost. He said the GAO study was "inaccurate, incomplete, misleading and ineptly prepared" (Thomas, 1995). In fact, two of the states cited in the GAO report, Tennessee and Louisiana, have issued their own studies refuting the findings of the GAO report.

In his June 1995 testimony before the U.S. House Subcommittee on Crime (Thomas, 1995), Dr. Thomas called the public sector's cost-savings challenge "weak." Listing his arguments, he said the very existence of a contract with a governmental entity suggests confidence that cost savings will be achieved. Second, he stated that it is general knowledge that private sector fringe benefits, particularly retirement benefits, "are less generous than those made available to public employees." Last, he said that the private sector "is not obliged to comply with a broad array of costly bureaucratic requirements government has imposed upon itself" in such areas as employee selection, promotion and termination, and costs of goods and services procurement. Dr. Thomas went on to say that it should be surprising only if a public/private contract failed to produce at least some cost savings. "In short," he said, "the real question is how great the costs savings of contracting are likely to be rather than whether there will be any cost savings."

According to Dr. Thomas, some states require by statute cost savings from privatized operations. In a 1994 report (Thomas, 1994), Dr. Thomas points out that the state of Texas precludes contract awards "absent an assurance of operating cost savings of at least 10 percent." The state of Florida, in requesting bids for the operation of two 750-bed facilities, received twelve proposals. Each contained legally binding commitments for cost savings equal to, or greater than, 7 percent. Experience has demonstrated construction cost savings of up to 25 percent and operational savings of between 10 and 15 percent.

Private contractors can also cut costs in other areas. For example, Wackenhut's chief executive officer, George Zoley, is quoted in *Investor's Business Daily* (1996) saying that governments can cut construction costs from 20 percent to 40 percent by contracting with private companies. He credits the savings to cutting red tape, using in-house architects and designs, which are less costly and more quickly constructed. Zoley was quoted as saying, "We can build in 12 months what it takes government 24 to 36 months to construct."

John Naisbitt, in his *Trend Letter* (1995), said that competition between private companies competing for public contracts is what creates the cost benefits and can create "dramatic savings." To reduce public employee groups' opposition to a privatization effort, Naisbitt recommends that government bid out the jobs to at least five qualified private firms and the public agency currently providing the services. Indeed, it has been historically demonstrated that monopolies, whether in the private or public sectors, are inefficient.

Finally, it is frequently difficult to compare accurately publicly operated juvenile facilities with private facilities. This is due primarily to differences in accounting procedures. For instance, comparing per diem costs or costs per day per youth—the most easily understood measure—is often deceiving because frequently not all cost factors are included in public reports. One example is capital costs for juvenile facilities, usually excluded from cost figures for publicly operated programs. Other costs are also frequently "backed out" or simply ignored in public program reports. Keeping these factors in mind, when equally compared, privately operated programs are shown consistently to operate more efficiently than public programs.

ACHIEVING DESIRED EFFICIENCIES

As discussed earlier, truly privatized public programs–where government turns over the keys to a private company–are rare. Most so-called privatized programs, including both juvenile and adult corrections programs, are actually public/private partnerships.

The public sector maintains a monitoring function over the private operation, ensuring that agreed-to standards are maintained and expected outcomes achieved. In theory, this relationship allows the standards and objectives of the original, public program to be maintained while gaining fiscal and operational efficiencies of the private sector. In practice, however, this is a difficult marriage requiring both sides to cooperate and focus on outcomes to make it work.

Frequently, as in most any other enterprise, success or failure depends largely on the personalities of the key management personnel representing the public and private entities. When two people dedicated to the success of a program are able to focus on outcomes, establish and maintain open and honest communications, and manage operations with outcomes in mind, programs are successful.

Early signs of potential failure are an unwillingness to change the old public culture, micromanagement, misunderstanding of, and failure to meet, the public sector's reporting requirements, bureaucratic snafus and a lack of effort to reduce or correct them, unclear lines of responsibility, and overexpectation of progress or near-term results. The solution to more than 90 percent of the problems we have faced in public/private partnerships is open and honest communications, a simple, and yet frequently difficult, objective to achieve in the highly politicized arena of corrections.

NEEDED: A RELATIONAL BREAKTHROUGH

Earlier, I listed one of the unanswered questions: Have the public and private sectors established a new interface that will allow public/private programs to flourish? My answer at this moment is no. The reason is far deeper than I have time to discuss here but goes to long-held political beliefs, social structure, self-preservation, deeply ingrained cultures, tradition, and, probably the largest issue, the fact that privatization has a "union-busting" image among public employee groups. When reduced to common denominators, what is best for the young people, while used as an emotional hammer, is seldom one of the serious discussion points.

Certainly, one might say it is easy for you, from the private sector, to argue that. Your job or your program is not necessarily on the line. My response is that, as a society, we can no longer afford to focus on "my program" or "my job." We have a rapidly expanding segment of our juvenile population that is increasingly out of control, preying on our society. Large chunks of real estate in our major cities, including Miami and Los Angeles, are economic wasteland because high juvenile crime rates keep businesses and customers at bay. In many of these areas public necessities such as public transportation and telephone services are not available, and even police and fire protection is seriously impacted. That is today.

If predictions are true, tomorrow will be much worse. Demographic experts predict that the new baby boomlet is right now feeding more juveniles into crime and that this new breed of criminal will be much younger and far more violent. Unless we can put our political differences aside and join forces, putting the best people from both sides of the public/private debate on the case, we will have much more to be concerned with than any particular job or program. Unless we put all of our efforts into creating programs, building facilities, training treatment professionals and operating programs that effectively redirect today's violent juvenile, our political disagreements will be irrelevant.

THE QUALITY OF SERVICE

If the arguments over cost savings of privatization are complex, quality of service issues are not much better. Again, the perceived level of quality provided in a public/private setting depends on which side of the argument is addressing the issue. Published reports from public organizations supporting privatization point out improved or equal quality in most areas, including food service, response to maintenance issues, and improved efficiencies in the use of personnel.

Those opposed to privatization in any form point out lower pay and fewer benefits, less qualified staff, reduced staffing leading to safety issues, and morale problems, all leading to reduced quality of service. In fact, however, the contracting public agency that sets the level of quality by contract and then monitors the service provided by regular performance audits. Failure to maintain specified levels of performance, including all phases of operation from education, to food quality, to safety, can mean termination of the contract.

One of the few definitive studies of quality issues again comes from Charles W. Thomas. In his 1994 presentation (Thomas, 1994), Thomas uses three measures: renewal of government contracts with private firms, private providers operating under consent decree or court order as a consequence of suits brought by prisoner plaintiffs, and compliance with standards of the Commission on Accreditation for Corrections of the American Correctional Association.

Under his contract renewal argument, Thomas assumes that contracts between public entities and private providers "would be terminated for cause or not renewed if contracting units of government were dissatisfied with either the cost savings being realized or the caliber of services being provided by independent contractors" (Thomas, 1994: 15). Thomas' review of contracts let since the mid-1980s revealed only one contract terminated. Our experience at Rebound closely follows those findings. Contracts with fifteen of our largest public agencies have been renewed annually for up to seven years. Rebound has had only two contracts terminated since our founding in 1988, and both of those ended by mutual agreement.

Thomas' second indicator is the number of consent decrees or court orders filed against private operators as a result of suits brought by inmate plaintiffs. According to Thomas, nearly three-quarters of American jurisdictions have major facilities or entire systems operating under consent decrees or court orders. None of those are a public/private facility. All of the corrections operations under court decree or orders are operated by public entities.

His third indicator is based on independent assessments of compliance with standards set by the Commission on Accreditation for Corrections of the American Correctional Association. He points out that the correlation between accreditation and the level of service is not perfect, because correctional facilities are not required to be accredited. However, he points out that more private sector operators have and are seeking accreditation than are public programs. He reports that of seventy-eight private facilities, more than 32 percent are already accredited, and another 38 percent are pursuing accreditation or plan to do so once their program is operational.

Thomas' final indicator points to a study conducted by Charles H. Logan (Logan, 1992). In that study, Logan researched institutional records of the Prison Social Climate Survey developed by the Federal Bureau of Prisons for a study of quality of life in the New Mexico Women's Correctional Facility, operated by Corrections Corporation of America (CCA), the Eastern New Mexico Correctional Facility, which housed the female prisoners prior to the opening of the CCA facility, and the Federal Correctional Institution in West Virginia. Logan's conclusion was that the private prison in the study outperformed the state and federal prisons, often by quite substantial margins, across nearly all dimensions (Logan, 1992: 17). Thomas concludes his discussion by stating that cost savings afforded by private/public partnerships in no way undermines quality and in many cases actually improve the quality of service.

While Thomas' and Logan's studies were based on adult facilities, our experience in the juvenile sector again follows their findings closely. In fact, even more factors are audited in juvenile programs than in adult systems, including development of social skills and recreational and educational achievement. Although it is difficult to measure our success against publicly operated programs, due primarily to a lack of available documentation from public programs, the general satisfaction of our agency clients indicates we are meeting or exceeding goals and quality standards.

ENSURING THE SUCCESS OF PUBLIC/PRIVATE PROGRAMS: STEPS TO TAKE

The *Wall Street Journal* (1995: A16), in an editorial, concluded, "Private prisons will have to be part of the solution to the nation's exploding prison population." The commentary pointed out that it can take up to four years to build a typical jail and cost $80,000 per cell, while the private sector can build the same facility in one-half the time at 60 percent of the cost. Notwithstanding one's position on privatization or public/private partnerships, it is evident that, in a time of overextended government budgets and unbridled growth in the number of criminal convictions and longer jail sentences, the public will demand solutions regardless of the impact on public jobs.

Today, public employees like those in Colorado may seem to have the irrefutable backing of a state statute or constitution, but given the choice of criminals loose on the streets for a lack of housing or a vote to change a state's constitution, I think the answer is clear. Survival of society will certainly supersede survival of public jobs or programs, especially if those public agencies are clearly not able to solve the problem. The answer is not in a continued debate between public and private sector providers.

The answer lies only in creating a system that focuses on the problem—young, violent juveniles who become mature, violent criminals—and then creates innovative programs that work. For that we need the best and brightest people, regardless of their political leanings.

As we argue the virtues and vices of public versus private juvenile programs, it reminds me of the U.S. space race with Russia during the early years. All three branches of the military services considered their rocket to be the best, the most powerful, the one to put the first American satellite into orbit. Stories of infighting between the navy and air force are enlightening. Dirty tricks were not out of the question. It was as if the reputation and very life of the particular service branch rested upon whose rocket would achieve the first world orbit. Thinking in Washington was that, indeed, out of this competitive process would emerge the best and most powerful launch vehicle. Then, in 1957, came the Sputnik, beeping its way around the world. Stunned and severely embarrassed, the three branches of service and government officials decided that only through cooperation was the United States going to catch up in the space race. Suddenly, national security took precedence over pride, wisdom overcame machismo, cooperation overcame competition. The rest is history.

I suggest that we in the corrections industry, whether adult or juvenile, are now at that same crossroad. Do we continue to concentrate our battles on the field of privatization versus public programs? Or do we need to look up and see what is happening outside our dusty battlefield? Do we need to consider seriously the consequences if we don't put partisan politics aside and take serious action soon?

Even the strongest critic of privatization and public/private partnerships will agree that "privatization" is here to stay. The times require it. If anyone understands the fickle nature of the voting populace, it should be those in the public sector. When it comes to survival, and the growth in crime is leading in that direction, voters will pick themselves over public programs any day. That same *Wall Street Journal* editorial I discussed earlier ended this way, "Citizens are demanding that government do more with less, and will no longer tolerate criminals going free because there isn't enough jail space. Given a choice between private prisons and the continued early release of criminals on the streets, we suspect the public will insist on going private" (*Wall Street Journal*, 1995). Clearly, there need to be a softening of positions and a meeting of the minds.

Arthur J. Maurice, director of the New Jersey Policy Research Organization, said, "Though never easy, change is a staple in every aspect of today's society. To keep government in the status quo will incur costs for all of us who depend on government, costs which we as taxpayers and consumers may be increasingly unwilling to pay" (Maurice, 1995: A13). Rather than continue our efforts to hold strong to our positions, we need to begin discussions and negotiations that can lead to more cooperation and improved services. Certainly there are many valuable theories and concepts already on the table and ready to be considered.

One of those has been offered by David R. Henderson, a research fellow with Stanford University's Hoover Institution. In a recent *Wall Street Journal* (1995: A11) guest column, Henderson agreed that opposition to privatization from the public sector needs to be "neutralized" by new concepts that may even make them advocates of privatization. He says that could be achieved by "offering a share of the net gains from privatization to potential losers." He cites the genius of Margaret Thatcher, who privatized the National Freight Corporation, "turning over 82 percent of newly created stock to current and former employees."

Another Thatcher privatization move sold government-owned public housing units to current tenants, discounting the cost based on the tenants' length of stay. Henderson said the government benefited by ending the fiscal drain on the treasury immediately and receiving income from the sales. The new owners lost their opposition to privatization and became a pressure group for private ownership of housing.

In closing, Henderson said, "The wrong way to privatize is to don green eyeshades and try to maximize the government's gain. The right way is to anticipate who might lose and to use some of the gains to win their support—50 percent of something is a whole lot better than 100 percent of nothing."

Certainly, this is only one way to address the concerns of those who perceive privatization as a losing prospect. The point is, there are creative ways to improve public services and to expand the capacity in our corrections systems that can minimize the impact on public sector jobs and programs. We're talking about a bigger pie, not smaller pieces from an existing one. Today's corrections systems need more trained people, not fewer; more programs, not less. Because a program becomes a public/private partnership does not mean fewer jobs.

More than 90 percent of Rebound's senior management group, including program directors, come from extensive backgrounds in public sector positions. As we and other private providers expand services and build new programs, there will be a need for more managers, more teachers, and more program directors. A sad reality of corrections is that the demand is far exceeding the supply and will for the foreseeable future.

Both public and private providers of juvenile programs must end our "interservice" bickering and come together to solve a problem that is slowly but surely beginning to envelop our entire society. We must move quickly. The anticipated increase in the number of juveniles needing our services and the mood of Congress, the legislatures, county and city governments, and the taxpaying public do not allow for the continued luxury of a slow, evolutionary process.

As Rebound explores new juvenile service opportunities throughout the United States and around the world, we are actively searching for ways we can work creatively and more effectively with public programs. We are willing to be the first to extend the olive branch, to begin discussions that lead to solutions, partnering, and teamwork. Our core values were created expressly for that purpose. What may sound like a form of martial arts, ICADO, actually represents a set of simple, yet exacting, standards that direct the way we serve our clients at all levels. It stands for:

Integrity, honesty and high ethical standards,
Continually striving for excellence,
Accountability in everything we do,
Decisions based on the best interests of youths, and
Open communications.

Josh Billings, a nineteenth century American humorist, said that "common sense is the knack of seeing things as they are, and doing things as they ought to be done." It is our hope that common sense will be at the core of every decision each of us makes as we seek solutions to juvenile delinquency and explore new opportunities to help young people make the right choices in their lives.

REFERENCES

American Correctional Association. (1992). *Overview of Privatization in Juvenile Corrections*. Washington, DC: Office of Juvenile Justice and Delinquency Prevention, Office of Justice Programs, March 31.

Corrections Journal. (1996). September 9.

Henderson, D. R. (1996). "Privatization Logic: Divide the Spoils and Conquer the Opposition." *Wall Street Journal*, September 13: p. A11.

Investor's Business Daily. (1996). March 4.

Logan, C. (1992). "Well Kept: Comparing Quality of Confinement in Private and Public Prisons." *Journal of Criminal Law and Criminology*, no. 83.

Maurice, A. J. (1995). "Privatization Works." *Asbury Park Press*, August 9: p. A13.

Naisbitt, J. (1995). *Trend Letter* 14, no. 8, April 13.

Thomas, C. W. (1995). "Testimony Regarding Correctional Privatization." Subcommittee on Crime of the House Committee on the Judiciary, Washington, DC, June 8.

Thomas, C. W. (1994). "The Transformation of Correctional Privatization from a Novel Experiment into a Proven Alternative." Presentation at the national convention of American Legislative Exchange Council, Tampa, FL, August 4.

Wall Street Journal. (1995). "Private Lockup." no. 6, Western Edition, July.

Chapter 7

Electronic Monitoring in Los Angeles County: A Case of Public-Private Partnership in Community Corrections

Sheldon X. Zhang

Most discussions on privatization of corrections focus on transfer of prisons and other custodial facilities into private management or ownership. This chapter describes a public-private partnership in Los Angeles community corrections, in which the private sector operates a home detention program while the public agency oversees its administration and the enforcement of government regulations. After a bumpy, two-year development, the program is now growing strong. It has provided valuable experience and knowledge on building a delicate partnership between the public and private sectors based on mutual needs and benefits.

The idea of private corrections is not new. Involvement of private organizations in the confinement and rehabilitation of offenders dates back to the eighteenth century (Curran, 1988). However, correctional tasks have traditionally been viewed as the responsibility of the public sector. Over the last two decades, rising crime rates, especially violent offenses, have prompted the public to call for "tough" sanctions for criminals. Legislators responded to the popular sentiment by initiating a series of changes in policies ranging from mandatory sentences to longer incarceration (Morris and Tonry, 1990; Skolnick, 1995). By 1990, virtually all new sentencing law was designed to increase the certainty and length of prison terms, to incapacitate the active criminal and to deter the rest (NCCD, 1992). The recent adoption of "three strikes" legislation in many states further indicates the continued decrease of public tolerance toward criminals.

Legislatures have significantly outpaced the construction of new facilities to accommodate the increasing mandatory and lengthy sentences. As early as 1983, criminal justice administrators identified prison and jail crowding as the most important issue facing them (Gettinger, 1984). Many jurisdictions across the country have been under court orders to reduce jail or prison overcrowding (Fyfe, 1991; Jolin and Stipak, 1992).

From 1970 to 1990, jail and prison population increased by nearly four times (NCCD, 1992). The Bureau of Justice Statistics (1992) reported that for the first time in U.S. history the number of men and women in prisons topped 1 million. This figure does not include the jail population, which, when last counted in 1992, amounted to 445,000 (Skolnick, 1995). By 1990, one out of every forty-six adult Americans was under some form of correctional supervision. This is twice the rate of correctional control that existed in 1980 and nearly three times the level in 1974 (NCCD, 1992).

The renewed interest in privatizing correctional services was a direct result of this rapid population growth in the nation's jails and prisons and skyrocketing costs involved in incarcerating the convicts (Johnson and Ross, 1990; Bowman et al., 1993). During the last sixteen years, the California prison population has increased sixfold, at a huge cost to the taxpayer. The prison budget has increased 400 percent in the past decade (Skolnick, 1995). Conventional government efforts have been rendered inadequate, to say the least; and taxpayers seem unable to keep up with the seemingly unending jail construction. It was estimated that California will spend 18 percent of its budget just to implement the "three strikes" legislation (Rydell et al., 1994).

One solution is to transfer part of the burden to the private sector, which includes contracting out the management and operation of correctional facilities, or the direct investment from the private industry in the construction of new facilities. The private participation in the incarceration of criminals is thought to reduce administrative cost, raise efficiency and increase the number of available facilities.

Another solution, which has received little attention in the discussion of privatizing government services, is searching for punitive and safe alternative sanctions to divert jail-bound offenders to community corrections. Historically, the justice system has had two options in dealing with convicted offenders-incarceration and probation. Both have been used excessively, with few intermediate sanctions (Morris and Tonry, 1990). In recent years, a wave of so-called intermediate sanctions has swept through the country, which include such alternatives as intensive supervision, shock incarceration and house arrest with or without electronic monitoring (Byrne, 1990).

The central component of these intermediate sanctions is intensive probation supervision (IPS), which has been widely implemented as a community-based alternative (Petersilia and Turner, 1990; Byrne, 1990). IPS is primarily designed to reduce prison overcrowding and place more restrictions upon those prison-bound offenders who would otherwise receive routine probation, which at the current state of local correctional budget often amounts to little more than suspended sentence or unsupervised community release.

Electronic monitoring (EM) arrived on the intermediate sanction's scene to enhance the intensity of traditional probation supervision. EM, in and of itself, is not a sanction but a means to ensure compliance with a curfew order or home detention. Since first judicially approved electronic monitoring appeared in 1983 in New Mexico, EM has received increasing interest and acceptance as an option for probation supervision across the country (Jolin and Stipak, 1992). By 1990, all fifty states had some EM programs, and the offenders being monitored reached a total of more than 12,000 (Renzema and Skelton, 1991).

There are two main reasons for the rapid growth in EM. First, the justice system's frantic search for alternatives to incarceration has created sufficient incentives for advances in electronic monitoring technology. Second, overcrowded jails and prisons have created a market with immense profit potential (Kastenmeier, 1986; Johnson and Ross, 1990). Entrepreneurs have been quick to cash in on this opportunity to pitch aggressive sales on this supposedly safe, punitive, and inexpensive solution.

THE INTRODUCTION OF ELECTRONIC MONITORING IN LOS ANGELES COUNTY

As the nation's largest probation agency, the Los Angeles County Probation Department currently supervises 90,000 adult offenders and 21,000 juvenile delinquents. They make up 42 percent of the state's probation population. In the past ten years, the number of offenders held in the county jail more than doubled, and so did the probation population. Community corrections is no longer just for petty offenders or misdemeanants; more and more convicted felons are released early or directly placed on probation due to jail crowding. In Los Angeles, 10 percent of the probation population are violent offenders, and more than one-third have been convicted on felony charges.

The rapid growth of the offender population has severely limited the agency's capacity to provide effective supervision. A large number of adult probationers are placed on automated "bank caseloads"-a computerized case management system that contacts offenders through correspondence and provides virtually no actual supervision. The regular caseload size has reached 300 per officer. Probation officers often find themselves trying to catch up with court-mandated paperwork rather than carrying out supervision activities. Probation in many cases ceases to be a punishment.

The county of Los Angeles has a history of contracting the private sector for certain services such as food preparation, laundry services, clerical support, and medical as well as mental health care. Most of these are auxiliary to the functions of the justice system. In 1986, Los Angeles County Probation started using electronic monitoring in its intensive probation supervision.

Several such programs have since been initiated either to alleviate overcrowding in the county jail or to divert jail-bound offenders to home detention programs, all of which were supported by federal and state grants on experimental or demonstration bases. In most of these programs, probation officers directly monitored offenders placed on house arrest, with technical assistance from the private industry. It soon became clear that there were no funds or staff to sustain these programs internally on a permanent basis, even though electronic monitoring had proven to be a valuable supervision tool. Meanwhile, many private companies launched aggressive marketing campaigns directly into the county's courthouse. Some were successful in persuading judges to send home detention cases to their private monitoring programs.

These companies operated on a freelance basis. There were no established standards to go by. Because participants paid a fee to the private company, it was not always in the company's best interest to report a violation for fear of losing a client. Some less than ethical companies would not report curfew violations as long as clients paid their bills. When found out, they would simply fold the business and open it in another area of the county under a different name. In addition, since no government agencies were involved, these private companies had no access to offenders' criminal records. As a result, no proper screening and investigation were done on participating offenders; an individual with an extensive criminal history could appear before the court on a low level misdemeanor charge and be granted home detention based solely on the circumstances of the present matter.

In response to the growing concerns over the lack of regulations in this emerging industry, the Los Angeles County Probation Department, in conjunction with other parts of the justice system, evaluated the situation and decided that a public-private partnership would be the best way to continue and improve this new alternative sanction. The need for such a partnership was obvious. The most compelling reason was budgetary. Home detention with electronic monitoring has proven to be a highly flexible alternative sanction that can be applied to a wide spectrum of offenders in a variety of sentencing contexts (Zhang, *et al.*, 1994). Depending on the specific needs of the offenders, it can be used as a punishment or a surveillance mechanism or both. However, labor-intensive case management and the technical support required for the monitoring equipment were beyond the financial capabilities of the local government. On the other hand, private companies were already providing electronic services to the courts on a limited basis but had no access to the backgrounds of the people they were monitoring. Nor do they have sufficient legitimacy to serve extensive correctional duties. Therefore, to maintain the services from private companies and ensure public safety, the most logical course would be a partnership.

In October 1992, a public-private home detention program, known as the Electronic Monitoring Service (EMS), was initiated by the Los Angeles County Probation Department. The program was designed to provide judges with an additional tool to impose punitive and restrictive sanctions on low-risk offenders. Participants are mostly petty offenders and misdemeanants who would otherwise be placed on summary probation or automated bank caseloads, which is basically a suspended sentence. Technically, these offenders should serve up to a year of jail time or a combination of jail and probation; given the current overcrowding situation, chances for them to go to jail or receive meaningful probation supervision are almost nil.

What makes this program unique is that it costs the county government nothing since the funding comes from fees paid by participating offenders. Elsewhere in California or in states such as Texas and Nevada, government agencies pay private companies for their electronic monitoring services since it is much cheaper for offenders to serve their jail time at home than in public facilities. In Los Angeles, the monitoring companies have also paid the cost of the Probation Department staff involved in oversight of the program. In addition, the program has established an innovative " indigent fund" to ensure equal service for offenders of all income levels. The established minimum cost of an offender in the EMS program is fifteen dollars a day or the offender's hourly wage rate, whichever is greater. All private companies have used a sliding scale based on the offenders' ability to pay.

Participants are screened prior to their enrollment in the program, and the private companies follow specific guidelines in monitoring their activities. Offenders with a history of, or conviction for, violent or sex crimes are excluded from the program. Also excluded are offenders convicted of selling or manufacturing drugs.

By its fourth year this public-private partnership had a current average of 800 cases per month. More than 90 percent of the offenders in the program have successfully completed their home detention sentences. Statistics are being collected for future analysis to determine, among other things, which types of offenders are most likely to perform well on EM, the impact of the program on offenders' life, and what types of offenders are most likely to recidivate. However, as far as the goal of the administration is concerned, the program has saved a significant amount of money for the county government by diverting jail-bound offenders. In 1995 alone, the program saved the county an estimated $15 million in the cost of jail beds.

The establishment of the partnership has not been a smooth one. Much of the first two years was spent on "defining" the joint venture and establishing countywide and even statewide standards in this new service industry. As a result of this program, there is now a standard operational manual in Los Angeles County that specifies the responsibilities of all partners in similar ventures. Also, as a result of this and several other consorted efforts, state legislation was introduced and passed in 1994 regulating similar business activities in California. Private companies can no longer operate without a license from the chief correctional officer of the local government; nor can they solicit business directly in a courthouse or from any judicial officers.

VENDOR SELECTION AND CRITERIA ESTABLISHMENT

The selection of vendors to provide monitoring services has been an experience of great significance for the Probation Department. The private sector and the government agency had to work with, and adapt to, each other's style. The checks and balances among the milieu of needs for profit and efficiency, accountability and bureaucracy often require understanding, patience, and even tolerance.

Initially, all vendors believed that there should be only one company to handle the entire county to maximize profit. The Probation Department decided to contract three vendors for several reasons. The first concern was that the size of the county, with its 8 million population, would require multiple providers to cover eleven superior court areas and thirty-one municipal court districts. A more important issue, however, was that such arrangement would prevent monopoly and keep prices down and the quality of services up. Another factor in the decision was that multiple companies can better provide continual service with little chance of interruption. Should one company fail for financial reasons or terminate service because of a labor dispute, the other two could pick up the slack.

The Probation Department first sent out a request for proposal (RFP) to solicit qualified vendors. All interested and qualified companies attended a bidder's conference. The evaluation process consisted of two phases. The first included an evaluation of the cost to the offender, the amount of financial support offered for the government agency's oversight cost, and the soundness of the proposed monitoring services. At the end of this phase, all proposals received a composite score and were ranked accordingly. In the second phase, the top six rated contractors were invited to make a presentation to the review committee. The review committee then recommended three vendors to the chief probation officer who made the final decision.

In all previous monitoring programs involving probationers in Los Angeles County, the role of the private companies was rather limited. They operated the equipment and reported violations, leaving the rest of the work, such as verifying curfew violations and filing proper paperwork, to probation officers. In the current EMS program, the Probation Department contractually requires the private companies to extend their services. In addition to monitoring, these vendors complete receiving procedures from the court; notify the appropriate authority of client enrollment; provide literature and referral materials (counseling centers, employment programs, etc.) to meet client needs; track and report offenders' adherence to other conditions of the court besides curfew hours, such as payment of fines or restitution; testify before court regarding monitoring system if needed in any judicial proceeding; and provide other services deemed necessary to the operation of the program. The vendors must also provide court-ordered breath alcohol testing via in-home monitoring units. Clearly, in this partnership the private companies are required to take on more responsibilities than just logging activities and reporting curfew violations.

WORKING WITH DIFFERENT STYLES

The public agency has to follow many legal mandates and procedures. This accountability entails many expectations that are not in the standard protocol of private business. For the private sector, the top priority is to increase clientele and profit and to run the business smoothly. Due to a lack of coordination between the players in the partnership and a clear understanding of each other's expectations, there have been many glitches since the program was conceived.

Soon after the program began, the issues of ambiguous responsibilities and overlapping authorities emerged. Initially, two offices within the Probation Department were involved in the program. The Office of Program Services, which spearheaded the project, provided direction to the private companies and monitored their activities; the Office of Pretrial Services was in charge of background investigation, assessing offenders' risk level and making recommendations to judges on suitability for participation in the program.

The ultimate authority was placed in Program Services, but Pretrial Services was not without a measure of control in determining the procedures of the program. Because of the involvement of two offices from the public sector, the vendors often voiced a feeling of frustration at not knowing who was in charge. For instance, vendors were required to submit identical information to both offices; which office was responsible for handling curfew violations was not clear to the vendors.

After a year of internal politics, restructuring took place in the Probation Department; and the entire oversight responsibilities and administrative duties were shifted to the Office of Pretrial Services. Furthermore, a steering committee was formed, involving representatives from both public and private sectors, to improve bilateral communication and make procedural decisions. The ambiguity has since been reduced.

Another problem involved uniformity in information gathering. The monitoring companies were required to use a computer system compatible with the government agency's. It took some time for the vendors to comply with this provision. During the early stage of the program, the two involved offices were interested in developing their own data sets and requested the vendors to submit specific information. This process frustrated the vendors, who had no idea what else their public partners might ask. Since the two government offices were not specific about the information needed and the format of the report due to lack of experience in such ventures, the three initial vendors submitted their own unique monthly reports. The judges, in turn, received reports of various formats. Eventually, both sides were able to agree on a format. With the advance in telecommunication technologies, the current monitoring company plans to set up a computer network in Pretrial Services, which enables the public agency to monitor all program activities instantaneously and download any information it needs.

Because of legal mandates and accountability, the public agency maintains the most control over the direction of the program, thus causing uneasy feelings on the part of the private sector about this unbalanced power structure. In the mid-1990s, the private companies, regardless of their abilities and resources, had to stretch to meet various demands imposed by their public partner.

For instance, during the initial stage of the program, the three private companies had to pay 20 percent of their gross revenue or $6,800 (whichever is higher) to cover the cost of the probation staff involved in supervising the EMS program. After six months, both sides still could not agree on the definition of "gross revenue" or even what format to use in compiling financial reports. The Probation Department soon came to realize that such an arrangement would be vulnerable to clientele fluctuations, thus limiting the flexibility to expand its oversight functions. As the first year's contract came to term, the Los Angeles County Probation Department moved to require the participating companies to guarantee the total support of its staff involved in the oversight of the program. The private vendors, of course, had to comply in order to secure the business.

This unbalanced power structure also affects other areas of the private business activities. For instance, participating companies cannot use information on the joint partnership freely in their advertising campaigns. They must not only clear their advertising material and correspondence regarding the program with the government agency but also adhere to certain bureaucratic protocols in their contacts with other public agencies and private companies.

Working with a government agency means having to deal with bureaucracy, which seems to have grown with time and developed a life of its own in this public-private venture. As the program has become more established, so have the procedures that govern various aspects of the partnership. Both partners in the venture complain about the excessive amount of paperwork and the slow decision making process, but neither seems able to do much about the situation. In the name of accountability, every change in procedure, as minor as a modification in a form, has to be approved through proper chain of command and documented carefully. Often what can be resolved in a simple phone call in the private sector will take weeks,, if not months, for a decision from the government agency. More than two-thirds of the workload in the government oversight agency involves processing paperwork. The private companies are required to submit identical copies of reports to both the court, which has jurisdiction over monitored offenders, and the Office of Pretrial Services, which,in turn, uses the same information to report to the court again. When judges want to find out about an offender's performance in the program, they turn to the government agency, supposedly only a program oversight function, rather than to the company that actually does the monitoring.

There are also other problems for which no easy solutions are in sight. For instance, the EMS was designed for low-risk offenders, but some judges simply ignore this provision and order EMS for offenders found to be "unsuitable or ineligible" by Pretrial Services. These autonomous judicial officers have created many awkward situations, and the Probation Department must obey court orders. However, by contract, the private companies monitor only participants deemed "suitable." Therefore, they are reluctant to take "unsuitables" who might undermine their program, but the correctional services that they provide are bounded by legal restrictions.

THE FUTURE OF THE PARTNERSHIP

Most privatization literature revolves around two key issues: cost-effectiveness and the quality of services. A frequent contention is that the government is plagued by bureaucratic red tape and inefficiency, but the private sector can profit from leaner organizations and flexible personnel and procurement policies, as well as more timely reaction to external demands (Janus, 1993). For the public-private partnership in Los Angeles County, cost-effectiveness is an irrelevant issue because the program is self-sustained; and the services are provided free of charge to the government.

Other financial issues have potential implications for the future of this partnership. A major concern is the program's ability to sustain itself with fees collected from participating offenders. Contracted by a government agency to provide correctional services, the private sector cannot " reserve the right not to serve." Private monitoring companies are not allowed to reject any cases handed down from the court. Recently passed legislation in California further bars judges and pretrial investigators from recommending offenders to home detention programs based on the offenders' ability to pay. In other words, the financial consideration of the private sector is effectively excluded from the judicial process.

In Los Angeles, the potential participant population was the main reason for the private companies to accept this rather "unfair" arrangement with the government agency. Initially, two measures were planned by both sides to prevent a financial failure: (1) establishing the indigent fund and (2) increasing the number of participants.

The indigent fund is an internal accounting arrangement to allow companies to charge more to those who can afford to subsidize poor offenders. It avoids possible discrimination against poor offenders who would otherwise be sent to jail, while well-off ones can pay for the monitoring services. However, the fund can be depleted quickly if a large number of poor offenders are sentenced to this program. It is estimated that it takes about four offenders who pay the regular fee (fifteen dollars per day) to support one indigent offender who can afford nothing. Fortunately, so far the majority of offenders referred to the program have been able to pay the regular fee. Disparities in payment so far range from fifty cents to $150 a day. Another proposal to prevent the depletion of the indigent fund would permit offenders to pay in installments and extend the payment period for a longer period of time so the total fees can be collected. Thus far, there has been no need to adopt this proposal.

However, efforts to increase referrals to the program have not been successful. Even with frequent seminars and presentations to judges and defense attorneys, the total referrals per month remain around 800, in a county where more than 300,000 arrests are made each year for various petty offenses and misdemeanors. It is not clear why the enrollment has remained low. Some blame the ineffective role the public agency plays in promoting the program to judges and defense attorneys. Others think that judges these days have so many sentencing options from which to choose that it increases the competition for the EMS. Still others, who claim that defense attorneys play a key role in recommending and negotiating sentences for petty offenders, charge that the public defenders, who represent indigent offenders, are reluctant to recommend the monitoring service for clients who cannot afford to pay for their defense counsel.

Whatever the reason, the low enrollment and the burden of supporting the public agency staff involved in the program have placed all three initial companies under severe financial burden. After two years of struggle, one company withdrew from the contract due to insufficient referrals, and the other two were merged and taken over by an out-of-state company. The restructuring has caused enormous confusion to the courts and offenders. The company going out of business left no employees to transfer ongoing caseloads to the other company, and no offenders in the program were notified of the change of monitoring company. Records and reports were either missing or not filed properly, seriously undermining the integrity of the supervision.

In face of this harsh financial reality, the Probation Department must accept the current monopoly, acknowledging that the current level of referrals can sustain only one company at a profitable level. To avoid future interruption of the EMS, another company has been selected as a backup. In case of a service disruption (due to bankruptcy or labor dispute), the current monitoring company is required to give a thirty day notice to the government oversight agency and to initiate the transition process.

In addition to the financial well-being of the private partner, the quality of service is also an issue. It is generally accepted that private operation might hold down costs by paying less in salaries and benefits (Patrick, 1986). Not only are government salaries higher than those in the private sector, but governments offer retirement and sick-leave benefits that far exceed what the private sector generally offers (Logan and Rausch, 1985). Lower wages are normally associated with lower skills (Patrick, 1986).

Although monitoring offenders by checking instrument signal readings and placing check-up phone calls does not require much training, many legal issues cannot be handled by private companies dealing with offenders in a complex justice system traditionally managed by trained officers. This is an especially pertinent concern when the sole reason for the private sector to become involved is financial gain. The minimum standards required by the government agency would become maximum standards for the private sector (Robbins, 1986). Corners might be cut to save money. It is not hard to envision, when profit is down, that the services that are most expensive and yield the least profit are likely to be trimmed. For instance, initially, most offenders on EMS were under supervision by both active (continuous) and passive (programmed contact) monitoring devices to ensure the highest level of surveillance. The active system costs twice as much as the passive system. Now program participants receive one or the other.

In the first four years, it was noticed that the telephone contacts and/or visits with clients were not always documented. Unauthorized leaves/entries/tampers reported by monitoring devices were not always recorded and explained in case notes. There was also a lack of follow-up in noncompliance cases. When some clients' phones were found disconnected, no follow-up reports were filed to the courts advising on the possibility of resuming monitoring. Although problems of this nature have mostly been attributed to the inexperience of the private sector working in the justice system, they certainly indicate that some corners may be trimmed to save money and staff time.

Close supervision from the government agency, therefore, becomes imperative to ensure proper business conduct. To maintain close oversight, the Probation Department staff have conducted unannounced audits of case files and randomly checked business records of the contractors. This has so far proven to be effective in keeping the private sector in compliance with the contract requirements and with the performance expectations of the public agency.

DISCUSSION

Traditionally, public and private sectors work rather independently of each other. The partnership in Los Angeles County can be best visualized as the intermediate range between the two ends of a continuum (Cox and Osterhoff, 1993). History has shown that neither the public sector nor private industry, when acting alone, has the capacity or resources to solve all correctional problems. A partnership enables utilization of the strengths of both sectors and reduction of the hazards and deficiencies that occur in each if operating separately.

Staffing flexibility and prompt reaction to outside demands are two distinct advantages of private involvement in correctional services. Such flexibility allows experimentation with innovative programs; their evaluation, without making permanent commitments to their staffing; and minimizing traditional bureaucratic constraints of the public sector. It also allows development of specialized services to cater to special needs of the correctional system, and it can be rapidly deployed to a greater geographic area with little of a public agency's boundary concerns (Mullen, 1985). A public-private partnership can extend or reduce its operation to meet the special needs of this intermediate sanction, thus reducing the instability inherent in most innovative programs.

It has not been an easy adjustment for the private companies to operate under the direction of the Los Angeles County Probation Department. The private companies have incurred considerable cost to comply with various government imposed contract provisions, such as twenty-four hour monitoring and sophisticated computer software. The initial optimism about instant financial success is being replaced by more realistic expectations and better understanding of the limits of the partnership.

Considering the Los Angeles County experience, it appears that several key points need to be observed if a public-private joint venture is to be implemented successfully:

1. The initial planning of the program must include all affected personnel and agencies from the court to probation, from line staff to management. The level of participation from involved personnel directly affects the operation and outcome of the program. Continuous cooperation and strong commitment from the leadership of each agency are imperative.
2. Responsibilities must be clearly defined for all partners in the contract, including where to turn for direction in case of conflict. This is especially true when more than one public agency is involved, since the government usually takes charge of the oversight of such partnerships.
3. It is important to be specific in assessing the needs and performance expectations of each party. Be sure to include provisions for evaluation and on-site monitoring, including access to all financial records. Goals must be clearly defined, with specific and attainable measurement that allows evaluation. Systematic and detailed data collection should be established early.
4. Affected offender population must be clearly defined and researched to determine if sufficient participants exist to justify the size of the planned operation and to clarify the kind of impact it will produce on the population.

Public-private ventures can be a cost-effective solution to alleviate government's fiscal pressure. Despite many ups and downs, the public-private partnership in Los Angeles County is still valuable, if not fully successful. Although most of the administrative arrangement restricts the private partner, such restriction is necessary for the program's legal and ethical obligations. It seems unavoidable that a government agency maintains close control over this program, which is gaining momentum and legitimacy in intermediate sanctions. The government agency also shares the responsibility to nurture and promote this innovative program, since the success of the public-private partnership ultimately depends on the number of referrals to it from the court. Without sufficient participants, the program is doomed.

REFERENCES

Bureau of Justice Statistics. (1992). *Correctional Population in the United States.* Washington, DC: U.S. Government Printing Office.

Bowman, G. W., S. Hakim, and P. Seidenstat eds. (1993). "Introduction." In G. W. Bowman, S. Hakim, and P. Seidenstat, eds., *Privatizing Correctional Institutions.* New Brunswick, NJ: Transaction.

Byrne, J. M. (1990). "The Future of Intensive Probation Supervision and the new Intermediate Sanctions." *Crime & Delinquency* 36, no. 1: pp. 36-41.

Cox, N. R. Jr., and W. E. Osterhoff (1993). "The Public-Private Partnership: A Challenge and an Opportunity for Corrections." In G. W. Bowman, S. Hakim and P. Seidenstat, eds., *Privatizing Correctional Institutions.* New Brunswick, NJ: Transaction.

Curran, D. J. (1988). "Destructuring, Privatization, and the Promise of Juvenile Diversion: Compromising Community-Based Corrections." *Crime & Delinquency* 34, no. 4: pp. 363-378.

Fyfe, J. J. (1991). "Some Hard Facts about Our Wars on Crime." *Washington Post National Weekly* 24, April: pp. 8-14.

Gettinger, S. (1984). "Assessing Criminal Justice Needs." *National Institute of Justice Research in Brief.* Rockville, MD: National Criminal Justice Reference Service.

Janus, M. (1993). "Bars on the Iron Triangle: Public Policy Issues n the Privatization of Corrections." In G. W. Bowman, S. Hakim, and P. Seidenstat, eds., *Privatizing Correctional Institutions.* New Brunswick, NJ: Transaction.

Johnson, B. R., and P. P. Ross (1990). "The Privatization of Correctional Management: A Review." *Journal of Criminal Justice* 18: pp. 351-358.

Jolin, A., and B. Stipak (1992). "Drug Treatment and Electronically Monitored Home Confinement: An Evaluation of a Community-Based Sentencing Option." *Crime & Delinquency* 38, no. 2: pp. 158-170.

Kastenmeier, R. W. (1986). "Corrections and Crowding." *Corrections Today* 48: pp. 38-42.

Logan, C. H., and S. Rausch (1985). "Punishment and Profit: The Emergence of Private Enterprise Prisons." *Justice Quarterly* 2: pp. 303-318.

Morris, N., and M. Tonry (1990). *Between Prison and Probation: Intermediate Punishments in a Rational Sentencing System.* New York: Oxford University Press.

Mullen, J. (1985). *Corrections and the Private Sector.* Washington, DC: U.S. Department of Justice.

NCCD (National Council on Crime and Delinquency) (1992). *Criminal Justice Sentencing Policy Statement.* San Francisco: NCCD.

Patrick, A. L. (1986). "Private Sector-Profit Motive vs. Quality." *Corrections Today* 48: pp. 68-74.

Petersilia, J., and S. Turner (1990). *Intensive Supervision for High-Risk Probationers–Findings from Three California Experiments.* Santa Monica, CA: RAND.

Renzema, M., and D. Skelton (1991). "The Scope of Electronic Monitoring Today." *Journal of Offender Monitoring* 4: pp. 6-11.

Robbins, I. P. (1986). "Privatization of Corrections." *Federal Probation* 50: pp. 24-30.

Rydell, C. P., F. A. Allan, and P. C. Jonathan (1994). *Modeling the Costs and Benefits of Three-Strike Laws.* Santa Monica, CA: Rand.

Skolnick, J. H. (1995). "What Not to Do about Crime: The American Society of Criminology 1994 Presidential Address." *Criminology* 33, no.1: pp. 1-15.

Zhang, S. X., R. L. Polakow, and B. J. Nidorf. (1994). "Varied Uses of Electronic Monitoring: The Los Angeles Experience." In J. O. Smykla and W. L. Selke, eds., *Intermediate Sanctions: Sentencing in the 1990s.* Cincinnati: Anderson Publishing.

Chapter 8

Policy Considerations in the Privatization of Local Detention Facilities

Sarah Armstrong and David Moulton

Jail populations are rising at a rate comparable with that of prisons, though the total numbers are a little smaller. From 1978 to 1990 the average daily jail population in the U.S. rose from 158,000 to 408,000. The rated capacity of the jails was 389,000, so they are as a group overcrowded by about 5 percent, despite the addition of more than 21,000 beds in the previous twelve months alone. The problem is worst for the large systems. Of the 508 jurisdictions in 1990 with a jail population of over 100 (which held 80 percent of all jail inmates), 142 were under court orders to limit their populations (Bureau of Justice Statistics, 1991: section 2 passim).

The experience of California is instructive (and disturbing): from 1980 to 1988, nearly $1.5 billion in bonds was approved for jail construction, yet there was a shortfall of 11,000 beds by 1990. Average construction costs were about $50,000 per bed, and operating costs far exceed construction costs over the life cycle of the facility (National Institute of Justice, 1990: 1-11).

Between fiscal year 1984-1985 and fiscal year 1989-1990, adult detention costs in California grew by 110 percent, while county general-purpose revenues (which provide nearly all of the funds for jail operations) grew by only 58 percent. Justice expenses, along with health and social services, are assuming an ever-larger share of local revenues and threaten to overwhelm the entire local government system. Public safety costs, already 56 percent of general revenues in 1984-1985, would consume 65 percent by 1994-95 if they continued to grow at this rate.[1] Obviously, there is not much more room to grow.

A number of factors contribute to this growth, a modest increase in crime being unfortunately not the most important, but amelioration of the problem requires major changes in the justice system and most probably in society as a whole. In the meantime, local authorities see themselves as confronted with two enormous challenges: how to construct enough beds to meet the demand, and how to pay for operating them.

The cost of many types of governmental operations has led to increasing interest in privatization of services in the hope that they can be rendered less expensively by entrepreneurs. This cost increase is painfully apparent for corrections, one of the few government services whose budget growth appears to be nearly immune to fluctuations in revenue and general economic health.[2] Although the existence of this phenomenon implies that economists and policy planners should examine why such rapid growth is occurring, much more attention has been paid to accepting the growth and focusing on limiting its costs, for which privatization is one of several options.

The decision to privatize a correctional facility, given that it demands a substantial proportion of existing fiscal resources, has become a not uncommon phenomenon following the industry pioneering of the Corrections Corporation of America (CCA). The U.S. General Accounting Office estimated that in late 1990 nearly 10,000 prison beds and over 6,000 local jail beds were operated by private contractors.

The debate accompanying the development of private prison contracts is not over and continues to be intense. The decision to fully privatize at the local level, in jails, is much more complex yet has received almost no attention in privatization literature. This chapter identifies these complexities as a first step towards assessing how such variables will affect the jail privatization decision. The authors assume during the course of this chapter that privatization of local jails means the total privatization of jail operations, not simply of individual services such as medical care or food service. Finally, this chapter does not intend any implications for jail construction.

The function and purpose of the local jail add a couple of important ingredients to the mixing bowl of the debate. These two issues are the focus of this chapter: a jail houses both unsentenced and sentenced persons and the local jail is an integral part of the criminal justice adjudication process and, both directly and indirectly, the local political system. The first issue introduces the problem of a diverse and quickly changing inmate population. The second issue has implications for the political and authoritative importance of the jail as a tool of society.

FRAMING THE DEBATE: PUBLIC VERSUS PRIVATE SERVICES

In a nonsocialist economy the reason that government performs a task at all is that private enterprise does not do it. This may be because there is not a private market for the service, there is no anticipated profit associated with the service, the service is generally felt to be a moral or social duty of government, or some combination of these.

There is no natural private market for a jail. It is a public good, spreading its benefits to all regardless of whether they purchase it directly. Who could voluntarily support a jail? Certainly not the inmates who are the direct "consumers" of the jail nor the victims of crime who would benefit from the incapacitation of their aggressors. The innumerable nonvictims of crime would benefit from the removal of the criminal from the community yet would not be inclined to pay directly for it. Unquestionably, then, it must be the government that ensures that a jail is supplied, though this, of course, does not mean that the government itself must construct or operate it.

Privatization in this context is the contracting out of public functions to private contractors. Suppose that private enterprise can supply a service more cheaply than the government; does this imply that it ought to do so? Not necessarily, especially if cost is not the only determinant of the value or effectiveness in producing the service. Should the lowest bidder win the right to sit on the Supreme Court? If the service that is provided by government can be exactly duplicated by a private contractor, then the contractor should be hired at less cost. Is it really the same service?

A business is in business to make money. This is not an ignoble end, but it is a clearly defined one. A government, in contrast, provides a service because it is felt to be in the public interest. This is much less clearly defined, but, obviously, it is not the same as turning a profit. (There are, of course, intermediate positions between these two poles that both business and government entities take, as well as hybrids of combined business and government activity. For simplicity of discussion, public and private are viewed here as opposites, although in reality each may share the goals of the other to some degree or work jointly on a single project).

When privatization is undertaken, it is the task of the government (as contracting agent) to devise a way by which public interest and private profit will lead to the same result. The problem is that the purely private enterprise will find it more profitable to provide the contractually required services while cutting corners in areas that are not specified in the contract yet are perceived as in the public interest. If some aspect of the operation is important, it must be included as a performance goal. In other words, an effective foray into privatization requires an ability to document explicitly all required outcomes for the given task. Successful privatization cannot be based on the entrepreneur's goodwill alone, just as successful government service cannot be based on cost-effectiveness alone.

John Donahue provides a useful guide to measuring how differences in function affect the decision to privatize a jail. In his book, *The Privatization Decision: Public Ends, Private Means* (1989), he has suggested criteria for deciding whether to privatize any service or keep it in public hands. First, can the activity ("task at hand") be specified precisely, and its delivery accurately evaluated? Second, can the process of choosing a contractor be made reasonably competitive?

These criteria appeal to common sense. If the government can define what it wants, it can purchase that service. Evaluation of the product ensures that the service contracted for was actually delivered. The competitive market will drive down the cost of supplying the service; here an important consideration is preventing the contractor from developing a monopoly position.

What is a jail's purpose, and what is the service it provides? Ultimately it is to support the justice system's response to crime, but jails have two immediate goals that are more easily observed. One of these purposes is the housing of persons who have been arrested and not yet sentenced or released. Ideally, they are kept healthy, housed safely, transported back and forth to the courts as the case is processed, and made available for attorneys, visitors, investigators, and so on.

The second immediate role of the jail is to confine for a period of time those who have been sentenced. Here again the product is visible-house inmates securely and humanely, as for pretrial inmates. For these measurable outcomes privatization would seem to be a candidate for consideration.

Of course, there is more to a jail than these simple outcomes. Jails should, if possible, contribute to the reduction of crime, but this goal is so distant, with so many other contributing factors, that it becomes impossible to isolate the influence of the jail on the crime rate. Moreover, there is not general agreement on how to reduce crime. Many authorities feel that crime can be lessened by deterrence, making jail an unpleasant and unattractive option for a potential offender (Kalmanoff, 1976). Somewhat in conflict with this viewpoint are humane treatment and rehabilitation so that when inmates are released they will at least not be more inclined to misbehave than when they were arrested. An intensely practical requirement is that jails need to encourage in the public the belief that they are fighting crime right now. These goals are not easy to specify in a contract, nor is it clear how they should be ranked with the previously cited tangible goals of incarceration.

Jails and prisons share the goals of responding to crime and gaining public acceptance. Their real difference arises out of the variations in function of the jail and the prison. These were identified earlier as the housing of both unsentenced and sentenced populations in the jail and the position of the jail as a local element in the criminal justice system, whereas prison deals with the output of that system. Thus, application of the criteria that affect the jail privatization decision should focus on function and procedure in achieving both short- and long-term goals.

In his book, *Bureaucracy: What Government Agencies Do and Why They Do It* (1989), James Q. Wilson provides a useful context for digesting Donahue's criteria. He categorizes activities and products as inputs and outputs. An activity that involves an emphasis on procedure and that does not produce a readily quantifiable product or a clearly identifiable outcome, such as the operation of an embassy, is an example of an input-oriented activity. An output-oriented task is one in which the emphasis is on ends, not means. Road construction results in a visible and measurable product. The government is not concerned with all of the details of how a road is produced if it meets the specifications of smoothness, durability, and so on.

Donahue contends that privatization will be less satisfactory when the outcome (output) is not easily measured and when the way in which a program is carried out is as important (input-oriented) as the output. As with the ambassadorship, there are many important government functions where not all of the outputs are measurable. Jail operations do not stand out as either singularly input-oriented or output-oriented. Both procedure and outcome are necessary for effectiveness of service. Producing the outcome of delivering an inmate to court while maintaining a record of no escapes is important. Meeting this outcome by holding all prisoners in twenty-four hour restraints is not a humane means of achieving these ends. Likewise, keeping sentenced inmates in a resort setting on an island in the Caribbean, even if it were cost-effective and entirely secure against escape, would not elicit community support.

Both means and ends are important to the private jail issue, an important conclusion for designing contracts to carry out privatization. The decision to privatize a county jail should include careful examination by the local authority to determine whether its ends can be defined accurately enough to be quantified and whether the means can be articulated well enough for the contracting agency to monitor them.

ISSUES IN PRIVATE JAILS

Pretrial Release

Let us now consider the policy issues that might affect future decisions to privatize and provide a means of evaluating jail operations that have already been contracted out. Jails and prisons perform many of the same functions. They must house, clothe, and feed inmates; provide hygiene and medical services; maintain order; and keep records of inmate movements. Often they try to provide inmate work programs, education, and other rehabilitative services. In physical layout jails and prisons may be quite similar.

The jail, however, differs from the prison in several significant ways relevant to the question of privatization. The job of the prison is to hold felony prisoners until the conclusion of their terms. It has a relatively homogenous population: inmates are sentenced, facilities or zones are generally of one broad security level (minimum, medium or maximum), and the turnover of inmates is not too fast, as most sentences are longer than a year. The primary function of a jail is to hold arrestees before trial or other disposition of their cases. Many convicted persons-both misdemeanants and felons with combined jail/probation-also serve short sentences (up to a year or so) in jail rather than in prison.

The jail handles a population that is more diverse in many ways: both unsentenced and sentenced offenders are housed; there is a wide spread among the severity of charges, from vandalism to first degree murder (and a moderate number of jail inmates-perhaps five to ten percent of the admissions-have no local charges but are held for other jurisdictions); and there is a constant turnover of inmates being booked and others being released. Average lengths of stay are quite short, typically, about one week, though they range from a few hours to a year or more.

Pretrial release is an issue that is of major importance and is qualitatively different from those faced by prison operators. The majority of persons who are arrested and booked into jails are in fact not held. Those who are charged with lesser, non-violent offenses are usually released after booking on their promise to reappear for the appropriate court hearings. Some go out on bail or bond, but more common are jail citations or "release on own recognizance" (ROR), for which no cash bond is required.

The extent of pretrial release varies greatly by jurisdiction, but in jails where there is an overpopulation problem almost all misdemeanants and perhaps half of the felons are released. Some of the less serious offenders will return to serve their sentences in the jail if they are convicted.

Thus, pretrial release is an issue of importance. However, the decision to release or detain does not rest upon the jail administrator alone. Several offices-law enforcement, prosecution, defense, courts, probation, as well as the jail itself-can be involved in the release decision at various points. Jail population management requires cooperation among these system elements, which are, to some extent, natural antagonists. Judges and prosecutors have the largest role in the release decision, and they are, in general, elected officials who are not obligated to compromise their independence in performing their duties as they see fit or, in particular, to consider the managerial problems of jail overcrowding.

There are other release decisions to which similar considerations apply: pretrial diversion, as to substance or spousal abuse prevention programs, and sentencing alternatives such as house arrest, work, or restitution programs. Inmates who serve their sentences in the jail typically receive credits for work time or "good time" (i.e., no misbehavior) that shorten their sentences. To some extent prisons also allow early releases, but the modes of release are fewer and statutorily determined.

Jail operators are inevitably involved in release decisions of these sorts. While individual release decisions are frequently made by formula, the policies establishing the formulas are not routine. Even in the release decisions there is some room for judgment. Since private operators are usually compensated according to the number of beds occupied, will this affect the decision to release?

There is scant empirical evidence on this point. It nonetheless presents an issue that should be explored fully before privatizing. The contract should be specific as to who makes release or diversion decisions and who monitors the contractor's performance in these areas. It may well be preferable for release decisions to be totally retained by the county. CCA's contract to run a jail and jail annex in Bay County, Florida, (450-500 beds) includes provision of a county employee who monitors the contract and reviews all release decisions made by CCA personnel operating the jail. This shows one possibility of accounting for potentially subjective decisionmaking, though it may not totally solve the problem.

However, the contract cannot spell out how a contractor will behave in making policy decisions on pretrial release issues, since these are unknown until they appear. All that can be specified is the extent to which the operator will participate in the decision-making process, if at all, and even then the dynamic between the contractor and members of the public sector cannot be predicted. Retaining control over pretrial release decisions, as in Bay County, also restricts the possibility of CCA's devising innovative ways of making safe releases and managing jail population.

The Jail's Role in the Criminal Justice System

The jail houses persons at the front end, at the conclusion, and at all the stops in between in the adjudication process. Of great importance to criminal justice planners is the fact that the local jail plays a crucial role in the overall criminal justice system of its jurisdiction. While the prison is, of course, also an element in the criminal justice system, it is separated both in location and in operational responsibility from county functions. The jail can be better compared to a point on a circle, and the prison to an end point of a line; even this simplifies the interactive relationship of the jail relative to the rest of the system.

During a defendant's pretrial incarceration, there is intense activity among agencies in the adjudication process. At some point an attorney is retained by, or assigned to, the defendant; the defendant may meet with his attorney and various investigators of the case; a pretrial release unit may meet with the inmate for interviews; and so on. This introduces a key issue for consideration: can a private operator replace a public entity in this inherently legal and political environment?

The jail has a dynamic position in the flow of criminal justice. It receives offenders off the street, moves them to pretrial release or to court, receives sentenced persons returning from court, and may either hold them or send them to probation or prison. Aside from the population handling-issues that come out of this (such as the fact that the jail probably has much less diagnostic history on its inmates than the prison will have), the jail's position raises questions of interrelationships among various criminal justice agencies.

For a variety of reasons there is a tendency to fill all the jail beds that are available, and more. The system actors with the most control over the jail population are not formally obliged to restrict jail admissions. Jail expansion, if unrestrained, would consume all of a county's resources. Fiscal responsibility demands that the jail population be managed by choosing which of the offenders should be detained and which must be released. Because of the independence of the players this must be accomplished at least partly by voluntary agreements.

The traditional jail operator in most counties is the sheriff. Besides his or her role in law enforcement, the sheriff must play the dual role of administrator and politician in the running of the jail. The sheriff oversees population management to ensure that safety and security are maintained and at the same time interacts with the county for funding and with other criminal justice officials to coordinate use of the jail in order to limit the powerfully negative effects of crowding.

For example, the state of Florida mandates the convening of a group called the County Public Safety Coordinating Council, which comprises the top officials from all county criminal justice agencies, including the sheriff and state-funded positions of state (district) attorney, public defender, circuit court judges, and state probation administrators, among others.[3] California, Washington, and several other states mandate similar bodies). The council is instructed to seek strategies of effectively managing its resources, of which the jail is the largest and most prominent example. These are people who interact professionally on a daily basis and determine criminal justice policy for the jurisdiction.

How would the replacement of the sheriff by a private contractor affect this council? One of the major issues facing it is the determination of the appropriate and affordable number of jail beds. (The legal issues associated with such a change are not considered here.) Historically, opponents of prison privatization have pointed to the problems of tying a profit incentive to housing an ever larger population. The private operator of a jail would have little incentive to limit jail crowding and encourage reductions in jail populations if payment was tied to the number of inmates held and their length of stay.

A staff attorney with the American Civil Liberties Union's (ACLU) National Prison Project described this concern to a U.S. congressional hearing on the privatization of corrections.[4] The ACLU worried over the absence of tight monitoring ability, claiming that there is "not yet in place a mechanism that makes private authorities.responsible for their actions in the same way that government authorities can be held accountable under current law."[5]

As public policy planners, we would take the ACLU's repetition of this common claim one step further. Aside from the mechanisms needed to create accountability in the smooth operation and conditions of the jail itself, mechanisms to smooth the flow of coordinated criminal justice planning are not at all clear once a private operator enters the scene. This role of the jail operator has been particularly neglected, and its importance underestimated.

The coordinating councils provide a forum for consumers of the jail to plan intelligently their shared use of a scarce resource; it is the only stand against the natural incentives to increase incarceration that exist individually for criminal justice officials. For public officials there is a strong incentive to put offenders in jail but little incentive to take them out or to avoid its use in the first place. Instead of money, the driving force for the criminal justice administrator - the district attorney, the judge, the sheriff-is public pressure and interest. Public sentiment in the United States continues to support criminal justice personnel who are perceived as "tough on crime," which translates into higher incarceration rates, criminalization of more activities, and longer sentences. The release of a single inmate who commits a particularly dastardly crime can thus have a devastating effect on professional careers but, far worse, result in long-term reverberations on strengthening rigid crime policies.

There is no simple message that can be sold to the public to change increasingly more punitive outlooks on criminal activity. There is incentive among elected officials and other government officials within this framework to be accountable to more than the public's sense of outrage at crime; there is also that other great scourge: taxes. Unfortunately, the public in recent years has given local officials conflicting directives. At the same time that public support has rallied around stringent crime bills, such as the indefinite prison incarceration option for habitual offenders in Oregon or California's "three strikes" law (1994), bond issues for local jail construction are regularly defeated at the polls (e.g., California, 1996). This, at least, provides some disincentive to jail crowding among county officials: Limited funding demands that not everyone that the public would like to see off the street is kept off the street. Availability of jail space is quickly met by an increased demand for its use that overshadows any proportional relationship between crime rates and jail population size. Unfortunately, the public does not seem willing to reduce its demand, although it has been historically unwilling to pay the price for its supply.

Where does the private operator fit in all this? Buckingham Security Limited's now defunct contract in Butler County, Pennsylvania, reveals the pitfalls in failing to address the jail's systemic and political functions.[6]

Butler County, like Bay County, Florida, is small, with a low crime rate. The local jail was 100-bed facility when it was transferred to private management.[7] Buckingham's contract and operation of the jail in its first year demonstrate how operational ambiguities can be worked out in local jail privatization. Although it at first resisted, Buckingham took on all of the county employees who had operated the jail under direct county management. A county employee also monitored the contract, providing the jail with a modicum of public authority, both in the eyes of the inmates who did not experience a change in their "keepers" and by the public who still perceived great county involvement through the county monitor. Despite glowing evaluations, higher staff pay, and improved morale following the contract's first year, the jail was returned to county management within two years. Tensions with the local union representing the correctional officers and consequent loss of support by the county commission effectively ended the otherwise uneventful contract with Buckingham (Logan, 1990). How would Buckingham have fared if it played a larger role as an "equal" agency in criminal justice negotiations among other officials, or if it had cultivated political relationships with county commissioners that other county officials find necessary?

How or whether specifications of this role could be included in a contract with a private jail operator is not clear. Applying Donahue's framework, it appears, however, that it may be impossible. The more the outcome is unknown, and the more the contracting government agency cares about how something will be done, the less easy it is to contract out the activity (Donahue, 1989). The political needs of the jail operator are an important element of the total job description but, like most political needs, are constantly changing.

A reviewer of this chapter suggested that privatized jails should hold only sentenced inmates. Some jurisdictions-not all-do maintain separate pretrial and sentenced facilities. While there are still many release decisions to be made for sentenced inmates, we agree that a privatized sentenced facility would face fewer problems than would a full-service jail.

CONCLUSIONS AND NEXT STEPS

This chapter is a preliminary attempt to identify the additional variables intrinsic to a discussion of the merits of privatizing local jails. These are, first, the implications of a pretrial population, which adds an element of increased inmate movement and turnover, wide variations in charge type, uncertainty as to behavioral characteristics, differences in length of stay in jail, and, ultimately, pretrial release decisions. Second, the system role of the jail and the ensuing political nature of its operation and management transform the debate of privatizing local corrections into a fundamentally policy-oriented one.

The hope of this chapter is not to conclude the debate but to continue it. To this end, identification of the added complexities of local corrections precedes a discussion of legal and contractual issues, which continue to be well voiced among the debaters of the private prisons question. In evaluating whether to privatize or not, we have found that the local political atmosphere forces this decision to be considered and made at this point on a case-by-case basis as the conditions that would generalize the appropriate ideal for privatizing a local correctional facility cannot exist in an environment of such complexity and ambiguity.

There are still unresolved issues in the general debate over the privatization of corrections. This includes issues of accountability, legality, and a subject touched on but not thoroughly examined by this chapter: competition. Finally, the possibility of contracting a jail out to a nonprofit organization alters the boundary of the discussion altogether.

We can only observe from experience in the field that, without the operation of the jail as a shared scarce resource, nothing a county might do, including privatizing, will save it from indefinite crowding and lawsuits.

NOTES

1.The assessment by California's association for county administrators is one of the first times these administrators have addressed the corrections issue with such a sober outlook (Simpson, 1991: 1-4).

2. In the recession-plagued state of California, the Department of Corrections is the only department whose budget was increased for fiscal year 1993-1994.

3. Florida Statute #951.26, as amended in 1992.

4. ACLU attorney Edward Koren, during the hearings ("Sessions," 1986: 7, 14).

5. Ibid., 7.

6. See Logan (1990: 19-37) for the best synopsis of the experiences of the private jail.

7. Florida ranks among the top three states with the highest incarceration rates, number of facilities, and number of inmates per capita nationwide (Bureau of Justice Statistics, 1991: 612-618).

REFERENCES

Bureau of Justice Statistics, U.S. Department of Justice. (1991). *Sourcebook of Criminal Justice Statistics. Correctional Population in the U.S., Section 2.* Washington, DC: U.S. Government Printing Office.

Donahue, J. D. (1989). *The Privatization Decision: Public Ends, Private Means.* New York: Basic Books.

Kalmanoff, P. (1976). *Criminal Justice: Enforcement and Administration.* Boston: Little, Brown.

Logan, C. H. (1990). *Private Prisons: Pros and Cons.* New York: Oxford University Press.

National Institute of Justice. (1990). "Jail Construction in California." *NIJ Bulletin,* August.

Simpson, R. P. (1991). *Jailhouse Blues: Hard Time for County Taxpayers: A Study of The Rising Cost of Incarceration in California.* California Counties Federation. Sacramento, CA.

Wilson, J. Q. (1989). *Bureaucracy: What Government Agencies Do and Why They Do It.* New York: Basic Books.

Chapter 9

Privatization Lessons from Hospital and Prison Experiences

Van R. Johnston

Managers and administrators have been under significantly mounting scrutiny to increase productivity and the delivery of quality services while defending themselves against growing budget constraints. Taxpayer revolts, debt limitations, and recessions have only added pressure to attempts by administrators to optimize cost-effectiveness. Clearly, this sort of stress causes public sector officials to review their mixes of alternatives while attempting to balance their budgets and satisfy their clients and constituents. It also provides an opening for enterprising entrepreneurs to explore potential opportunities for providing public sector services on a contractual basis.

Whether the privatization option is, in fact, better than a more traditional public sector agency approach with updated or streamlined management techniques may simply be a matter of debate. When faced with such increasing demands, the evidence is that public officials have opted for a mix of privatization alternatives in increasing numbers. Certainly, there are concerns for equity, due process, public participation, sovereignty, and effectiveness with theirconnotations of public sector values (Nagel, 1989). When public budgets were so harshly constrained in the 1980s, however, managers and other decision makers in the public arena found themselves choosing private sector oriented privatization options and worrying about the consequences later (Palumbo, 1986).

Economic considerations, usually raised as questions of efficiency in professional management circles, are powerful (Carver, 1989; Donahue, 1989). They are often translated into practicality-oriented arguments when privatization alternatives are considered. Justification for practical privatizing efforts usually ranges from the cost of service provision itself to satisfying short-term project needs, dealing with increasingly limited state and local government budgets, and improving service quality and government operations (O'Brien, 1989). Efficiency and economy are relatively simple to identify in such a context (Moe, 1987).

State and local governments often find themselves being forced to live in a changing world where economy and efficiency must not only count but, indeed, be showcased. At the same time, traditional public sector values and interest groups force their way into decision makers' choices as well. Concerns for equity, security, and union positions simply do not cease to exist. The result is that an increasing number of those who analyze privatization efforts and programs at the state and local levels, among others, are claiming that we really are at a place and time where we have some sort of blend of public and private sectors. Various terms are used to describe this state of affairs, including "sector blurring" and "twilight zone" (Bozeman, 1987; Moe, 1987).

Managers in the public sector have become increasingly aware of their dilemma. Efficiency-based productivity formulas are often interpreted as optimizing cost criteria but with some significant risk of jeopardizing legal, safety, political, and other significant rights (Kautzky, 1987; Palumbo and Maupin, 1989). A lot can disappear in transitioning from a public sector model to a private one. In making such adjustments, state and local administrators have experienced serious conflicts in attempting to cope with the problems of integrating their new roles, limitations, risks, and responsibilities with those that they've more traditionally identified with (Thompson, 1983; Kolderie, 1986; Sullivan, 1987; Moe, 1987; Donahue, 1989; Palumbo and Maupin, 1989).

State and local officials, managers, and administrators in Colorado have experienced and experimented with a variety of privatization efforts in the last two decades. They have lived through the preceding trauma and concerns. They have had some unique, notable, and exhilarating results. Moreover, they have had some marginal results, some failures, and even collapses. There have been a lot of lessons along the way. Most would call Colorado's privatization experience progress. Some would not.

Two specific areas of privatization experimentation will be examined. One is in the area of health care. The case is that of University Hospital, and it is an intriguing and complex learning experience. The second is a multi-iterative attempt to cope with getting tough on crime but being unwilling to pay the price. It was a struggle between and among state and local authorities, on one hand, and private sector entrepreneurs, on the other, to deal with a prison overcrowding crisis precipitated by a change in the state law.

The context for both cases is one in which Colorado found itself immersed in a serious recession. Colorado began experiencing serious fiscal problems at both the state and local levels in the early 1980s when the economy collapsed. The primary reason for the downturn was the energy bust. The state did not have a very diverse economy. The bust occurred, and tens of thousands of energy industry employees left the state. The exodus seriously impacted the tax structure. Without a diverse economic base, serious fiscal stress was experienced at both the state and local levels of government.

As agencies and governments struggled to cope, privatization-based alternatives increased in terms of perceived potential viability. As state and local officials attempted to deliver their services while trying to be as fiscally frugal as possible, the privatization experiments became a reality. The two explored here are the privatization experience of University Hospital and the multi-iterative privatization thrusts that have occurred, successfully and otherwise, with the prison system at both the state and local levels.

UNIVERSITY HOSPITAL

University Hospital is the teaching facility for the University of Colorado (CU) Schools of Medicine, Pharmacy, Dentistry, and Nursing. CU's affiliated Health Sciences Center also has over 850 scientific laboratories, which contribute biomedical research findings that can be used to assist patients at University Hospital. In 1985, a four-year reorganization study was undertaken to explore more efficient and effective options for delivering services at University Hospital.

University Hospital has a quality faculty and is recognized for a number of scientific achievements, including expanding its research output dramatically during the decade of the 1980s. There have been many serious problems, however. For years, there has been a financial deficit. The number of indigent patients kept increasing, with consequences for the budget. The state purchasing system has been cumbersome, and many argued that it affected both teaching and research by restricting opportunities to buy cutting-edge equipment at this potentially prestigious hospital. There was also a problem with borrowing capital, as a state organization, for necessary improvements.

Perhaps most noticeably, there was a chronic staffing problem that centered on inadequate state salaries. The hospital's nurses, feeling the financial squeeze as acutely as any other group, revolted in 1988 with a mass resignation. Two-hundred and fifty-six nurses quit their jobs to protest what they believed was an intolerable situation (Barrow, 1991). This event became the catalyst for a reorganization that went into effect October 1, 1989. A coalition of hospital administrators, faculty physicians, the CU Board of Regents, and state legislators launched an assault on the hospital's operational and fiscal problems with a privatization effort, packaged as House Bill 1143. The sponsors of the bill in the Colorado General Assembly were Representative Chris Paulson and Senator Jeff Wells (Kilkenny, 1991).

Holding up caveats against this adjustment were the attorney general, Duane Woodard, and the Colorado Association of Public Employees (CAPE). The attorney general argued that public assets would be transferred to private control and that the bill therefore violated two sections of the state constitution prohibiting such a transfer. CAPE argued that the hospital privatization bill was an attempt to evade civil service protection measures for over 1,500 employees (Morson and Newcomer, 1990). They geared their case to assert that the constitution wouldn't permit the state to reorganize itself into private subsidiaries.

The governor, Roy Romer, let the legislation turn into law without his signature. The effect of the adjustment was that almost 2,000 classified employees were forced out of the state civil service and into a new corporation-based personnel system. A Denver district court found the legislation to be constitutional. CAPE appealed to the state Supreme Court, which found the legislation to be unconstitutional on Christmas Eve 1990 (Roberts, 1990).

During the fifteen months that University Hospital (UH) operated as a private hospital, a number of significant operational and fiscal problems were improved upon. UH turned around its cash position from a deficit of $3.8 million in June 1989 to a surplus of $2.4 million in June 1990. It also collected $7.8 million of outstanding debts. A new purchasing system was brought on-line, as was a new patient billing system. UH also put together a new hospital executive leadership team that had been recruited from prestigious teaching and research hospitals to support the implementation of its new administration. It then successfully recruited new nurses and other health care professionals. New personnel and pay systems were brought on-line with subsequent reports of success. New and expanded programs were also developed, which included an AIDS program, a new bone marrow transplant unit, a sports medicine program, cardiology developments, and other success experiences. Furthermore, employee and patient satisfaction survey results both showed improvement (Barrow, 1991).

With the words "we find that the statute violates Article XII, Section 13, and is unconstitutional beyond a reasonable doubt, we reverse" (Colorado Supreme Court, No. 89 SA476, 1990), the Colorado Supreme Court decided on December 24, 1990, that the legislature cannot simply turn the hospital, which is a public asset, over to a private corporation. If the regents still control the facility's board of directors, the personnel system is still really public, too (Morson and Newcomer, 1990). Estimates ranged from $10 million (Gavin and Schrader, 1990) to $25 million (Gavin, 1990) if the state would have to convert University Hospital to a public agency again. There was also very serious concern regarding all the new programs, systems, and gained efficiencies, not to mention the morale and turbulence problems involved.

Nurses' pay went up approximately two dollars per hour during the fifteen months of privatization. Nursing and other staffing concerns improved dramatically (Schrader, 1990).

The director of Institutional Relations at the University of Colorado Health Sciences Center has expressed serious concern for potential staffing problems that could come out of the Colorado Supreme Court decision. He argued that noncompetitive salaries, for instance, create rippling financial problems throughout the institution. He also noted that only a relatively few (21 of 822) nurses remain as state workers; and only 270 of 2,200 full-time employees are civil service. Retirement system and Social Security problems could be extreme, especially for those who withdrew state retirement investments. Recruiting would be a major problem. Purchasing would also be seriously affected (Barrow, 1991).

Regina Kilkenny, associate director of public affairs for the University of Colorado Health Sciences Center, analyzed a new bill introduced in March 1991 designed to deal with the Supreme Court's concerns for constitutionality. CU's goal would be to create a constitutional, private, nonprofit organization. University Hospital believes this really is possible with the appropriate adjustments. Among these significant adjustments will be an option for past employees to choose between the current private-oriented personnel system or the public civil service system. Future employees would not be given a choice and would work for the private, nonprofit corporation.

The bill Kilkenny analyzed was introduced in the state Senate on March 18, 1991. It is Senate Bill 225, sponsored by Senate majority leader Jeff Wells, a Republican from Colorado Springs. The bill, as implemented, would create a new nonprofit corporation to operate University Hospital.

The main features of this new bill, designed to eliminate the concerns of unconstitutionality found in the old House Bill 1143 by the Colorado Supreme Court, are as follows: $60 million debt limit is set for the corporation; the university would be required to provide $3.2 million in each of the first two years for the medically indigent; and hospital employees would not be forced to switch to the private corporation from the public personnel system (Editors, *Denver Post*, 1991).

Colorado's University Hospital is one of five state universities to have divested its hospital by 1990. The others are Arizona's University Medical Center in 1985, Florida's Shands Hospital in 1979, Maryland's University Medical System in 1984, and West Virginia's University Hospital in 1985. The targets are typically financial enhancement, more management flexibility, and increased responsiveness to changing environments (Johnston, 1990).

In 1991 and 1992 legal action was taken against University Hospital again. The Colorado Association of Public Employees challenged several aspects of UH's reorganization plan. Most seem to think that the struggle, at that point, was directed more toward fine-tuning the level of privatization of University Hospital than of any total success by either party. Something approaching a public authority would appear to have been a more optimal organizational structure than either the formerly fully public University Hospital or a completely private corporation.

LESSONS FROM PRIVATIZING UNIVERSITY HOSPITAL

The University Hospital privatization experience in Colorado not only offered a number of discrete lessons along the way but also demonstrated a multi-iterative evolutionary learning process. Concluding that remaining public would keep the organization from excelling and from becoming the entity it wanted to become, it also determined that a break with tradition was needed to free itself from the restrictive bonds of the public agency syndrome.

The shackles on growth and development that University Hospital found itself bound by included a rigid civil service system and low state wages that frustrated employees and created morale and recruiting problems. UH also found itself constrained by a traditional low-bid purchasing system. Imagine the frustration of perceiving one's organizational image as a world-class research and teaching institution, while having to utilize a low-bid purchasing system to acquire minimum specification equipment. The experience of living through such situations drove UH to struggle even harder for reform and reorganization. When over 250 nurses went on strike at one time, it proved to be the catalyst needed for transforming change.

The coalition of legislators, administrators, regents, board members, doctors, nurses, and staff did its front end work reasonably well. The legal planning wasn't the best, however. Nonetheless, like other privatization efforts, the frustration was so great that the transition would proceed anyway. Attorney general Duane Woodard warned that these were constitutional issues that needed to be addressed and dealt with. He wasn't listened to until the state Supreme Court decided that the privatizing reorganization was, indeed, unconstitutional.

In the meantime a great deal of progress was made. In the short period of fifteen months, for instance, financial controls were established, debts were collected, capital was raised, new programs started and expanded, salaries increased (e.g., nurses' salaries went up $2.00 per hour during this period), morale improved, and recruiting was successful. The reorganized institution was beginning to live up to its image of itself. New vitality and enthusiasm seemed ubiquitous.

Then came the Supreme Court decision. Noting UH's tax based funding, a requirement to take care of the state's indigent, evasion of its civil service responsibilities, and a personnel system still dominated by the regents through control of the board, the Supreme Court determined that, without changes in the constitution, UH would remain a public agency. The Colorado Association for Public Employees was behind the suit. It had lost in the district court in Denver but won the battle when it got to the Colorado Supreme Court.

University Hospital could remember how desperate its existence had become before the reorganization and how exciting, stimulating, and productive professional life had become after the changes. It recommitted itself to the reorganization and to meeting the court's concerns head-on. It also found a sponsor in 1991 in Senator Jeff Wells for SB 225, supporting the reorganization. Other states were also reporting successful hospital privatization experiments, including Arizona, Florida, Maryland, and West Virginia. Such successful experiences provided even more encouragement for the CU Hospital.

University Hospital is pursuing its vision of a transformed institution. Its goal now is a compromise entity known as a public authority. This configuration gives it significantly more control over its destiny while allowing it to break free of its more stringent and traditional public sector shackles. One major state organizational adjustment of note was that the state created a new Colorado Department of Health Care Policy and Financing, which would solve the indigent care problem raised by the Supreme Court (Gavin, 1992).

Among the many lessons University Hospital learned along the way was that it did not want to remain as it was when it started to reorganize, as a traditional state agency, with all the restrictions, while trying to become a world-class research and teaching institution. The value of longer-range and more precise and comprehensive legislative planning and lobbying became a lesson due to the Supreme Court decision. The experience of the exciting professional success unfolding from the transition was inspiring and left UH determined to persevere. The vision was working, with necessary modifications. Persistence was paying off and would continue to yield positive results. The transformation had, indeed, produced greater management flexibility, an increased capacity for responding to changing environmental conditions, and more professional financial management. Perhaps most importantly, University Hospital learned that its vision of its transformed and privatized self was very close to being right on target. The collective sentiment is that the successes have been well worth the effort. There are a lot of important lessons to be learned from this University Hospital experience.

PRIVATIZING PRISONS IN COLORADO

Colorado has had a few significant experiences with prison privatization. Each was quite different. There were some successes and some failures resulting from each experiment. Along the way we have learned a number of lessons. The prison dilemma was also exacerbated by the economic recession precipitated by the energy bust.

The severity of Colorado's prison problems developed primarily out of a series of sentencing law changes that began in 1977. Since those tougher laws were passed, the prison population was figured to increase to 7,256 by 1990 from 4,400 in 1987. It must be recognized that no funds were allocated for developing that increased capacity. From this situation alone, it is evident that facilities needed to be found quickly to house the extra 2,850 inmates.

The state's legislators got tough on crime and, at the same time, held the line on increasing taxes as much as possible. The result was a significantly growing need to either build several new prisons by the early to mid-1990s or find other facilities appropriate for prisoner confinement (Colorado Division of Criminal Justice, 1987).

Colorado then refused to accept its prisoners at state penitentiaries. The backup was handled at several county jails. Arapahoe and Denver Counties sued to help alleviate the problem and to collect the real costs of over forty dollars per prisoner per day. The counties' cases were handled by Arapahoe County. Because of the court cases the state began taking responsibility for the majority of its own prisoners. Colorado prisons were eventually actually forced by a court order to clear state inmates out of county jails by January 1, 1989 (Pankratz, 1988).

Jails at the local level were being used to confine and maintain individuals sentenced to a term of imprisonment in a correctional facility. The Colorado Department of Corrections was authorized to reimburse any county providing such service sixteen dollars per day for maintaining a state prisoner in a county jail (Morrissey, 1987).

Besides using local county jail facilities for state purposes, then, the counties were concerned with recovering significant amounts of money being spent to maintain state prisoners. The American Civil Liberties Union also promised law suits on the overcrowding issue but waited for a quite a while to see which way the state would decide to act on this issue. Colorado was becoming increasingly aware that it had serious problems regarding overcrowding in its correctional facilities.

The Colorado Department of Corrections also experienced a number of lawsuits itself. The most significant case regarding the state's prison population and the issues of living conditions and overcrowding was *Ramos v. Lamm* (1986). In this collection of cases the federal court actually took jurisdiction over the operations of the state prison system. Because of the lawsuit, the Colorado Department of Corrections had to pay millions of dollars to upgrade the condition of its physical facilities and to improve the health care system for its prisoners (Kautzky, 1988).

In 1985, Colorado passed the most significant legislation affecting Colorado's exploding prison population, HB 1320, the 1985 modified presumptive sentencing law. This law is popularly known as the "Mielke bill." "Mielke" significantly lengthens the sentences given the prison population in Colorado. The Colorado State Division of Criminal Justice projections indicated a 77 percent increase in the prison population between 1987 and 1995. The length of stay increased most dramatically due to the Mielke bill. It has been the driving force behind the exploding prison population projected for Colorado (Colorado Division of Criminal Justice, 1987b).

The Colorado Senate voted to lighten prison sentences in Colorado in order to ease the pressure of severe prison overcrowding. It also voted for an electronic lotto game to pay for new prisons. Jeff Wells, state Senate majority leader, was the sponsor of both bills. He explained that even with both of these significant changes, the prison system in Colorado would still have serious difficulties (Diaz, 1988).

Governor Romer vetoed the lotto bill, arguing that encouraging gambling was not the way to solve the state's prison overcrowding crisis. The governor wanted to increase taxes on alcohol and cigarettes to raise at least some of the needed revenue (Sanko, 1988). Following the veto, state representative Paul Shauer promised to fight to override the veto (Roberts, 1988). Lotto was approved shortly thereafter (Roberts and Diaz, 1988), and ticket sales began on January 24, 1989. Early estimates indicated that lotto resources would likely be below previous worst-case estimates, however (Fulcher, 1989). The seriousness of the prison crisis continued to accelerate, requiring a serious analysis of all available alternative resolution strategies.

There have been two significant experiences with prison privatization in Colorado. The first was an effort by Harvey Prickett, president of American Correctional Systems at Ault, Colorado. It failed. Another, at Brush, Colorado, did not succeed at first. It has since become a real contributor to the state in terms of delivering prison services. Colorado is increasingly willing to look at such private sector options since its prison system became significantly overcrowded, primarily due to substantially more harsh prison sentences given since the 1985 presumptive sentencing law (HB 1320, the Mielke bill) was passed.

The first case was based in Ault. Ault is a small town about twenty miles east of Fort Collins, Colorado, an economically depressed area. It is also the location selected by private entrepreneur Harvey Prickett, president of American Correctional Systems, Inc., of Fort Collins. Prickett started a joint venture to build a private, 500-bed prison, which he planned to become part of the Colorado prison system.

Prickett recruited the Bechtel Group, Inc.'s, Bechtel Civil, which had recently renovated the state's "old max" prison at Cannon City. He also joined forces with Daewoo International (America) Corporation. The Ault Public Building Authority was the overall manufacturer in this case. Shearson Lehman Brothers of New York was to provide funding after the preliminary capital project was completed. Prickett recruited Colorado State University to provide the inmates and guards education services. His strongest argument for the facility was that it would meet or exceed all of the American Correctional Facility standards. Prickett's project looked promising in the beginning, then ran into problems with the state government. Prickett did not make a convincing case to the legislature. Neither did he and his entrepreneurial group convince Governor Roy Romer, who indicated that Prickett's project was not what the state was interested in and refused to include it in the options for prison system expansion in Colorado. Ground for the private prison at Ault had already been broken, however. When Daewoo heard of the governor's rejection of the project, Daewoo pulled out quickly, and the project collapsed.

The second case deals with Rebound! Colorado. Originally, it was called the High Plains Corrections and Training Center. It was a facility built in Brush, Colorado. Designed as a facility that could meet the needs of the Colorado Division of Youth Services, it was to be cost-competitive. Cost efficiency was to be based on better cash flow, lower administrative costs, and higher employee morale. High Plains was built as a model "speculative" prison. Its population was targeted to be the juveniles committed to the state's Division of Youth Services. There was, however, no contract. The Division of Youth Services was not interested in High Plains, and it became an empty private facility without paying clients.

The legislature, however, later had a change of heart and provided preliminary funding for the effort. By the end of 1989, High Plains (renamed Rebound! Colorado) had 100 juvenile inmates. By mid 1990, this private sector youth prison found a niche in the overall prison system by providing facilities for both Colorado inmates and detained youths from other states who are taken in on a contract basis. The experience with Rebound! Colorado is being watched very carefully. This experiment will very likely be built upon as Colorado expands its operations toward the private sector as it struggles with an increasingly serious prison overcrowding crisis.

At a 1990 privatization presentation of the Colorado chapter of the American Society for Public Administration, both Betty Marler, a senior administrator with the Colorado Division of Youth Services, and Jane O'Shaughnessy, CEO of Rebound! Colorado, stated that Rebound! Colorado had found a viable nitch and was doing a good job as a private prison. Therefore, this could be a prototype for the future in Colorado (O'Shaughnessy, 1989). We must be cautious, however, because this is a youth prison and not close to a full-scale maximum security operation (Johnston, 1990).

Colorado has been forced by the overcrowding crisis situation to consider all available alternatives. Privatization therefore will likely become more of a possibility as it continues to develop and demonstrate successful projects. Colorado decides to move more significantly toward private ventures in this arena, it should carefully pre-structure a meaningful request for proposal system to ensure the strongest possible bidders are approached. It could also prepare an encompassing and highly focused model contract so it can control the entire operation. It should also develop a first-rate monitoring and evaluation system to ensure satisfactory implementation of the contract over time.

Privatization is viewed as an increasingly viable alternative that could lead to efficient provision of mandated prison services, while seriously monitoring and controlling costs. The classic efficiency and economy arguments are made and debated, for example, by Carver (Carver, 1989) and Donahue (Donahue, 1989). Colorado's Corrections Department executive director noted that privatization "is a reflection of private sector opportunity to take the advantage of reluctance of taxpayers to absorb the costs of incarcerating the substantial increase of offenders resulting from harsher sentencing policies. The willingness of citizens to support the increase in the certainty and severity of sentencing has historically not been matched by financial enthusiasm for addressing the attendant costs" (Kautzky, 1987).

Palumbo warns us that we should be cautious when utilizing privatization to help solve prison problems. He notes that there are many serious and unresolved questions. He gives us a corrections example: "There are enough serious questions to warrant caution in moving forward with greater profit-making involvement in corrections, but, given the nature of policy making in American politics, the likelihood is that we will back into greater use based on ideological and expediency grounds and then try to work out the complicated ethical, moral, constitutional and management questions later" (Palumbo, 1986).

It is very likely that Colorado will continue to experiment with privatization in order to optimize efficiency, economy, and administration. These experiments demonstrate the increasing pressures on government officials. This pressure is perhaps most intense on those struggling at the state and local levels who are attempting to apply frugal fiscal practices while searching for innovative and creative ways to deliver mandated services.

PRISON PRIVATIZATION LESSONS

There is a variety of significant lessons to be learned from Colorado's experiences. Perhaps the greatest is that if state and local governments decide to get tough on crime, they need to be responsible enough to provide the economic, political, legislative, and administrative support to get the job done right. Otherwise, there will be a surfeit of legal, fiscal, and managerial problems to cope with along the way. Not providing the infrastructure for implementing the Mielke legislation (HB 1320), which just about doubled criminal sentences, is a good example of this shortsightedness.

The state also received lessons from not accepting its prisoners and forcing them back onto the local jurisdictions. It was sued and lost and forced by the courts to expand the prison system. It instituted a lottery, shortened sentences, privatized where it thought possible, and squirmed in a number of other ways to cope with this dilemma.

The state was also sued in *Ramos v. Lamm* for overcrowding and unhealthful living conditions. Because the state did not show appropriately responsible behavior, the courts took over operation of the prison until "old max" was renovated. Several millions of dollars were spent on upgrading the facility and the health and safety infrastructure. The excess population incarcerated therein was appropriately dispersed.

The attempt to establish a private prison at Ault collapsed. Harvey Prickett and his Fort. Collins-based American Correctional System did their private sector homework reasonably well. Bechtel Civil is one of the best firms in the world. Shearson Lehman was lined up for financial assistance. Colorado State University was going to supply training. Even the international Daewoo Corporation wanted to be involved. What Prickett and his associates failed to do was their public sector homework. They failed to convince the governor and the legislature. Therefore, no commitment, no contract, no prisoners, and no funding. This all leads to no operation and no profit.

Another significant example of the importance of breaking even financially in privatizing ventures is the High Plains Correction and Training Facility at Brush, Colorado. Originally, the facility was built as a speculative prison for youthful offenders. The entrepreneurs did not work their plans out with the Governor, with the legislature, or with the Colorado Youth Authority. When the physical plant was ready, the Youth Authority said it was more of a traditional prison emphasizing incarceration. The Youth Authority emphasized rehabilitation. No communication, no contract, no youth offenders, no profit. High Plains went out of business.

Finding new financial backers for this private venture in Boston, the project was renamed Rebound! Colorado. The company did its lobbying and marketing homework this time and won state support on the order of $1 to get started. It is successful. The lessons were learned in this case.

Other areas in the prison system requiring learning and diligence include unions, contracts, sovereignty, ethics, and administrative efficiency. What happens if private sector guards unionize and go on strike? This is an area involving health and safety, and contingency plans are needed. More professional and comprehensive contracts are also needed. Request for proposal procedures could also be established. Sovereignty issues can arise when government turns its duties over to contractors.

What about ethics? Is it ethical for private sector guards with vested interests to be able to determine time off for good behavior when their income could be affected? This is a conflict of interest. Trading government protections and standards away for the lowest private sector bids may not be appropriate in many cases for a wide variety of reasons. We do need to learn lessons from our experiments and experiences. It looks as though we may have to live through multi-iterative learning loops until we are able to navigate optimally in this new dimension of the merging sectors.

PRIVATIZATION LESSONS AND THE FUTURE: LEARNING TO LEARN

In retrospect both cases analyzed in this chapter, although fraught with difficulties and obstacles, demonstrated the net benefits of privatization. Both ventures endure and have passed the test of time. The University Hospital model has proven itself in terms of providing financial stability and efficiency.

Rebound! has also demonstrated the effectiveness of the privatization option and continues to operate successfully. An examination of Rebound!'s recent record is found in another chapter in this book.

Privatization is no longer a new experience for the practitioners and theorists in both the private and public sectors who are struggling to optimize cost efficiencies, on one hand, and quality delivery of services, on the other. We have learned at all levels of government, including state and local, that we can contract out basic services such as food and laundry and gain significant cost reductions. As the level of service gets more complex, however, experience has demonstrated that the savings are not quite so clear. When we approach fully privatized operation of public sector service agencies and units, many serious questions and issues remain unclear or yet to be resolved.

Public sector managers and administrators have traditionally labored under far more restrictions than their private sector counterparts. As a result they've developed an image of being less efficient and business-like (Holzer and Rabin, 1987). The Reagan administration's Grace Commission Report on cost control produced almost 2,500 waste reduction recommendations for government administrators. During a period of heavy emphasis on economy and efficiency, deregulation, contracting out, and more comprehensive privatization projects, keeping public sector values such as equity, service, numerous protections, and due process in mind can become increasingly difficult. By the mid-1980s, as an example, over forty states were under court order or were subject to litigation to improve either prison operations or conditions. In order to cope, there was an increasing number of recommendations to privatize, including one from the President's Commission on Privatization that was targeted for the state and local levels as well as the federal government (Linowes, 1988).

Critics of privatization can be found in academe and among practitioners in both the private and public sectors. Classic opponents include the American Federation of State, County and Municipal Employees, the American Bar Association, the National Sheriffs Association, the American Civil Liberties Union (Donahue, 1989), and numerous local, state, and federal professional organizations. They warn that privatized operations often get very political and frequently involve questions regarding skimming and ethics. They also deliver caveats about fraud, lack of competition, less accountability, and service interruptions due to a variety of market-based causes. In the long run, they argue, there is significantly impaired control over the quality of service (Palumbo and Maupin, 1989; O'Brien, 1989).

Some argue eloquently that government has a responsibility to provide its services safely and humanely and at reasonable costs. There is a public trust involved that government does not have a right to abdicate. DiIulio quotes James Madison to make such a point. "In framing a government which is to be administered by men over men, the great difficulty lies in this: you must first enable the government to control the governed; and in the next place oblige it to control itself" (DiIulio, 1987). DiIulio goes on to admonish that unless public management does a better job of determining its role and managing its organizations to deliver optimally its services, its viability will increasingly crumble (DiIulio, 1989).

Others provide similar warnings. Palumbo notes the dangers involved in following expediency and ideology toward profit making and efficiency when the trade-offs can involve significant constitutional, ethical, and management problems (Palumbo, 1986). Along with Maupin, he warns that questions regarding safety, legal rights, and political matters need to be dealt with responsibly (Palumbo and Maupin, 1989). Kautzky and Mande (Kautzky, 1987; Mande, 1987) also commented on the inclination of citizens to demand significant and comprehensive responses to public problems and then squirm to avoid the fiscal responsibilities that come with these decisions.

There is no question that privatization is here to stay. It has even become increasingly difficult in many cases to determine what services ought to be public or private. We are also witnessing the growth and development of an intermediate sector, some sort of hybrid of the private and public sectors. Bozeman, Moe, and Stanton refer to the phenomenon variously as sector blurring and the twilight zone (Moe, 1987; Bozeman, 1987; Moe and Stanton, 1989). Without question we will need to learn to navigate optimally in this new dimension. Perhaps most importantly, we need to learn to learn from our experiences with privatization. The lessons gleaned from our hospital and prison privatization experiences are likely to prove most valuable in making these adjustments as we approach the millennium.

REFERENCES

Barrow, B. (1991). *FACTS: University Hospital Reorganization House Bill 1143, 1989.* Denver: University of Colorado Health Sciences Center.

Bozeman, B. (1987). *All Organizations are Public: Bridging Public and Private Organizational Theories.* San Francisco: Jossey-Bass.

Carver, R. H. (1989). "Examining the Premises of Contracting Out." *Public Productivity and Management Review* 13, no. 1, Fall.

Colorado Division of Criminal Justice. (1987a). "Sentencing Trends in Colorado." *CDCJ Bulletin*, August 1.

Colorado Division of Criminal Justice. (1987b). "What Causes Correctional Populations?" *CDCJ Bulletin*, December 15.

Colorado Supreme Court, No. 89 SA476 (1990).

Diaz, J. (1988). "Senate Approves Lotto Games to Pay for New Prisons." *Denver Post*, March 22.

DiIulio, J. (1987). *Governing Prisons: A Comparative Study of Correctional Management.* New York: Free Press.

DiIulio, J. (1989). "Recovering the Public Management Variable: Lessons From Schools, Prisons, Armies." *Public Administration Review* 49, no. 2, March/April.

Donahue, J. D. (1989). *The Privatization Decision: Public Ends, Private Means.* New York: Basic Books.

Editors. (1991). "University Hospital Bill Introduced." *Denver Post*, March 19.

Fulcher, M. P. (1989). "Estimates of Income from Lotto Shrinking." *Denver Post*, January.

Gavin, J. (1990). "New Law Urged for University Hospital: Move to Reprivatize Iffy." *Denver Post*, December 29.

Gavin, J. (1992). "Statewide Health." *Denver Post*, February 22.

Gavin, J., and A. Schrader (1990). "Storm Warnings Out for University Hospital 'Disaster.' " *Denver Post*, December 27.

Holzer, M., and J. Rabin (1987). "Public Service: Problems, Professionalism and Policy Recommendations." *Public Productivity Review*, no. 43, Fall.

ISC/Rebound! (1991). *Colorado Pre-Parole Facility: Overview.* Henderson, CO: Group 4 International Correction Services, and Rebound! Colorado.

Johnson, J. (1988). "Politics, Power Struggles: A Part of Divestiture Battle for University Hospitals." *Hospitals*, June.

Johnston, V. R. (1990). "Privatization of Prisons: Management, Productivity and Governance Concerns." *Public Productivity and Management Review* 14, no. 2, Winter.

Kautzky, W. L. (1987). *Privatization-An Analysis*. Colorado Springs: Colorado Department of Corrections.

Kautzky, W. L. (1988). *Report on Colorado Correctional System: A Blueprint for Public Safety, 1987-1988.* Colorado Springs: Colorado Department of Corrections.

Kilkenny, R. (1991). "University of Colorado Hospital Privatization." (Unpublished.).

Kolderie, T. (1986). "The Two Different Concepts of Privatization." *Public Administration Review* 46, no. 4, July/August.

Lane, G. (1991). "Adams Will Act on Prison." *Denver Post*, March 20.

Linowes, D. F. (1988). "Privatization: Toward More Effective Government." President's Commission on Privatization.

Mande, M. (1987). *Getting Tough on Crime in Colorado.* Colorado Division of Criminal Justice.

Moe, R. C. (1987). "Exploring the Limits of Privatization." *Public Administration Review* 47, no. 6, November/December.

Moe, R. C., and T. H. Stanton (1989). "Government Sponsored Enterprises as Federal Instrumentations: Reconciling Private Management with Public Accountability." *Public Administration Review.* 49, no. 4, July/August.

Morrissey, D. F. (1987). Report to the Colorado General Assembly on CRS 17-1-112, *Privately-Operated Prisons: Legal Issues.*

Morson, B., and K. Newcomer (1990). "CU Hospital Public, Court Says." *Rocky Mountain News*, December 25.

Nagel, S. S. (1989). *Higher Goals for America.* Lanham, MD: University Press of America.

Newell, T. (1988). "Why Can't Government Be Like Government?" *Public Productivity Review* 12, no. 1, Fall.

O'Brien, T. M. (1989). *Privatization in Colorado State Government.* Colorado Office of the State Auditor.

O'Shaughnessy, J. (1989). *Rebound! Colorado.* Brush, CO: High Plains Youth Center.

Palumbo, D. J. (1986). "Privatization and Corrections Policy." *Policy Studies Review.* 5, no. 3, February.

Palumbo, D. J., and J. Maupin (1989). "The Political Side of Privatization." *Journal of Management Science and Policy Analysis* 6, no. 2.

Pankratz, H. (1988). "State Packs Prisons at Deadline." *Denver Post*, December 29.
  Ramos v. Lamm, 713 F.2d. 546 (1986).
Roberts, J. A. (1988). "Romer Vetoes Lotto, Presses.Override." *Denver Post*, April 14.
Roberts, J. A. (1990). "University Hospital Privatization Overturned." *Denver Post*,
  December 25.
Roberts, J. A., and J. Diaz (1988). "House Overrides Veto of Lottery Bill." *Denver Post*,
  April 20.
Sanko, J. (1988). "Romer Vetoes Lotto Bill." *Rocky Mountain News*, April 14.
Schrader, A. (1990). "Ruling Stirs Worries at University Hospital: Administrators Fear
  Hospital Staff Exodus." *Denver Post*, December 28.
Sullivan, J. J. (1987). "Privatization of Public Services: A Growing Threat to
  Constitutional Rights." *Public Administration Review* 47, no. 6,
  November/December.
Thompson, D. L. (1983). "Public-Private Policy: An Introduction." *Policy Studies
  Journal* 11, no. 3, March.

Chapter 10

Privatization as a Viable Alternative for Local Governments: The Case Study of a Failed Michigan Town

Robert T. Kleiman and Anandi P. Sahu*

Many local governments in the United States fell on hard times and encountered deep fiscal problems in the late 1980s and early 1990s. In 1991, the extent of default on bonds issued by local municipalities reached record levels-more than 200 municipal bond issues, valued at approximately $4.6 billion, went into default. As federal assistance to local government dwindled in this period, credit ratings of municipal bonds deteriorated, and local tax bases were eroded, a movement

* The authors would like to thank Louis H. Schimmel, former receiver, city of Ecorse, Michigan; Rick Eva, controller of Ecorse; and Bob Daddow of Gordon & Co. for supplying detailed information regarding the privatization efforts; and the Heartland Institute, Michigan, for inducing the authors to undertake the research initially.

toward greater efficiency in resource use began in earnest. One form that the thrust toward efficiency took was privatization.Even though a surging economy in the last half of this decade temporarily solved the local government financial problem, the political pressures to cut taxes and maintain the movement toward greater efficiency have incorporated privatization as an effective device to control costs and achieve more efficient operations. The recent experiences in moving toward more privatized local government can be instructive as to the possibilities and limitations of privatization.

Ecorse, a small Michigan town located south of Detroit, acquired the unfortunate distinction of becoming the first community in the history of the State of Michigan (and in the entire United States) to be ordered by a court to be placed in receivership. While in 1986 Ecorse teetered on the verge of economic bankruptcy due to excessive government spending, at the end of August 1990, the deficit had disappeared, and the city reported a small surplus as a result of the reforms introduced by the court-appointed receiver. To many, Ecorse represents a grand experiment in privatization, as a vast majority of city services were privatized. The dramatic turn in Ecorse's fortunes holds an important lesson for numerous small (and some large) cities that share Ecorse's problems.

In this chapter, we analyze the fiscal experience of Ecorse leading to receivership and subsequent privatization of almost all government services to survive as a municipal entity. This study critically evaluates the costs and quality of services newly provided by the private sector.

BACKGROUND ON ECORSE AND THE ROAD TO RECEIVERSHIP

Ecorse is a 2.2 square mile community of approximately 12,000 people located in the Downriver area of Detroit. Downriver is typical of rustbowl communities that dominate the industrial heartland of mid-America. From a peak of 20,000, the city's population had slipped to approximately 12,000 by 1986. More than half of the residents are senior citizens living on fixed incomes in tract houses built after World War II for the returning GIs and factory workers. The town is divided evenly between blacks and whites and separated by a wide band of railroad tracks, with blacks living largely to the west, and whites to the east. Less than one-half of the city's adult residents have graduated from high school.

The city enjoyed good times throughout the 1960s and early 1970s. Great Lakes Steel and Dana Corporation provided a sturdy tax base, and the city offered good public services in combination with low property tax rates. For example, the city had a total of fifteen playgrounds. In 1970, Ecorse's property tax rate of 47.86 mills was below the state average of 48.62 mills.

The downturn began when Great Lakes Steel reduced its local workforce from 13,000 to 5,000, and Dana Corporation relocated its operations. Rather than cutting the budget, city officials raised taxes to maintain the level of services. By 1975, the city's property tax rate had risen to 53.71 mills, more than 2 mills higher than the statewide average. By 1985, it had zoomed to 73.07 mills, considerably above the state average of 54.47 mills.

As a result of the high property tax rate and diminished business activity, Ecorse's property values plunged 50 percent between 1976 and 1986. Property tax increases of 20% were unable to make up for the lost revenue, and real property tax receipts fell more than 40 percent. Furthermore, per capita income dropped from just about the state average to nearly 20 percent below the average. The state-equalized value of Ecorse's property plummeted from $235 million in 1980 to $165 million in 1986. Even as tax revenues fell, city officials failed to change their spending habits by curtailing expenditures to take into account the declining revenue base. Instead, they financed local services by increasing local property tax rates. This strategy worked for a while, but eventually the higher tax rates discouraged business investment, further eroding the potential for an increased tax base.

Ecorse also had a tradition of turmoil at city hall. Throughout its history, Ecorse has experienced recall elections and charges of official misconduct. Critics argued that the city couldn't escape red ink because officials wouldn't take friends and supporters off the municipal payroll. By the early 1980s, Ecorse had twice the number of employees per capita as neighboring Lincoln Park. Symbolic of the budgetary mismanagement was the $45,000 paid annually for an animal control officer, the need for whose position could be disputed easily.

Ecorse didn't really begin to confront these problems until 1982, when the City Council asked chief Wayne County Circuit Court judge Richard Dunn to take over the police department. The judge balanced the budget over the next couple of years by ordering Ecorse to sell bonds to cover the debts, but he didn't renegotiate contracts. In 1984, the city failed to pay its Police and Fire Fighters Pension Plan contributions and bills owed to utility companies and other vendors, resulting in an overall deficit of $4.0 million for the 1984/1985 fiscal year. In 1985, Judge Dunn ordered the city to post a $4 million judgment bond to pay off that debt and balance its budget for the 1985/1986 fiscal year.

Although Ecorse did sell bonds for $4 million, the city ran up a $4.5 million deficit for the 1985/86 fiscal year. During this fiscal year, Ecorse stopped paying its bills to such creditors as Detroit Edison and the Detroit Water and Sewage Department in 1986. Judge Dunn then ordered the city to submit a balanced budget for the 1986/1987 fiscal year by July 1, 1986.

When the city failed to adopt a 1986/1987 budget even by December 1986, the Judge ruled the city in violation of Michigan's Uniform Budgeting and Accounting Act (Public Act 621 of 1978). In the midst of the court proceedings, the mayor and a few other city officials took off for an out-of-town, taxpayer-paid trip to a municipal officials' convention. On December 3, 1986, Judge Dunn then appointed Louis Schimmel, director of the Municipal Advisory Council of Michigan (a municipal bond firm), as court-appointed receiver after city officials failed to comply with a court order to balance their budget. Ecorse became the first city in Michigan history to be placed in the hands of a court-appointed receiver.

Schimmel faced a formidable task. In the thirty months prior to his appointment, Ecorse had spent $9.6 million more than its tax revenues. Even after the $4 million bond issue, the city still had an unfunded liability of $5.6 million. It also owed the city of Detroit approximately $1.5 million in back water bills. It was funding the police and fire pension system through the city's general fund. In addition, the city was engaging in unauthorized interfund borrowings by transferring funds earmarked for such purposes as roads and water to other funds. The 1986 audit report of the city's accounting firm, Ernst and Whinney, commented, "the City of Ecorse is in serious financial condition and to date, no visible solutions have been presented to correct this situation. Further, the City's ability to borrow to meet immediate cash needs is limited and the City likely will not have sufficient cash to discharge its liabilities in the normal course of business."

Ecorse's road to receivership is portrayed in Table 10.1 which chronicles the revenues and expenditures in Ecorse's General Fund account for the 1980 through 1987 fiscal years. As this table reveals, from a small surplus in 1980, Ecorse's deficit (as a per cent of revenue) increased to almost 47 percent in 1987. The increasing deficit was the obvious result of declining revenue and rising expenditure levels. With every passing fiscal year, the city's steps toward receivership quickened.

Table 10.1
Ecorse's Road to Receivership

Year	Ecorse's General Fund (in millions of dollars)							
	1980	1981	1982	1983	1984	1985	1986	1987
Revenues	7.12	6.82	6.68	6.45	6.30	6.25	6.25	6.21
Expenditures	6.79	7.46	7.80	7.73	7.19	7.68	8.82	9.12
Deficit	(.33)	0.64	1.12	1.28	.89	1.43	2.57	2.91
Deficit/Revenue (%)		9.4	16.8	`19.8	14.1	22.9	41.1	46.9

AN OVERVIEW OF PRIVATIZATION

As noted by Donahue (1989), extreme views have been expressed in the privatization debate. On one hand, "proponents are fond of invoking the efficiency that characterizes well-run companies in competitive markets and then, not troubling with any intervening logical steps, trumpeting the conclusion that private firms will excel in public undertakings as well" (Donahue, 1989: 215). On the other hand, "it is perverse to reject privatization simply because some enthusiasts favor it for the wrong reason" (Donahue, 1989: 215-216).

However, an openness to privatization by no means implies contempt for government bureaucracy. "Productive efficiency is simply not the cardinal virtue of civil service organizations. Public agencies characteristically are structured to guarantee due process and administrative fairness, to ensure that all considerations get proper weight and that no citizen's rights are violated" (Donahue, 1989: 216). We thus need to examine the privatization issue carefully.

The central theme of the privatization proposal is to increase the productivity of government and thus to reduce costs by transferring production of government services or the ownership of assets to private firms. Privatization is an alternative to government production of goods and services that relies more on the private institutions to satisfy residents' needs and less on government. As noted later, it is an important management tool that offers employees incentives to be efficient and utilizes the expertise of private firms that perform the same functions as governmental agencies.

The term "privatization" has been applied, in the context of the U. S. economy, to three different ways of increasing the activity of the private sector in providing public services: (1) private sector choice, financing, and production of a service; (2) deregulation of private firms providing services; and (3). public sector choice and financing with private-sector production of the service selected.[1] With the first, the entire responsibility for a service is transferred from the public sector to the free market, where individual consumers select and purchase the amount of services they desire from private suppliers. As an example of the first definition, solid-waste collection is provided and produced by private firms in some communities. The second version of the privatization means that government reduces or eliminates the regulatory restrictions imposed on private firms providing specific services.

The third version of privatization refers to joint activity of the public and private sectors in providing services. The concept is that consumers collectively select and pay for the amount and type of service desired through government, which then contracts with private firms to produce the desired quantity and type of service. Although the government provides for the service, a private firm produces it. The idea here is that contracting with private firms to produce goods and services may also reduce costs.

Up until the mid-1980s, most privatization efforts at the state and local levels were applied to either routine housekeeping services in which government itself is the customer or public services with well-defined, tangible outputs. Although many communities have experimented with privatization of final services consumed by taxpayers, Ecorse is unique to the extent to which these services have been privatized.

HOW CONTRACTING OUT CAN REDUCE COSTS

Proponents of privatization argue that government producers have no incentive to hold down production costs, whereas private producers who contract with the government to provide service do. The lower the cost incurred by the firm in successfully satisfying the contract, the greater the profit that it makes. Competition among potential private suppliers to obtain this contract is expected to bring government the lowest possible cost for the specified level of service.

On the other hand, the absence of competition and profit incentives in the public sector is not likely to result in cost minimization. As summarized by Pack (1987), competitive bidding by profit-maximizing firms for a well-specified output greatly increases the likelihood that the product will be produced at the lowest cost.

The major cause of the cost differences between the private and governmental sectors is employee productivity. Lower labor costs may arise either from lower wages (which means that the government was paying wages higher than necessary for a given skill) or from less labor input (which means that the government was hiring unnecessary workers). Government agencies are normally less productive per paid labor hour than private firms due to such factors as excessive staffing levels, relatively generous vacation, holiday, and leave policies, inadequate capital equipment, and inferior management and labor practices. Moreover, in relation to its private sector counterparts, government tends not to reward individual initiatives or punish aberrant behavior contributing to the lower productivity.

Private firms may also more readily experiment with different production approaches, whereas government tends to stick with the current approach since changes often create political difficulties for elected officials. In addition, private firms may use retained earnings to finance research or to purchase new capital equipment, which lowers unit production costs. On the other hand, government may not be able or willing to allocate tax revenues to these purposes as easily, given the many competing demands for a portion of the government's budget.

Another fundamental reason for the cost disparity is attributable to the greater efficiency associated with a private sector firm operating in a competitive environment. Private owners have a strong incentive to operate efficiently, while this incentive is lacking under public ownership. If private firms spend more money and employ more people to do the same amount of work, competition will lead to lower margins, lost customers, and decreased profits. The disciplining effect of competition, however, does not occur in the public sector. Government agencies tend to operate in a noncompetitive environment and therefore can overcharge for services and provide unwanted services.

Public employees have a vested interest in having the government grow. Higher government expenditures lead to increased staffing levels, larger salaries for department heads, higher status, and more perquisites. However, private ownership produces the public benefits of lower costs and high quality only in the presence of a competitive environment. Privatization can not be expected to produce these same benefits if competition is absent.

One reason for the growth in governmental spending is the desire by producers to supply more services. An elected official who promotes higher spending levels gains the enthusiastic support of the beneficiaries of the government's largesse. In addition, larger government leads to larger staffs as well as a greater number of favorably inclined service users who can be pressed into service during election campaigns.

Some would argue that the idea that government has no incentive to hold production costs down may be too strong because local officials face competition from potential candidates and communities face competition from other communities for both residents and businesses. If the government's costs for a service in one community are higher than they need be, then taxes in that community are also higher than they need be. Accordingly, households or businesses might move to those communities with lower costs for a given level of services. However, since economic competition is presumed to be more effective than political competition, it may be more accurate to argue that the incentive to hold cost down is greater for a profit-maximizing, private firm than it is for a governmental entity.

WHY CONTRACTING OUT MAY ENCOUNTER DIFFICULTIES

Potential problems with the private provision of government services might arise from the bidding process, the precise specification of the contract, and the monitoring and enforcement of the contract. First, competitive bidding may not provide the service at lowest cost to the contracting government if there are only a few potential suppliers, and the government has a limited idea about the level of total costs, or ineffective contract management exists.

Furthermore, there is concern that potential suppliers may initially offer a price to the government that is less than actual production costs to induce the government to privatize the service or to win the contract. Subsequently, the contractor would then demand a higher price after the government has dismantled its own production system. Such lowballing in the bidding process may be reduced if the local government requires relatively long-term contracts, or it is easy to switch contractors.

The second potential difficulty with privatization concerns the specification of the service to be provided in the contract. It is particularly difficult to characterize output for some services. If society is not certain what "good" education is and how to measure it, for instance, how can government contract for it?[2]

The third potential problem concerns monitoring the service quality provided by the private firm and enforcing the contract when problems arise. Monitoring the performance of the private supplier creates costs, which may be substantial, for the government. In addition, there must be a remedy if the supplier does not provide or stops the service. For example, suppose that the contractor underestimates the production costs so that the price charged the government is not sufficient to cover all production costs, resulting in losses for the firm. This could result in serious implications in the case of many services such as police and fire protection, if the firm shuts down. Therefore, Sappington and Stiglitz (1987) have suggested that government should consider both the probability that intervention will be necessary and the costs of intervening if necessary.

ECORSE'S GRAND EXPERIMENT WITH PRIVATIZATION

Many political observers have suggested that Ecorse represents a grand experiment in that almost all of the city's services were privatized. To date, no city has undertaken the privatization of city services to the extent that Ecorse did.

Schimmel moved quickly to balance the city's 1986/1987 budget. His first major action as receiver involved dismissing forty paid political appointees. He eliminated the salaries of ten elected part-time officials (including the mayor and the City Council), fired the mayor's secretary, and forced the mayor to pay for his own car. He also wiped out positions for school crossing guards, nurse, community center director, civil defense director, sanitation inspector, and purchasing agent. He made the city stop funding the local secretary of state's office, which is normally funded by the state.

His second major act was privatizing the thirty-four member Department of Public Works. Schimmel negotiated a generous buyout and pension plan for public works employees and eliminated the department. As a result, one firm was hired to perform all of the town's road, water facilities, and sewer maintenance at an annual cost savings of approximately $35,000. To ensure that the public works department was not reconstituted, Schimmel sold the public works building and associated equipment to the private company now handling the work. The city received approximately $385,000 in proceeds (or a gain of $296,452) from the sale of the building and equipment.

Schimmel wanted to contract out even for police and fire services. Since state law prohibited privatizing police and fire services, he asked Wayne County and Detroit to provide these services for a fee. However, they refused. Undaunted, Schimmel proceeded to renegotiate the contracts of both policemen and firefighters.

He offered a strong incentive plan to retire eleven of the force's twenty-nine officers, which they accepted. By replacing highly paid veteran officers with fresh recruits who started out at $16,500, the city was able to save an estimated $300,000 per year. Under the new agreement, minimum manpower requirements and minimum shift requirements went out the window. Five police officers were replaced with lower-cost telecommunications clerks. In all, the police force was cut from more than fifty to twenty-nine. New police and fire chiefs were later hired at salaries about 25 percent less than their predecessors had made.

Through attrition, Schimmel also reduced the number of firefighters by half a dozen, replacing them with part-time, five dollar per-hour civilians. The use of part-time firefighters is a system employed by many newer suburban cities and townships and is much less expensive than having a full-time force sitting around twenty-four hours a day, seven days a week.[3]

Schimmel also persuaded the police and fire unions to agree to cut out overtime-a device they had used to increase their salaries from approximately $30,000 to $50,000 and, in some cases, more-unless he approved it. Excessive overtime payments to police and firefighters were responsible for much of the city's overspending. Schimmel also did away with personal days across the board. With regard to sick days, any employee absent for more than three consecutive days would need a doctor's slip. In addition, the city converted to a health maintenance organization plan, which resulted in cost savings of more than $0.5 million per year.

The receiver reorganized the policies of the police pension fund, which had been drastically underfunded. The city's Police and Fire Pension Fund was frozen, with all new employees being placed in the Michigan Municipal Employees Retirement System (MMERS). Additionally, thirty existing employees were transferred from the city's Police and Fire Pension Plan to MMERS.

The American Federation of State, County, and Municipal Employees (AFSCME) represented the majority of Ecorse's other workers. Since AFSCME employees hadn't made extensive use of overtime, job reductions were necessary to reduce costs. The union voted to cut its payroll by more than one-third of its workers. The membership approved the contract by a 2-1 margin, and some people who subsequently lost their jobs actually voted to ratify the agreement.

Garbage collection was already being handled by the private sector. However, Schimmel put the contract up for competitive bidding and reduced the cost from $30,000 to $13,400 per month. Motor vehicle maintenance, tree trimming, water meter reading, street and sidewalk repairs, and weed cutting were also contracted out to the private sector at considerable cost savings. In addition, the duties of the animal control officer were contracted to Ecorse's neighboring city of River Rouge at significant cost savings.

The city boat launching facility, which had lost money under government control, was privatized and is now turning a profit for the private sector operator. Moreover, surplus buildings and abandoned city lots were sold. The arena, named after a local politician, now houses the business of an entrepreneur. The receiver also shut down the ice rink,[4] library, and six of the city's parks and cleared the remaining parks of antiquated equipment in order to save on liability insurance. Schimmel also canceled city ambulance service, leaving Ecorse residents to use private companies.

In order to alleviate the city's cash shortage, the receiver was able to obtain an emergency loan in the amount of $1 million in 1987 from the state of Michigan. He also obtained property tax and state revenue sharing anticipation notes in amounts approximately equal to the city's legal borrowing limit for such debt (50 percent of the estimated property taxes and state-shared revenues). Furthermore, an additional 2.5 mill judgment tax levy was assessed to partially fund the city's delinquent 1987 contribution to the Police and Fire Pension Trust.

The city also preserved cash by renegotiating payments to the Detroit Water Board and Detroit Edison far lower than what Ecorse was initially assessed. The dispute over the water bill developed when it was discovered that a city master meter had been out of commission for an extended period of time. Ecorse negotiators argued that Detroit water officials had estimated the bill using data that were outdated. As a result, Schimmel persuaded Detroit's water department to accept $1.1 million in payment for $1.6 million in overdue water bills. With respect to the delinquent electricity bill, Ecorse negotiators convinced Detroit Edison not to pursue late charges. The savings to the city amounted to $15,000.

In summary, Mr. Schimmel accomplished four major initiatives during his tenure:

1. Straightened out the chaotic system of financial record keeping;
2. Settled all pending labor grievances and litigation.
3. Eliminated unnecessary personnel and services.
4. Privatized nearly all remaining necessary services by contracting them out.

In all, the city's labor force which once numbered 140, was reduced by more than 60 percent. Few departments remained unscathed from Schimmel's budget cutting. Other than police and fire personnel, the city had only seventeen employees at the end of Schimmel's reign in 1990.

Despite the cuts, Schimmel did not ignore capital maintenance. Six hundred and fifty thousand dollars worth of street paving and drainage projects were completed, including a $25,000 repair of the police department garage floor. In addition, the city also completed numerous demolition and board-up projects of abandoned buildings. New street lighting on Jefferson Avenue, one of the city's major streets, and in other parts of the city was also undertaken. New water meters were also installed throughout the city, eliminating losses in revenue.

Under Schimmel's tenure, new ambulance, fire engine, and follow-up vehicles for the fire department were purchased. New computer, phone, radio, and copy equipment was also acquired for the city's police, fire, court, and finance functions as well as for other city departments. In addition, a combined, expanded, and centrally located center for Ecorse's senior citizens was set up.

The budget-cutting measures and style of Schimmel rubbed many in the town of Ecorse the wrong way. Elected politicians and affected unions were unhappy and portrayed Schimmel as an economic czar. Many in the community have criticized the $100,000 salary paid yearly to Schimmel and the $60,000 paid to city controller Rick Eva. In addition, they argued that Schimmel shouldn't have been allowed to slash budgets since no one elected him to do so. Although this is true, the judge who approved his plan was elected which created voter accountability. Schimmel's sweeping powers were never fully tested in court. Although the City Council filed a suit in 1987 challenging the receivership, the suit was thrown out on a technicality, and the council did not pursue an appeal.

Results of the Reforms
Ecorse has clearly demonstrated the advantages of contracting out government services to the private sector. Private companies bidding for public contracts

must be competitive. They have the power to weed out incompetence and inefficiency and can respond to changing conditions much more quickly than bureaucracies. The contractor knows that if his services are not good, the contract can be terminated or will not be renewed. Therefore, properly employed, privatization results in better government service at less cost to taxpayers.

As a result of the reforms introduced by Louis Schimmel, the $6 million budget deficit in Ecorse was eliminated, and the city audit report showed a $95,000 surplus in the city's general fund for the fiscal year ended June 30, 1990. In addition, the city has repaid $200,000 of the $1.0 million loan obtained form the State of Michigan in 1987, well in advance of its due date. Moreover, except for a judgment levy imposed by the court, the entire turnaround was achieved through spending cuts and efficiency gains, not through tax increases. Schimmel stepped down as receiver of the city at the end of August 1990.

It is important to examine overall cost savings and their sources. For Ecorse, the Department of Public Works (DPW) was the major operation for the city. As a result, cost savings due to privatization efforts have been divided into DPW privatization and all other privatization efforts. Table 10.2 provides a comparison of costs for DPW operations for the three years preceding privatization and the three years

Table 10.2
Comparison of Costs Before and After Privatization

Item	Before ($)	After ($)	% Change
General Fund - DPW	2,638,904	1,015,578	61.5%
Local Street Fund	146,571	453,282	+209.3%
Major Street Fund	70,945	507,538	+615.4%
Water and Sewer Fund	1,419,832	1,653,037	+16.4%
Total of the Above	4,276,252	3,629,435	+17.9%
Less: Unique Cost Items:			
Water & Sewer Fund Costs	(1,419,832)	(1,653,037)	+16.4%
Estimated St. Renovations			
(1989 and 1990 Local and Major Street Fund)		(761,000)	N/A
DPW Costs Incurred	2,856,420	1,215,398	-57.5%

after (without adjustment for cost escalation due to inflation). An examination of this table reveals that the city's DPW operations costs were reduced by an eye-catching 57.5 percent. Moreover, it did not come at the expense of neglected maintenance. In fact, both Local Street Fund and Major Street Fund allocations were increased by 209 percent and 615 percent, respectively.

We have examined the extent of total savings from DPW privatization and all other privatization efforts. The calculations are presented in Table 10.3. In order to arrive at the total savings, we have added to the DPW cost savings the additional savings due to renegotiating the rubbish collection contract, reductions in engineering area, reductions in parks and recreation areas, and privatization of the city's boat ramp. The total savings to the city of Ecorse due to privatization efforts amount to about a $1 million per annum. Even without adjusting for the effects of inflation, the cost savings amount to a staggering 55 percent over the annual costs incurred during the three year period preceding the privatization of city services. When adjusted for inflation, the savings rise to almost 63 percent. If the issue of the quality of life in Ecorse after the privatization is not taken into consideration (an issue that was not rigorously investigated in this chapter), the extent of efficiency gains from privatization is noticeably significant.

Not only was the deficit eliminated, but, more significantly, improved management practices were put into place that provided a new system of delivering city services at a much lesser cost. These changes will enable the city to save millions of dollars in the coming years over what it would have spent had the changes not been made. Moreover, Ecorse's current savings as a result of privatization will increase each year if public-sector costs in other cities continue to escalate faster than the cost of private contractors. As reported by Koretz (1991: 26), "average compensation per state and local employee rose by 82% in the 10 years ended June, 1991-far faster than the 53% rise in consumer prices and the 61% increase in average total compensation garnered by private-sector employees."

Quality of Life After the Privatization

We have examined two important indicators of quality of life for the City of Ecorse and two surrounding communities, River Rouge and Detroit. Like Ecorse, both River Rouge and Detroit experienced fiscal difficulties and urban decay during the 1980s. River Rouge is approximately the same population size as Ecorse, whereas Detroit is almost a hundred times larger. We have compared the number of fires as reported by the state fire marshall's office (see Table 10.4) and the index crime rate compiled by the Michigan state police.

On the basis of reported fires (per 10,000 population), Ecorse does not seem to register a decline in the number of fires, whereas the number of fires remains stable for River Rouge and declines for Detroit. Similarly, the index crime rate increases for Ecorse between 1985 and 1990, and the crime rate declines for both River Rouge and Detroit. Although the increase in the number of fires and reported crimes appears to correspond with the greater privatization of city services, we should remember that these increases may be attributed to a variety of factors, including greater poverty, joblessness, and general urban decay.

It should should also be kept in mind that, by law, police and fire cannot be privatized. Even though, as mentioned earlier in the chapter, the receiver did introduce some cost-saving changes in police and fire departments, it is difficult to attribute the increase in the number of fires and reported crimes to these changes until one firmly establishes that the quality of police and fire services was adversely affected by the changes, an investigation we do not claim to have attempted in this chapter.[5]

Table 10.3
Savings Achieved by Privatization

Panel A: DPW OPERATIONS:

DPW costs incurred in 1986-88	$2,856,420
DPW costs incurred in 1989-91	1,215,398
Unadjusted reductions in costs	1,641,022
Adjustments for one-time costs in above:	
Vested vacation and sick pay	(150,000)
Severance payments	(21,812)
Adjustments for recurring costs and benefits not included in above:	
Longevity payments	60,000
Retiree health & life insurance costs	(300,000)
Property taxes	7,350
Savings Over A Three Year Period	$1,236,560
Minimum Annual DPW Savings	$ 412,187

Panel B: ALL OTHER PRIVATIZATION EFFORTS:

Pro forma costs of a rubbish contract for 1988-91 (at $350,000 per year)	$1,400,000
Actual costs incurred for 1988-91	(831,967)
Estimated Savings From Renegotiated Contract	568,033
Annual Cost Savings (Rubbish)	189,611
Annual savings due reductions in engineering area	150,000
Annual savings due reductions in parks and recreation areas	125,000
Annual savings due to privatization of the boat ramp	50,000
Annual Cost Savings (Non-DPW)	514,611
Total Annual Cost Savings (DPW + Non-DPW)[*]	926,798
Annual Savings as a % of 1986-88 costs	54.90%
Annual Savings Adjusted For Inflation[#]	1,060,626
Inflation Adjusted Annual Savings (in %)	62.82%

[*]Annual saving calculations are based on annualized DPW and rubbish collection costs for the 1986-88 period and the annual costs for engineering, parks and recreational maintenance, and boat ramp maintenance for fiscal year 1986 ($160,405; $200,761 and $25,000, respectively).

[#]Inflation-adjusted numbers are calculated by assuming that costs incurred by the city would have increased at the rate inflation (given by the Consumer Price Index) during 1989-91 period.

Source: Our cost savings calculations are based on data contained in the report by Gordon & Company, 1992.

CONCLUSIONS

Ecorse has clearly demonstrated the advantages of contracting out government services to the private sector. The city realized an inflation-adjusted annual cost savings of 63 percent as compared to the three-year period immediately preceding the privatization of city services. The Ecorse experiment shows that, if the bidding process for public contracts is competitive, privatized services have the power to weed out incompetence and inefficiency, and the private sector can respond to changing conditions much more quickly than can bureaucracies.

The techniques employed in Ecorse appear to have wide applicability to other communities. Efforts to maintain traditional modes of public service delivery using government agencies and government employees will eventually force elected officials in cities across the U.S. either to reduce the quantity or the quality of public services or increase taxes. As taxpayers are generally unhappy when new taxes are imposed, increasing efficiency is the obvious alternative. As Ecorse has demonstrated, privatization enables municipalities to bring the competitive incentive structure of the private sector into the delivery of public goods and services. Thus, the techniques employed in Ecorse could be adapted for application in other communities.

Table 10.4
Comparison of Fire Reports and Crime Indexes

Panel A: Number of Reported Fires (Per 10,000 Population)

Year	Ecorse	River Rouge	Detroit
1985	121	97	194
1986	129	97	205
1987	135	118	187
1988	176	72	209
1989	131	87	176
1990	167	98	175

Panel B: Index Crime Rate*

Year	Ecorse	River Rouge	Detroit
1985	6,132	10,075	12,565
1986	6,707	9,069	11,795
1987	9,386	9,471	11,632
1988	8,078	8,999	11,054
1989	7,870	9,123	10,572

* Index crimes are: murder, rape, robbery, aggravated assault, burglary, larceny, motor vehicle theft, and arson.
Source: Numbers in Panel A are calculated from data supplied by the Michigan state fire marshal's office and crime rates in Panel B are directly quoted from data supplied by the Michigan state police.

NOTES

1. The concept of privatization in countries retreating from experiments with socialism refers to removing certain responsibilities, activities, or assets from the collective realm. The United States, for much of its history, has so strongly resisted collectivism that there is not much of a socialized sector to dismantle.

2. One method of ascertaining the desired quality level of education is to let the consumers decide the educational choice through vouchers.

3. Insurers indicate that homeowners' fire insurance premiums haven't risen more than in neighboring communities. However, rates have risen slightly on commercial structures in comparison to other municipalities.

4. It may be argued that the closing of the recreational facilities diminished the quality of life in Ecorse. However, it should be noted that the ice rink was built when there were

children in Ecorse schools compared to an enrollment of about 1,600 in 1989. A similar argument exists for the underutilization of park services.

5. Note that despite cost-savings changes introduced into police and fire departments, the dollar amount spent on public safety increased by 32 percent between 1987 and 1990 according to annual financial reports prepared for the city of Ecorse by Ernst & Whitney. The increase in the expenditure may have been due to contributions to Police and Fire Pension Fund.

REFERENCES

Donahue, John D. (1989). *The Privatization Decision*. New York: Basic Books.

Ernst & Whinney. (1987, 1988, 1989, 1990). "Comprehensive Annual Financial Report, City of Ecorse, 1987, 1988, 1989 and 1990."

Gordon & Company. (1992). "Privatization Efforts-City of Ecorse, Michigan, Years Ended June 30, 1986 through 1991."

Hudgins, Edward L., and Ronald D. Utt. eds. (1992). *How Privatization Can Solve America's Infrastructure Crisis*. Washington, D.C.: Heritage Foundation.

Koretz, Gene. (1991). "Fat Paychecks Got States and Cities Deep in Hock" *Business Week*, September 23: p. 26.

Pack, Rotenberg J. (1987). "Privatization of Public-Sector Services in Theory and Practice" *Journal of Policy Analysis and Management* 6, no. 4: pp. 523-540.

Sappington, David E. M., and Joseph E. Stiglitz. (1987). "Privatization, Information and Incentives" *Journal of Policy Analysis and Management* 6, no. 4: pp. 567-582.

Chapter 11

The Cost and Production of Solid Waste Disposal Service

*Douglas K. Adie and James C. McDavid**

Waste management, which includes solid waste collection, disposal, sewage treatment, and landfill supervision, is one of the more important services supplied by local governments and is a particularly good candidate for privatization. An analysis of Canadian data shows that municipal governments spend a significant amount on waste management.

In the 1980s a survey of Canadian municipalities found that waste management accounted for 26.4 percent of local government contracts for services. Contracting out was widely used: 20.6 percent of local governments provided their own residential solid waste collection services, 37.3 percent operated mixed collection services, and 42.1 percent contracted out waste collection services entirely to private contractors (McDavid, 1985a).

A detailed survey of contracting-out practices in British Columbia in 1989 (McDavid, 1990) indicated that in a sample of 102 British Columbia communities, 58.2 percent contracted out commercial solid waste collection, and 54.6 percent contracted out residential solid waste collection.

*This chapter was written with the research assistance of Eric Clements.

Direct comparisons of the British Columbia (BC) subsample in the earlier cross-Canada survey (McDavid, 1985a) to findings from the more recent BC survey point to the fact that in British Columbia between 1980 and 1989, the percentage of municipalities over 10,000 population that contract out residential solid waste collection has more than doubled from 34 percent in 1980 to over 68 percent in 1989. Indeed, when municipal managers were asked what they expected the trend in contracting out services to be in the future, no one expected less reliance on contracting out. One quarter of all managers surveyed expected the role of contracting out to increase.

Continued fiscal pressures in the public sector in Canada have resulted in significant shifts of expenditures, first, from the federal government to provincial governments, and more recently, from provincial governments to local governments. The end result is that local governments are being forced to do more with less. Privatizing the production of municipal services will, if anything, become increasingly important in the foreseeable future.

PREVIOUS RESEARCH ON SOLID WASTE COLLECTION SERVICES IN CANADA

Research in Canada, comparing public and private production of solid waste collection services, dates back to Kitchen's (1976) study of scale economies in a sample of forty-eight Canadian municipalities with populations over 10,000. Among the predictors in his analysis was a dummy variable for public or contract production. It turned out to be highly significant, indicating that the cost per capita was less in municipalities served by private contractors. Unfortunately, because no samplewide average cost was given, it was not possible to determine the percentage difference between per capita public and private producer costs.[1]

Subsequent to Kitchen's study, several case studies (Bureau of Municipal Research, 1981; Savas, 1981) compared costs per household for public and private (contract) producers of residential solid waste collection services. Findings on the relative efficiencies were mixed. In Montreal in 1977, for example, public producers were 31 percent more costly per household than private (contract) producers (Savas, 1981). On the other hand, a five-year comparison of public and contract apartment collection costs in North York, Ontario, (per apartment) showed that while the contract costs were initially lower than public costs in 1974, by 1978 they were 18 percent higher (Bureau of Municipal Research, 1981).

McDavid conducted the first careful, systematic comparison of public and private residential solid waste collection costs across Canada in 1985. The study included a total of 109 municipalities and found that in 1980 contract producers of residential solid waste collection services were more efficient than their public counterparts. Public producers were 50.9 percent more expensive per household than contract producers. Furthermore, public producers in mixed settings (public and private producers sharing solid waste collection responsibilities) were only 11.7 percent more costly than private producers operating alone (McDavid, 1985a).[2]

McDavid' s (1985a) cross-Canada study found evidence that public-private cost differences were associated with differences in producer technologies. Private firms tended to use productivity incentives more frequently and to use larger collection vehicles to haul residential solid waste. The resulting productivity differences were marked. On the basis of tons collected per crewperson hour, private producers were 95 percent more productive than their public counterparts (McDavid, 1985a).

Since the McDavid study (1985a), several Canadian case comparisons have also been conducted (McDavid, 1985b; McDavid and Schick, 1987). The results generally support previous findings in Canada, namely, that private producers tend to be more efficient than public producers. For instance, Richmond, British Columbia, contracted its waste disposal service to a private collector in 1983, saving 39.8 percent per household over the previous year' s collection costs. When it converted, it sold all its municipal collection vehicles to the contractor, who then used them in Richmond. The contractor did not change service levels and continued to operate with two persons per collection vehicle, the same manning level as had existed prior to the changeover. The contractor increased crew productivity by 65 percent and cut the number of collection routes by 50 percent (McDavid, 1985a). Similarly, the West Vancouver conversion to a private contractor in 1981 resulted in savings of 19 percent in 1982. Productivity levels, measured in tons per crewperson per day, increased by 21 percent in 1982.[3]

COST ANALYSIS

In this chapter we use survey data collected in 1989 on twenty-eight municipalities in British Columbia, Canada, to analyze cost and production conditions for solid waste collection agencies, both public and private.[4] More specifically, we estimate the parameters for average cost and total cost. We are interested in comparing costs when the waste disposal service is provided by the municipality itself (public) or by a private contractor (contract).

The basic data are in the Table 11.1 where the municipalities are identified. The production method indicates whether collection service is provided by a municipality (public) or a private contractor (contract). This feature is accounted for in regressions with the dummy variable P, listed in Table 11.2 of independent variables. The variable P takes on the value 1 if collection services are provided by the municipality or 2 if by a private contractor. The number of households served, H; the average crew size, C; and tons per year, T, are defined in Table 11.2 of independent variables. They are, for the most part, self-explanatory.

Table 11.1
Data Table

Producer	Method*	Households	Crew	Tons / year	Location	Fee level	Collection cost	Disposal cost	Contr. Adm	Cost / ton	Cost / hhld
Burnaby	P	38,000	2	33,000	lane & curb	N/A	1,635,921	1,630,127	0	49.57	43.05
Campbell River	C	4,476	2	2,790	curb	48.00	164,386	133,861	3,628	58.92	36.73
Coquitlam Dist	C	19,644	2	19,512	curb	39.70	779,823	864,431	58,387	39.97	39.70
Delta	C	24,750	2	25,000	curb	40.00	800,000	0	?	32.00	32.32
Esquimalt	P	2,800	3	2,000	yard	N/A	160,000	30,000	0	80.00	57.14
Kamloops	P	19,300	1	22,400	lane & curb	N/A	734,500	342,100	0	32.79	38.06
Kelowna	C	19,320	1	19,320	lane & curb	45	869,380	43,469	?	45.00	45.00
Matsqui	P	14,200	1	10,564	curb	75	455,000	373,000	0	43.07	32.04
Mission	C	5,496	2	4,444	curb	55.4	197,197	136,378	0	44.37	35.88
Nanaimo	P	12,150	1	6,676	lane & curb	45.84	431,602	54,362	0	64.65	35.52
Nanaimo	C	4,000	1	2,261	lane & curb	45.84	128,866	21,535	806	57.00	32.22
N. Vancouver City	C	5,879	2	6,626	lane & curb	89.00	231,397	373,111	16,198	34.92	39.36
N. Vancouver Dist	P	19,000	2	21,000	curb	N/A	923,000	1,173,000	0	43.95	48.58
Oak Bay	P	6,000	3	2,500	yard	N/A	290,624	57,511	0	116.25	48.44
Penticion	C	8,000	1	6,200	curb	59.50	219,914	69,000	21,991	35.47	27.49
Port Alberni	P	5,600	2	3,300	lane & curb	N/A	252,000	88,688	0	76.36	45.00
Port Coquitlam	P	9,000	2	10,897	lane & curb	128.00	624,400	488,300	0	57.30	69.38
Port Moody	P	3,470	2	3,841	curb	104.00	280,000	192,300	0	72.90	82.35
Prince George	P	13,228	1	9,568	curb	50.04	406,162	33,488	0	42.45	30.70
Prince George	C	4,854	1	3,293	curb	27.00	131,061	11,525	?	39.80	27.00
Prince Rupert	P	3,900	3	5,600	yard	96.00	305,000	116,000	0	54.46	78.21
Richmond	C	27,772	2	28,040	curb	76.5	1,024,261	1,229,225	104,542	36.53	36.88
Saanich	P	27,500	3	16,000	yard	N/A	1,392,800	259,300	0	87.05	50.65
Surrey	C	52,000	3	52,000	curb	56.30	1,824,000	936,000	134,000	35.08	35.06
Vancouver	P	86,228	2	100,900	lane & curb	N/A	4,980,300	2,587,100	0	49.36	57.76
Victoria	P	13,105	4	6,749	yard	N/A	1,032,625	121,979	0	153.00	78.80
W. Vancouver Dis	C	11,000	2	11,833	curb	105.00	603,328	530,462	?	50.99	54.85
White Rock	P	5,000	1	3,600	curb	N/A	234,000	170,500	0	65.00	46.80

The location of collection, L in Tables 11.1 and 11.2, indicates an aspect of the quality of service and is treated as a dummy variable. L is given the value 1 for curb only; 2, for lane and curb; and 3, for lane, curb, and yard. As the value of L increases, an aspect of quality increases.

Table 11.2
Independent Variables

Variable	Definition
P	production method: assign value 1, for publicly run systems; 2, for contract with private disposal companies
C	crew size: the average number of workers on a truck (C: 1_3.3)
H	households served: this variable is used with AC_1 to determine the effect of scale on AC_1
T	tonnes per year: this variable is used with AC_2 to determine the effect of scale on AC_2
L	location of collection: this variable measures the quality of service in ascending levels of quality. Numbers are assigned to this variable as follows: curb only = 1, lane and curbs only = 2, lane, curbs, and yard = 3 The higher the number for this variable the higher the quality of service. It is also to be expected that AC will increase as L increases.

The location of collection is also used to adjust the quantity of collection services Q_1 and Q_2. Q_1 is the number of households served per year; Q_2 is the number of tons of garbage collected per year. The amount of solid waste generated per household per year hovers around one ton, so the units of Q_1 and Q_2 tend to be similar. In two of the twenty-eight, Q_1 and Q_2 are identical. Despite the correlation coefficient between Q_1 and Q_2 of .93, Oak Bay and Nanaimo collected only half the number of tons per year, as households, while Prince Rupert collected 40 percent more.

The fee level per household is what the household pays per year for waste collection if there is a charge. Where a charge is levied, the fee per household per year times the number of households yields total revenue. Fees are more frequently levied when waste is collected by a private contractor.

There are three types of costs, namely, collection costs, disposal costs, and contract administration costs. Contract administration costs only exist when the collection services are contracted to a private company, although in some contract cases these costs may not be distinguished. In this case, contract administration costs are included in the costs for collection since they pertain to the collection operation.

In Table 11.1, cost per ton, AC_1, is collection costs per ton. Cost per household, AC_2, is collection costs per household. Total costs, TC, are total costs of collection. Disposal costs depend on the local costs imposed for dumping by local dumps and are usually not under the control of the waste collection companies, be they public or private.

The ranges for average cost per household per year, AC_1, and per ton, AC_2, are as follows:

$30.24 <$AC_1$> $82.35

$32.00 <$AC_2$> $153.00

Average Costs of Solid Waste Collection

The two average costs, AC_1 and AC_2, are the two dependent variables in the first two regression equations. The equations are

$$AC_1 = a + b_1 P + b_2 C + b_3 H + b_4 L \tag{1}$$

and

$$AC_2 = a + b_1 P + b_2 C + b_3 T + b_4 L \tag{2}$$

AC_1 and AC_2 represent average costs per household per year and average costs per ton. The results of these two regressions are listed in equations 1 and 2 in Table 11.3[5] The summary statistics for these two regressions, namely, R^2, R^2_{adj}, and F, indicate that 50 and 64 percent of the variation in the dependent variables, AC_1 and AC_2, is accounted for by variation in the independent variables.

In Table 11.3, the constant terms for equations 1 and 2 are 45.54 and 40.05, respectively. The coefficient for each of the independent variables is also listed with the t-statistics underneath in parenthesis. The coefficients of primary interest are those of the variable P, the method of production.

The negative sign of the coefficients indicates that privatizing the production through contracting influences average costs in the expected direction (namely, reduces costs).

Table 11.3
Regression Results

| | | | Independent Variable (t-statistics) | | | | | | | | | | | Summary Statistics | | |
Equation Number	Dependent Variable	Constant Term	P	C	H	H_{adj}	T	T_{adj}	L	H^2	H^2_{adj}	T^2	T^2_{adj}	R^2	R^2_{adj}	F
2	AC_2	40.05 (2.29)	-13.21 (-1.73)	15.16 (3.08)			-.0004 (-2.47)		7.96 (1.34)					.64	.58	10.34
3	TC_1	136585 (2.05)			26.30 (4.66)					.0003 (4.76)				.97	.96	365.48
4	TC_2	183205 (2.61)					29.62 (5.06)					.0002 (2.80)		.95	.95	244.97
5	TC_1	121364 (2.04)				27.53 (4.84)					.0001 (4.9)			.97	.97	455.12
6	TC_2	169435 (2.53)											.0001 (2.51)	.96	.95	268.52

The t-values, namely -2.21 and -1.73, indicate that the estimates of the coefficients are significantly greater than zero at the 95 percent confidence level.

The coefficient of P in equation 1 is -11.38, which indicates that privatizing the collection service reduces the average cost per household per year by $11.38. The coefficient of P in equation 2 is -13.21, which indicates that privatizing reduces the average cost per ton of $13.21.These are genuine savings that accrue to contracting, even after all other factors are accounted for. The mean values of average costs over the twenty-eight municipalities are AC1 = $57.50 and AC2 = $46.55. These reductions reductions represent savings in costs per household per year and costs per ton of 20 percent and 28 percent, respectively.

The coefficients of the second variable, C (crew size), in equations 1 and 2 are 10.01 and 15.16, respectively, which suggest that the addition of one crew member to a truck increases the average costs AC_1 and AC_2 by $10.01 and $15.16 respectively. Both of these coefficients are also significant at the 95 percent level as indicated by the t-values of 2.99 and 3.08, respectively.

It might be useful to see if savings from contracting out are accompanied by savings from reducing crew size. A simple correlation between P and C answers this question. In actuality, the correlation between crew size (C) and production method (P) is -.072, which is of the expected sign (negative); that is, as P increases (collection is contracted out), crew size decreases, but this correlation coefficient is too small to be meaningful. It would seem reasonable to believe that crew size, C, is positively related to quality of services, L. The correlation between C and L is +.44, indicating a noticeable positive relationship between crew size and quality of service.

Is there a relationship between the production method (public vs. private) and the quality of service? There is, in fact, and it is negative (r = -.368). As collection is privatized, quality (as indicated by locations of collection) is reduced. The effect of privatization on average cost, however, controls for this effect. If the quality of service is reduced when collection services are contracted out, then there is a second cost savings of approximately sixty cents per year per household (which is rather small). On a cost per ton basis, however, the cost of reducing locations of collection by one saves $7.96, and these savings are in addition to the savings realized by changing the delivery method of waste collection services.

Both equations (1 and 2 in Table 11.3) indicate very small, but positive average economies of scale as the number of households and/or number of tons of waste disposal of increases over the ranges examined. For equation 1, the coefficient of H is negative, indicating that as each household is added to the routes, average cost per household falls by 1/100 of a cent. The t-value of -.79 indicates that this coefficient is not significantly different from zero. This average cost function used here with only a linear term for H does not provide a method to test for a U-shaped average cost curve.

From equation 2, the coefficient of T is -.0004, which indicates that increasing waste collected by one ton per year reduces cost per ton by 4/100 of a cent per ton. The t-value in this case in -2.47, indicating significance at the 95 percent confidence level. For each additional 10,000 tons per year disposed, the average cost per ton falls by four dollars over the range of sizes examined. This reduction is small, although it is realized on all units of waste disposed.

The coefficient representing the location of the pickup, L, in equation 1, namely, -.28, is also insignificant for the equation explaining average costs per household. The coefficient of the same variable for equation 2 is 7.96. This value suggests that as the locations of collection increase one grade, costs per ton increase by $7.96. For each quality jump, the costs per ton increase by almost $8.00 per ton.

Total Costs of Solid Waste Collection

The average cost functions are not the proper vehicle for testing for economies of scale or the curvature of the average cost curve. To do this, we need a total cost function with the quantity of services expressed with both a linear and a quadratic term. For instance, if the quantity of services is measured in either the number of households served per year, H, or the number of tons collected per year, T, the total cost functions are

$$TC = a + b_1 H + b_2 H^2 \qquad (3)$$

and

$$TC = a + b_1 T + b_2 T^2 \qquad (4)$$

Because different collection services, both public and private, provide different qualities of collection service, as measured by the possible locations of collection, it was thought that the quantities, either H or T, should be adjusted for this. To make this adjustment, the following computations were made. If the location of collection is the curb, no adjustment is made to H. If the location is curb and lane, or yard, H is adjusted by a factor of 1.05 or 1.075, respectively. These same factors are used to adjust tons, T, also.

These adjustments allow for two more total cost functions, namely:

$$TC = a + b_1 H_a + b_2 H_a^2 \qquad (5)$$

and

$$TC = a + b_1 T_a + b_2 T_a^2 \qquad (6)$$

where the subscript "a" indicates the adjustment. The coefficients for these four equations for total cost are estimated in equations 3-6 in Table 11.3.

From Table 11.3, equations 3-6 have R^2 and R^2 adj of .95 or higher indicating that more than 95 percent of the variation in total costs of collection is explained by either the number of households, H, and the number of households squared, H^2, or the tons collected by year T and the tons squared, T^2, or these variables adjusted for the location of collection.

From Table 11.3 the equations are as follows:

$$TC = 136,585 + 26.30H + .0003H^2 \tag{3}$$

$$TC = 121,364 + 27.53H_a + .0001H^2_a \tag{5}$$

$$TC = 183,205 + 29.62T + .0002T^2 \tag{4}$$

$$TC = 169,435 + 30.74T_a + .0001T^2_a \tag{6}$$

The results of these regressions are quite similar. All coefficients are positive and significantly different from zero at the 95 percent confidence level. Also the constant items and coefficients of the linear and squared terms are of the same order of magnitude. Since our concern is primarily with average costs rather than total costs, average costs can be calculated by the appropriate divisions. From equation 3

$$AC1 = TC/H = 136,585/H + 26.30 + .0003H$$

From equation 4

$$AC2 = TC/T = 183,205/T + 29.62 + .0002T$$

From the above two equations we can ask the question, Is there an optimal scale of operations where average costs per household or per ton are minimized? If so, at how many households or how many tons are AC_1 and AC_2 at a minimum? To compute the number of households serviced where AC_1 is a minimum,

$$let\ dAC1/dH = -136.585/H2 + .0003 = 0$$

Solving the above equation for H yields,

H* = 21,337 households

The coefficients of equations 3 and 5 indicate a U-shaped average cost function where average cost per household per year is minimized when the collection unit services 21,337 households. The average cost of collection per household per year in this case would be approximately $39.10.

Similarly, to compute the number of tons per year collected where costs per ton AC_2 are at a minimum,

let $dAC2/dT = -183,205/T2 = .0002 = 0$

Solving the above equation for T yields,

T* = 30,266 tons per year

The coefficients of equation 4 and 6 indicate a U-shaped average cost function where average cost per ton is minimized when the collection agency collects 30,266 tons per year. The average cost of collection per ton in this case would be approximately $41.72. Both these estimates for minimum average costs per household per year and per ton were made using all observations for both public and private providers.

CONCLUSION

What can we learn from the analysis of the data in this sample? The data yield more reliable results when used to analyze costs than when used to analyze production. Without regard for the numerous adjustments that can be made in production, simply changing the method of production from public to private provision results in dollar savings of between 25 and 40 percent on a per household per year or per ton basis respectively.

From the total cost function we learn that the average cost curve appears to be U-shaped, yielding a minimum average cost point of serving a household or of disposing of a ton of solid waste. The analysis suggests that under current production conditions, there is an optimal size of a collection unit. This is estimated to be a unit that collects from about 21,000 households or one that collects about 30,000 tons of solid waste per year. The minimum average collection costs per household per year are then $39.10, and costs of collecting a ton are $41.72.

NOTES

1. Kitchen's study, which reported an inverted U-shaped average cost curve, was flawed in several respects. First, because actual tonnages were not available, population was used as a proxy for this output measure. Second, the reported collection costs (obtained from the municipalities) included the cost of collection for both residential and nonresidential

addresses in varying proportions, even though their costs are quite different. Municipal officials then "estimated" the proportion of total output attributable to residential pickups so the study could focus on just residential collection.

In addition to the inverted cost finding, Kitchen found that larger average vehicle capacities tended to be associated positively with average costs. Both of these findings are questionable and have not generally been substantiated in subsequent studies. See Tickner and McDavid (1986) for a review of subsequent research.

2. A more careful econometric analysis of the cross-Canada study (Tickner and McDavid, 1986) showed that when a Cobb-Douglas cost function was estimated for public and private contract producers, and statistical adjustments for scale and service levels were made, the cost savings were still 28 percent comparing private contracted firms to public producers.

3. Comparisons between the West Vancouver and North Vancouver District (McDavid and Schick, 1987) indicated that the North Vancouver District experienced its efficiency increase in residential solid waste collection operation by changing the way its own municipal crews worked. From 1982 through 1984, the prospect of contracting out resulted in a changeover from three-person to two-person municipal crews. This reduced collection costs by 8.4 percent and increased tons collected per crew per day by 56.6 percent.

4. The data were collected on behalf of the City of Victoria's Engineering Department as part of a study of department efficiency. Municipalities were identified in British Columbia that were similar to Victoria so that the results would be helpful and applicable to Victoria in assessing the efficiency of the city's solid waste collection operations.

REFERENCES

Bureau of Municipal Research. (1981). *Providing Municipal Services: Methods, Costs and Trade-offs*. Toronto: Bureau of Municipal Research.

McDavid, J. C. (1985a). "The Canadian Experience with Privatizing Residential Solid Waste Collection Services." *Public Administration Review*, 45, no. 5, September/October.

McDavid, J. C. (1985b). "Privatization of Residential Solid Waste in Richmond, British Columbia." *Local Authority Management* 11, no. 2, September.

McDavid, J. C. (1990). "Contracting Out Public Works Services in British Columbia." In O. Yul Kwan, ed., *International Privatization: Global Trends, Processes, Experiences*. Saskatoon: Sask Institute For Saskatchewan Enterprise.

McDavid, J. C., and G. K. Schick (1987). "Privatization Versus Union-Management Cooperation: The Effects of Competition on Service Efficiency in Municipalities." *Canadian Public Administration* 30, no. 3: pp. 472-488.

Savas, E. S. (1981). "Intra-City Competition Between Public and Private Service Delivery." *Public Administration Review* 41, January/February: pp. 46-52.

Tickner, G., and J. C. McDavid (1986). "Effects of Scale and Market Structure on the Costs of Residential Solid Waste Collection in Canadian Cities." *Public Finance Quarterly* 14, no. 4: pp. 371-393.

Chapter 12

Playing Golf on Plush Private-Sector Greens

Raymond J. Keating

Considering how often government fails to perform adequately essential services such as police protection, education, and road maintenance, it boggles the mind that government would venture into the business of owning and operating golf courses. Nonetheless, federal, state, and local governments are all well entrenched in the golf business. The upkeep of fairways and greens rivals the upkeep of roads and bridges. However, absolutely no economic reason exists to justify this scenario.

THE ECONOMICS OF GOVERNMENT GOLF COURSES

None of the so-called market failure justifications for government intervention in the economy hold true in the case of golf courses. Theoretically, market failure exists when the market system does not achieve optimal allocativeefficiency. That is, potential gains remain unrealized. It has been long asserted that the remedy to market failure naturally is government intervention. However, this is largely an assumption. Clearly, many instances exist where government action due to real or perceived market failure does not necessarily foster improvement. Nonetheless, government action generally is prescribed when markets fail due to monopoly, public goods, external costs or inadequate information scenarios. Government ownership of golf courses fails to meet any of these tests for market failure.

Monopoly

The golf course market is not monopolistic. No threat exists that one supplier of golf courses will "corner the market." In addition, the notion that privately owned golf courses will necessarily exclude the majority of the public from playing the sport by becoming so-called clubs for the rich does not withstand even a cursory examination. Many golf courses are privately owned and accessible to the public at reasonable cost. With the ever-expanding popularity of golf, the financial incentive to increase the number of affordable facilities is great. The large demand for quality, reasonably priced golf facilities will not simply be ignored by golf entrepreneurs.

If one needs an example, simply take a look at American Golf Corporation. Under the guidance of golf entrepreneur David Price, American Golf owns, leases, or manages over 145 golf properties nationwide. In a January 1993 *Golf Illustrated* article, Price declared: "What I'm really trying to do is to make golf accessible to the average guy, and that type of marketing is what Sam Walton was all about with Wal-Mart. Because of American Golf's size, we can keep prices down, and that only benefits the little guy, the golfer who can't afford those so-called fancy $75-a-round courses." In fact, American Golf, the nation's largest golf management firm, services several aspects of the golf market, including resorts, private clubs, practice centers, and daily fee courses (Kiersh, 1993).

Public Goods

The consumption of public goods creates spillover effects, whereby individuals who did not pay for the good or service receive benefits. The classic example is defense spending. If a nation's defense was privately provided, then many would elect not to pay for defense, assuming that others would. Economists refer to this as the free-rider problem. Such a hazard does not come into play with golf courses.

External Costs

Nor does the external costs bogeyman pose a problem. Externalities adversely affecting parties exclusive of the market transaction involved in purchasing and playing a round of golf do not exist or, at most, are inconsequential.

Information

Inadequate information fails to justify government intervention in the golf market as well. All information as to quality, and so on, among golf courses is readily apparent to the public.

In fact, to the contrary, government intervention often distorts market signals and the transmission of information. In the marketplace, profits are analogous to flagsticks on the golf course. Just as the flagstick gives the golfer something at which to aim, the incentives of higher profits attract capital and labor to the most productive endeavors. Government intervention interrupts these signals, thereby creating either shortages through high taxation, for example, or surpluses through subsidies that would not necessarily exist in a free market. Rather than solving the market-failure problem of not achieving optimal allocative efficiency, government intervention often creates or accentuates it.

THE POLITICS OF GOVERNMENT GOLF COURSES

While economics does not support government involvement in the golf business, politics, as is so often the case, seems to dictate otherwise. From the politician's perspective, justification for government golf course ownership and operation is threefold: patronage, special-interest pressure, and government revenues. A mere cursory review of each justification, however, reveals faulty reasoning.

Patronage

First, the patronage issue can be discarded out of hand. A politician worth his or her salt in the often ethically dubious world of handing out government jobs based on political activities will manage to do so with or without golf-related positions being available. If government golf courses were privatized fully or operated by a private firm, then perhaps an elected official would have to find a job for his campaign treasurer's nephew at the local beach rather than on the golf course. (We shall leave the debate over privatizing beach management for another time.)

Special Interests

As for special-interest pressure, many golfers mistakenly believe that privatization will limit access to affordable rounds of golf. However, when considering the number of privately-owned courses open to the public at reasonable cost, as well as the already noted responsiveness of golf entrepreneurs, golfers' concerns would seem shortsighted and short-lived. In fact, the dynamics of the marketplace point toward great benefits for the average golfer under a privatization scenario. Very often, the upkeep of government-owned golf courses compares woefully with that of privately owned courses. The quality of government courses often rises and falls with the general fiscal tide of the respective governmental entity owning the facility. Incentives to maximize the return on a golf course, as with any venture, do not exist without private ownership and the profit motive. A private owner possesses every incentive to provide excellent service at the best price possible to ensure market share and profits. The same incentives do not exist for government bureaucrats.

Government Revenues

The issue of government revenues has become a prominent consideration relating to golf courses. As amazing as it may seem, many governmental entities manage to lose money owning and operating their own golf facilities.

For example, the U.S. Defense Department maintains an Office of Morale, Welfare and Recreation, which runs over 300 government-owned golf courses around the nation at an estimated per course loss of approximately $200,000 per year (Beckner, 1992). That amounts to an annual loss of over $60 million.

In addition, New York state owns and operates seventeen golf courses. A January 1993 audit of these courses by the State Comptroller's Office revealed that from fiscal year 1989-1990 through fiscal year 1991-1992, seven of these seventeen courses operated at a three-year cumulative loss of over $1.2 million (New York State Comptroller, 1993). New York even managed to operate Montauk Downs on Long Island, one of the most impressive and challenging course layouts in the entire state, at a hefty three-year loss of $234,650. Two other courses, Beaver Island in Erie County and Pinnacle in Steuben County, lost even more money, $349,152 and $321,182 over three years, respectively. All seventeen New York state-owned courses accounted for a cumulative, three-year profit of only $650,255.

Full-scale privatization of golf courses relieves governments of financial responsibility for these facilities; the respective governmental entities receive revenues upon the sale of golf courses to the private sector; and the facilities are placed on the property tax rolls. Governments also would reap tax benefits from added profits, incomes, and sales generated by these private sector golf ventures.

However, many politicians do not yet seem ready to embrace full-scale privatization of government-owned golf facilities. Instead, privatizing golf course operations is increasingly becoming a powerful fiscal tool. This competitive contracting step down the privatization path generally includes private golf management firms bidding for contracts or leases, with the winning firm paying either an annual license fee or a percentage of revenues or profits. At the very least, such privatization of golf course operations generates substantial revenues for governments at very little expense, while also reaping the rewards of private sector incentives. Lost to the government under limited privatization, though, are revenues from the outright sale of facilities and relief from ultimate financial responsibility, as well as the absence of property tax revenues that would have accrued under full-scale privatization.

GOLF PRIVATIZATION INITIATIVES

Increasingly, governments are turning to private sector alternatives for golf facilities. For example:

New York state merely needs to look to New York City for some ideas on the benefits of privatizing golf course operations. The city contracts out the operations of its fourteen city-owned golf courses. From 1983 through 1985, New York City reported losing over $1.5 million on golf operations (New York State

Comptroller, 1993). Officials report that the city now makes money on its golf courses; in 1991 alone, the city received over $1.7 million in license fees from its golf concessioners, primarily due to cost savings from not having to manage the courses in-house (New York State Comptroller, 1993).

In fiscal year 1991, the city of Detroit lost approximately $600,000 operating four of its six municipal golf courses (Zolkos, 1992). In late 1991, the city turned over the operations of these four courses to American Golf in return for $50,000 in 1991, $50,000 in 1992, and $100,000 in 1993, with the annual payment reaching $200,000 in 1995 (Zolkos, 1992).

The Reason Foundation, reported on the privatization of course operations in Houston, Texas. "Since 1989, Houston has privatized three of the city's six 18-hole golf courses to three different management companies: BSL Golf Corp., Lopez Management Co., and Paul Reed Golf. According to Director of Parks and Recreation Don Olson, 'They've done a very competent job.' Houston's Hermann Park Golf Course lost $40,000 during the final year of city operation. The course is now earning the city over $200,000 annually, and BSL Golf has earned a profit" (Reason Foundation, 1994).

In August 1992, Indianapolis mayor Stephen Goldsmith announced the privatization of golf course operations for the twelve city-owned courses. Goldsmith even left open the possibility for the outright sale of the courses one day. In particular, a nine-hole course may be sold to the private sector with a guarantee that it be expanded to eighteen holes.

Philadelphia has been leasing its six golf courses to a private firm since 1985. The twenty-five year lease requires that the firm pay the city 10 percent of gross revenues, while another 5 percent of gross revenues goes for capital improvements.

Suffolk County, Long Island, is privatizing the operations of its Bergen Point Country Club. Long-considered a poorly constructed course, Bergen Point will receive a $2.5 million capital infusion from Global Golf of East Northport, Long Island, and the county will share in 25 percent of the profits. According to Suffolk County parks commissioner Ed Wankel, "We now net $50,000. We hope to increase profits by $125,000 the first year" (Bennett, 1993).

California owns three golf courses, and in April 1989 it contracted out the operations of one course for a twenty year period (New York State Comptroller, 1993). The state required a minimum bid of 12 percent of gross revenue as rental payment and 5 percent of gross revenue for course capital projects; in the end, it received 18 percent of gross revenue for rental payments plus the 5 percent for capital projects.

CONCLUSION

As evidenced in this chapter, privatizing operations or leasing golf courses to private sector firms makes good fiscal sense, and elected officials at all levels of government and from all political persuasions are quickly coming to realize this. Government resources expended on golf course operations drop dramatically under a shift to privatization, while virtually ensuring revenue increases. This is quite a change for those governments currently losing money or barely earning a profit on their facilities.

For example, if New York state were only to privatize the operations of its seventeen state-owned courses, a similar per course return to that of New York City's for 1991 would bring in over $2 million in license fees in one year. This compares to the state's three-year operating profit of only $650,255 from 1989-1990 through 1991-1992. If the Department of Defense similarly privatized golf course operations, a comparative per course return to New York City's would translate an annual $60 million loss into almost a $36 million gain.

In the end, though, the final step of full-scale privatization should be taken. As noted, absolutely no economic reason exists for government to be in the golf business. If one argues to the contrary, then why stop with golf? Why not government-owned and operated bowling alleys, roller rinks, marinas and ski resorts?

Unfortunately, New York state, again, has actually said yes to the question of state-owned marinas and ski resorts. The state owns and operates twenty marinas. Over a two-year period, from 1990-1991 to 1991-1992, six of these twenty lost money, and the total operating profit for all twenty marinas stood at $604,781 (New York State Comptroller, 1993).

In addition, New York state owns three ski resorts: Gore Mountain, Whiteface Mountain, and Belleayre Mountain. If any assets were ripe for full-scale privatization, one would have to say ski resorts certainly are ready for the picking. Government-owned golf courses, marinas, and ski resorts merely amount to a middle and upper-income government recreational subsidy. If one believes that governmental action should be a last resort, only to be taken when the marketplace fails, then government golf courses, as well as marinas and ski resorts, clearly overstep such limits and should be privatized.

Full-scale privatization reorients government away from non-essential endeavors best left to the private sector, while increasing government's revenues through facility sales and an expanded tax base. Ordinary taxpayers may even see tax reduction, if their elected officials are truly visionary. Perhaps best of all, golfers play on well-kept courses with improved services.

REFERENCES

American Golf. (1992). "Military Golf Course Briefing for Citizens for a Sound Economy." December 1.

Beckner, P. (1992). *Wasting America's Money II: A Two-Year Snapshot of How Congress Spends Your Money.* Washington, DC: Citizens for a Sound Economy.

Bennett, A. B. (1993). "Privatization Works for Suffolk Parks." *Long Island Business News*, March 1.

Kiersh, E. (1993). "The Changing Face of Public Golf." *Golf Illustrated.* January.

New York State Comptroller. (1993). *Fiscal Performance of State Golf Courses and Marinas.* January 12.

Reason Foundation. (1994). *Privatization 1994.* Los Angeles: Reason Foundation.

Zolkos, R. (1992). "Government Golf Courses Are on the Upswing." *City and State.* August 10.

Part III

Obstacles and Side Effects of Contracting Out

Chapter 13

Implementing Privatization in the Public Sector

Allan C. Rusten

As a management consultant to city, county, and state governments over the past twenty years, I have observed and, in some cases, participated in a number of efforts by public sector managers to start down the road toward the privatization of government services and activities. Not surprisingly, that road is littered by at least as many failures as successes. While the circumstances of the situation vary from community to community, some common threads run through the pattern. The extent to which the following elements are present largely will influence the degree of success in attempting to implement privatization in the public sector.

1. The availability of data that describe and accurately measure the productivity and true cost of the service as currently provided by the government agency.
2. A comparison of those data with regional and/or national statistics to determine whether a disparity exists and, if so, the extent of that disparity.
3. A determination of the corrective steps, if any, that could be taken, short of privatization, to bring productivity and true costs into line with regional and national standards.

4. A full sharing of these data with the employees involved and with their bargaining agents and a sincere dialogue to address the central problem and the sub-issues that will accompany efforts to privatize
5. The development of specific plans to protect the interests of the employees and the vulnerability of the government if the service is privatized.
6. Carefully crafted and data-supported specifications to be used in publicly advertised requests for bids from vendors who wish to provide the service in question.
7. Detailed discussions with the bidders to address all the key issues, including issues the bidders may raise based on experience elsewhere.
8. The development of specific and detailed contracts or memoranda of agreement with the vendors and/or employee groups that agree to provide the services in accordance with bid specifications.
9. The constant and ongoing management, monitoring, and measuring of the productivity and true costs of the services being provided by the parties to the various service-delivery agreements and comparisons of those data where appropriate.
10. Ongoing public release and discussion of accurate data concerning the privatized service.

THE PUBLIC RELATIONS BATTLE

Too few local and state officials fully comprehend the pitched public relations battle that is about to be joined when they entertain the idea of privatizing selected services.

The first wave to hit them will be the affected employees, who may include their spouses and children in public demonstrations. Then will come the bargaining agent who represents the affected employees (or who now hopes to represent them). Depending on the size and sophistication of the union and its national stature, the union's participation may range from simple lobbying to high tech advertising campaigns, such as the media blitz AFSCME put on in the first year of the Rendell administration in Philadelphia. Eventually, there will also be harsh words and charges from minority groups that, more than likely, will be the hardest hit by any layoffs resulting from privatization.

To repel this onslaught, government leaders must be in a position to document the problem and explain its case to the public. That means having the facts at hand. It is shocking to know that many local governments, including those in larger communities than you would imagine, have no data and no records to document even the most elementary information.

For example, my firm has conducted numerous studies for municipalities concerning the productivity and costs of their solid waste collection operations. In far too many of these municipalities, there were no accurate data available on such elementary matters as the number of hours worked per week by collection crews, the number of residences being served citywide and by route, collection loads, haul distances, and seasonal workload differences. One very large municipality did not even maintain records as to the number of collection vehicles in service each day. Quite a few cities had no route maps for their collection crews. A municipality that suffers from those types of data gaps will lose the public relations battle if it suggests the possibility of privatizing its solid waste collection operations simply because some mayor or city manager intuitively believes that money can be saved by privatizing.

The claiming of savings and cost reductions from privatization represents another area in which public relations battles are decided. Too many governmental agencies are unable to determine the true costs of providing a specific service. Without that documented cost data base, you cannot compare the costs of alternative service delivery methods and cannot accurately determine the degree of savings that may be achieved through privatization.

Several years ago, our firm was hired by the Los Angeles Grand Jury to conduct an evaluation of Los Angeles County's program of contracting out services previously provided by county employees. At that time, the county's privatization program was the largest such program in the country, and the county was claiming that some $25 million had been saved through privatization.

Our evaluation concluded that privatization was an effective management technique that could result in substantial savings to the taxpayers. We were able to document approximately $10 million in savings. Because we were able to show only a level of savings far less than the savings claimed by the county, the local newspapers, employee groups, community groups, and others jumped all over the county officials for exaggerating their claims and possibly misleading the public. What should have been an impressive cost-savings accomplishment by the county instead became a public relations nightmare.

MANAGING PRIVATIZATION

The reason that public relations difficulties arise so frequently in many jurisdictions is that there is inadequate management of the privatization effort. The problem begins with the inability or unwillingness to devote the necessary time and effort to the collection and analysis of the necessary data. What you are doing now and how much it costs become essential, baseline data that are the foundation for all future comparisons and decisions.

In the case of Los Angeles County, the problem over cost savings occurred because there was no uniform or standard method for determining existing true costs. Each department was left to its own devices. Some departments included budgeted salaries in existing costs, even if some of the positions were vacant and were not going to be filled. Other departments counted only the filled positions. Some departments included the costs of privatization feasibility studies they had hired consultants to conduct, but other departments excluded these costs. Some agencies included indirect administrative costs in computing the total cost of delivering a specific service, while other departments included only direct cost.

These inconsistencies were found throughout the entire county process largely because of inadequate central direction of the program, weak monitoring of contracting activities, and poor measurement of privatization outcomes. As one county official told us during the evaluation, "We have 58 departments contracting in 58 different ways."

Each department head was essentially responsible for his contracting efforts: conducting the feasibility study, making cost comparison/savings projections, developing the request for proposal (RFP), writing the contract, monitoring the contractors, and evaluating the entire process. Because of this decentralized approach, a number of factors affected the degree to which various department heads participated in privatization efforts. These factors included the comfort of the department head in dealing with the contracting process, the extent to which a department head felt politically pressured in finding some way to privatize at least one activity, and the influence of the county's system of paying annual bonuses to department heads selected for outstanding management (contracting out being a priority criterion for such awards).

Interestingly, we found that among department heads in Los Angeles County who were the most adept at privatizing their various functions, privatization was regarded as a modern management tool with some important advantages. The advantages cited most frequently were:

1. It is easier to deal with an unsatisfactory contractor and his employees than it is to deal with county employees, their union contracts, and civil service regulations.
2. The presence of an outside contractor sets up a sort of healthy competition within the department that encourages county employees doing the same tasks to match or surpass the contractor's performance.

The second "advantage" requires more explanation. Those department heads in Los Angeles County who became the most adept, and were viewed as the most successful, users of privatization learned through experience never to turn an entire function over to a single contractor. In most cases, they would divide a function into two or three components (e.g., geographical locations, facilities, etc.), reserving one component for continued service delivery by county employees and the other component or components for service delivery by one or two contractors.

MONITORING THE CONTRACTOR

Just as individual departments in Los Angeles County, left to their own devices, varied their approach to the privatization program, so did they vary in monitoring the performance of contractors who were engaged in delivering services previously provided by county employees. The monitoring actually begins with the development of a contract that spells out precisely the duties of the contractor. It is the "scope of service" against which performance is to be measured. Here, too, we found that each department was free to do as it pleased. At the time of our evaluation, there had been no movement toward using identical or similar language or provisions in RFPs and contracts. The county's auditor-controller had issued "Guidelines for Monitoring" such contracts, but each department was free to use or ignore these guidelines.

One monitoring technique that was exceptionally effective for some departments was the "competition technique." For example, the Probation Department selected a food services contractor for one of its facilities and a different food services contractor for a second facility. With the two vendors competing against each other, the service costs of each actually decreased in each of three consecutive years. Another department, Parks and Recreation, made it a practice to contract out only a portion of a given service, leaving its employees to perform the same type of service at another location. Monitoring the contractor and measuring the contractor's performance included comparing the costs and outputs of the contractor with those of the county employees.

The approach generally taken by the Parks and Recreation Department was an effort to avoid one of the major pitfalls in privatization–becoming contractor-dependent. If an agency contracts out an entire function, displacing staff and equipment, the agency becomes vulnerable to the present and/or future contractors with respect to service levels and costs. Parks and Recreation made it a practice to retain 25 to 30 percent of its employees in a contracted activity. These employees were the department's backup in the event of contractor default or poor performance. Under these circumstances, the county workers could step in and perform the job until a settlement could be reached, or a new contractor hired. As mentioned before, the partial contracting mode also sets up a beneficial competitive situation.

Ensuring contractor accountability also was regarded by some departments in Los Angeles County as protection against contractor dependency. Some departments viewed the contractors as extensions of the county work force and included clauses in their contracts that gave the department the right to reject or remove personnel assigned to the contracted activity. Several departments also included penalty clauses in their contracts, permitting them to withhold payments in the event of substandard performance. These techniques are effective tools in monitoring contractor performance and in quality control.

A TYPICAL SUCCESS STORY

Having discussed the various problems and pitfalls that can sabotage an effort to privatize, let's look at an actual experience in which both the operation and the patient flourished. We were engaged by the Salt Lake City Public Works Department to examine its then-existing methods and costs of municipal collection of solid waste, find ways in which those methods might be altered to increase productivity and reduce costs, and determine the feasibility and effects of private sector collection of solid waste.

Our assessment determined that existing solid waste collection operations were relatively efficient and well managed and that in all recognized cost measurement categories Salt Lake City ranked close to the acceptable national average. Nevertheless, we did identify opportunities for increased productivity and reduced operating costs. Also, we urged the city to explore privatization possibilities through the development of specifications and the issuance of bid requests, but under conditions that would best protect Salt Lake City's interests.

We utilized a combination of available city data and our own original research to determine a number of critical factors such as:

1. The extent of route balancing and mapping of the city's ninety collection routes (eighteen in each of the five geographical sections of the city).
2. The number, types, ages, and utilization of the city's solid waste collection vehicles.
3. The average number of hours actually worked per day and per week by solid waste collection personnel.
4. Seasonal workload variances with respect to the average number of tons collected per month, per workday, and daily per crew.
5. Solid waste collection costs, including cost per ton collected, cost per service (collection stop), and cost per household annually and monthly.

Opportunities for Improvement

Although we found that Salt Lake City compared favorably with the national averages in all of the recognized cost measurement categories, there were sufficient indicators that solid waste collection operations could be made more productive and therefore more economical. Specifically, our data determined that collection crews were actually working less than an average of 5½ hours a day in the busy month (27½ hours per week) under a task system plan, whereas the national average under that arrangement is 30 hours per week. Under a task system, employees are free to go home after they have completed their assigned route or "task," regardless of the number of hours they have worked. They are normally paid for a full week for completing their tasks, not just for actual hours worked.

Another indicator of room for improvement concerned the number of service stops per crew. The number of stops was 466 per crew day in Salt Lake City as compared to the national average range of 510 to 600 services per collection crew per day. Finally, the seasonal workload variances indicated that productivity could be increased at least during the lighter workload periods of the year.

In light of these findings, we recommended, among other steps, that the following actions be taken in order to enhance the efficiency of solid waste collection operations:

1. Reduce the size of the eighteen solid waste collection crews from three to two persons during the lightworkload, four-month period from mid-October to mid-February.
2. Eliminate the permanent position of laborer on the three member crews and employ temporary laborers during the eight-month period of heavy and moderate workloads.
3. Develop specifications and then seek bids from private firms for the collection of solid waste in approximately one-half the city. The other half of the city should continue to be serviced by municipal solid waste collection crews so that the city will retain a protective capability to provide such service and so that it may use its service area as a

basis for evaluating and comparing the costs and service levels of the private contractor.

OUTCOMES OF PRIVATIZATION

The then director of public works for Salt Lake City, Jim Talebreza, stated that the program to enhance solid waste collections through productivity improvements and privatization "boasts a more than 200 percent gain in productivity at an annual savings of over $900,000."

The city modified our recommendations to some extent. First, it reduced its collection crews from three members to two, and it raised the number of required service stops from 466 to 500 per crew per day. Then, the city contracted out approximately one-quarter of the city's solid waste collection routes instead of the recommended one-half.

The private collector in its quarter of the city used three one-man crews, each of which collected 640 homes per day in an area where the city had previously employed four two-man crews. Having these data available for purposes of comparison, Talebreza said public works management then worked closely with the union to implement a similar one-man collection system in the remaining three-quarters of the city.

"Although management clearly had the right to implement the conversion without negotiation," Talebreza argued, "management felt it was prudent to capitalize on the cooperative spirit of the union." The end result was a formal agreement with the union.

To initiate the one-man collections, the city acquired six thirty-seven-cubicyard side loading trucks. The savings that resulted enabled the city to purchase four additional one-man side loading trucks ahead of schedule, completing the conversion.

Within a three-year period, Salt Lake City was able to reduce its solid waste collection force by forty-three refuse collectors, one supervisor, and four trucks, for a 70 percent reduction in manpower. Talebreza says that this reduction in manpower amounts to an annual savings of $995,000 in personnel costs alone.

Talebreza writes that two major factors contributed to the success of Salt Lake City's efforts. One was the development of "an adequate and accurate data base for analytical and comparative purposes." The other, he says, is that by contracting a quarter of the city's collection to the private sector, "We were able to compare methods and costs between the two processes, making it possible for everyone concerned to see that the City's proposed operational procedures were reasonable."

The Salt Lake City success story is not unique. It mirrors other successful efforts in other communities to privatize the delivery of government services. A close examination of each will reveal that virtually every one of them succeeded because it employed the ten elements that we identified at the outset, the crucial threads in the pattern of successful implementation of privatization in the public sector.

Chapter 14

Legal Barriers to Local Privatization

Nicholas Morgan

In 1982, the city of Chula Vista sought to contract with a private garbage collection company, but a competing company filed suit to stop the contract from being performed. In 1992, the city of San Diego sought to contract with American Medical Services to provide paramedic services to the city. The president of the local firefighters' union challenged the legality of the contract. In 1940, the city of San Francisco sought to contract with a private engineer to solve some of the city's transportation problems. The city's controller refused to release the funds.

Municipalities have a long history of contracting with private parties for the provision of various services. Opponents of privatization also have a long history of obstructing such contracts. Public employees, taxpayers, and reticent administrators all have various reasons to challenge the shift in service providers from public sources to private ones. Those challenges tend to have certain legal theories in common. Local privatizations will be successful largely to the extent that potential legal challenges are anticipated and resolved before anyone has an opportunity to file a lawsuit. While every municipality's attempt to contract out will necessarily differ in detail according to factors such as the service to be provided, the state laws in effect, and any municipal constitutions or charters, the national legal landscape is littered with four typical challenges.

First, opponents have tried to characterize contracts as monopolistic, not authorized by state law, and ineffectively supervised by the local governmental authority, in which case a contract may violate federal antitrust law. Second, opponents have tried to characterize contracts as "franchises," which are usually subject to a higher level of state or local regulation than a mere "contract." Third, opponents have tried to characterize private service providers as employees of local government rather than independent contractors. Employees are often required to comply with prohibitive civil service requirements. Finally, while personal services are often not subject to competitive bidding requirements, litigation has resulted from the argument that any service that could be provided by public employees is not "special" and therefore must be subjected to competitive bidding requirements.

Each of the challenges can be met, so long as the underlying principles are understood. Foremost among those principles is accountability. Local government wields powerful tools, typically including condemnation and taxation, that make crucial a level of accountability when a private party assumes the provision of services previously provided by local government. As discussed later, accountability can best be achieved, and potential legal challenges can best be anticipated, by including competitive bidding in the privatization process and by clearly defining the roles of the private and public actors.

ANTITRUST RESTRICTIONS

The court in *Tom Hudson & Associates, Inc. v. City of Chula Vista*[2] addressed the propriety of the city of Chula Vista's exclusive contract with a private trash collection company, granted without a competitive bidding process.[3] A second trash collection company, which had inquired into but not received the contract, brought a federal antitrust action against the city and the hired firm.[4] In *Tom Hudson,* the court ultimately found for the defendants,[5] but the case does illustrate a potential source of liability for cities granting exclusive franchises to private firms: antitrust law.

Federal antitrust law does not ordinarily apply to government or "state" actions.[6] However, in the late 1970s and early 1980s, the U.S. Supreme Court decided two cases, *Lafayette v. Louisiana Power & Light Company*[7] and *Community Communications Co., Inc. v. City of Boulder,*[8] that created potential antitrust liability for municipalities. The Court in those cases observed that municipal action is not always "state action." Under *Lafayette* and *Boulder,* municipalities now must carefully consider whether their activities are anticompetitive and run afoul of antitrust law. Subsequent cases have set down two guidelines, explained in *Tom Hudson*, to immunize municipalities and the private parties they contract with from antitrust liability.

Local Anticompetitive Action Must Be Supported by Affirmatively Expressed State Policy

In *Golden State Transit Corporation v. City of Los Angeles*,[9] a taxicab company challenged the city's regulation of taxicabs on antitrust grounds. For the city's anticompetitive regulation to be immune from antitrust liability, the city had to (1) demonstrate the existence of a state policy to displace competition with regulation and (2) demonstrate that the legislature contemplated the allegedly anticompetitive actions taken by the city.[10] The court cited a host of constitutional and statutory provisions permitting state regulation of taxicabs.[11] Then the court pointed to a statute that exempted from state regulation those taxicabs already regulated by a city or county.[12] This combination amounted to a "'clearly articulated and affirmatively expressed state policy' which allows municipalities to displace competition with regulation in the taxicab industry."[13] Therefore, the city's regulation of taxicabs was "state action" and not subject to an antitrust challenge.

In *Tom Hudson*, recall, the city of Chula Vista granted an exclusive trash collection service contract without a competitive bidding process.[14] Fortunately for the city, the California Government Code explicitly permitted cities to provide solid waste handling services by exclusive franchise with or without competitive bidding.[15] Because California had an affirmatively expressed policy on exclusive garbage collection contracts, the city of Chula Vista was immune from an antitrust suit. However, the privatization could just have easily been jeopardized by attacking the private contractor on antitrust grounds. Under certain circumstances, even a private party may acquire state immunity from antitrust liability.

Private Party Must Be Actively Supervised By Government to Acquire State Immunity From Antitrust Liability

In *California Retail Liquor Dealers Association v. Midcal Aluminum, Inc.*,[16] the Supreme Court addressed the question of when private actions can be considered "state action" for antitrust purposes. In *Midcal*, the state established a price control scheme for wine but left the price setting up to private wine producers and wholesalers.[17] The state merely enforced the prices specified by the private parties.[18] Midcal Aluminum challenged the scheme as violative of antitrust law. One issue before the court was whether the state's involvement was sufficient to establish antitrust immunity.[19] In finding that the state's involvement was insufficient, the court noted that the state did not "monitor market conditions or engage in any 'pointed reexamination' of the program."[20]   The state cannot simply promote private anticompetitive behavior without "pointed" supervision thereafter.

The *Tom Hudson* court recognized this principle. The city did grant an exclusive trash collecting franchise without competitive bidding; that is, it did promote private anticompetitive behavior. However, the city's finance department had to review, and the city council had to approve, all rate proposals from the trash collection company. The court held that this was sufficient government supervision to immunize the private party's actions from antitrust liability.

Conclusion

It is clear that municipalities can grant exclusive franchises to private parties and not violate antitrust law so long as strict procedures are followed. However, a simpler mechanism exists for avoiding antitrust liability. Had Chula Vista merely engaged in a competitive bidding process or made the contract nonexclusive, the argument could have been made that antitrust law did not apply because no "monopoly powers [had] been granted to a private person."[21] Where state law does not contemplate municipalities engaging in anticompetitive contracts with private parties, competition is a must. Even where state law does permit anticompetitive contracts, competitive contracting arguably avoids the necessity and cost of continued oversight.

One of the principal benefits of privatization is the cost savings the private sector achieves by virtue of being competitive. Awarding contracts without the benefit of competitive scrutiny will not likely result in the maximum cost savings. Why privatize, on one hand, and thwart a principal benefit of privatization, on the other?[22]

CONTRACTING AS A FRANCHISE

A franchise gives permission to a private party to do something that ordinary citizens cannot.[23] Franchise award conditions are typically more stringent than mere public contracts.[24] For example, San Diego's charter requires a two-thirds City Council vote followed by a referendum where a franchise is involved. Legal challenges of municipal contracts executed without the more exacting franchise requirements will center around whether the contract must be deemed a franchise as a matter of law.[25] The list of "franchise" services generally includes "the right to supply gas or water to a municipality and its inhabitants, the right to carry on the business of a telephone system, to operate a railroad, a street railway, city waterworks or gasworks, to build a bridge, operate a ferry, and to collect tolls therefor. And these are but illustrations of a more comprehensive list."[26] While definitions of "franchise" vary somewhat among jurisdictions, the outlines of a "more comprehensive list" of franchises can be determined from the general elements drawn from Court opinions on the subject.

Provision of a Vital Public Service

A franchise, generally, is a privilege granted by a governmental body to a private party to carry on a business of a public or quasi-governmental nature.[27] Franchises have been variously stated as involving provisions of "vital public services," "well-known services which are deemed public utilities," or "such services and functions as government itself is obligated to furnish to its citizens."[28] Outside of a state law or local charter provision specifying particular utility services that local governments must provide by franchise, what constitutes a "vital" public service is somewhat open to interpretation.

For example, in *Ponti v. Burastero*, involving a garbage collection contract, the court found that franchise provisions of a city charter must be complied with only when specifically named public utilities are being provided.[29] In *Copt-Air v. City of San Diego*, the court concluded that a franchise "ordinarily refers to such services and functions as government itself is obligated to furnish to its citizens and usually concerns such matters of vital public interest as water, gas, electricity or telephone services."[30] However, at the other extreme is *Finney v. Estes*, another garbage collection contract case out of Colorado where the court concluded that services requiring a franchise "never have been considered in the same classification or category with the removal of garbage done under the responsibility of a municipal corporation in performing an affirmative duty imposed thereon as a governmental function for the preservation of public health and safety. Having this imposed duty, a municipality can perform the function by its own employees or can farm the job out under contract."[31] *Finney* and *Copt-Air* seem to directly contradict one another.

Obviously, any services specifically required by constitution, statute, or local charter to be provided by franchise require a franchise. Likewise, it is safe to assume that a contract for the provision of a personal, as opposed to public, service will not require a franchise. However, beyond such obviously "public" and obviously "nonpublic" services, it would not be safe to rely on the nature of the service being provided as determinative on the issue of whether a franchise will be required.

Government Permission Is Required for Private Party to Perform Service

Where the nature of a service is not determinative on the franchise issue, courts will look to whether government permission is required for a private party to perform a certain service. Two broad categories of services exist requiring government permission to perform: services in prohibitively regulated areas and services requiring the use of public property. In both instances, a franchise may be required.

If the services are so heavily regulated as to require government permission before a private party could perform them, then a franchise will be required.[32] It has been stated:

Rights exercised by a citizen may, when the public interest requires, be withdrawn by the state, so as in effect to make them franchises to all practical purposes. Whenever any occupation or business is conducted in such a manner that the welfare of the people generally requires it to be regulated, modified, or restrained altogether, the legislature may affix to its exercise any conditions that legitimately tend to correct the evil; and thus, what was at one time a common right may be made the subject of a franchise.[33]

Typically, such statutory control over an industry will specify that a franchise is required. For example, in the early part of this century, Oklahoma required anyone engaged in the cotton ginning business to have a permit. The state heavily regulated the industry and declared by statute that it was a utility. Under such a regulatory regime, cotton ginning was a franchise.[34]

More typical at the local level is a service that requires government permission to perform only because it involves the use of public property. Ordinary citizens may not make use of public streets to lay cable or pipes. A franchise is required for these types of uses. However, not all uses of public property require a franchise. For example, a Nebraska court has held that a company that purchased water from a utility, treated it. and then supplied steam and chilled water via subsurface pipes to several buildings for heating and air-conditioning, did not need a franchise.[35] The court reasoned that the service was not of interest to the general public, did not interfere with the public's use of the streets above the pipes, and was subject to termination by the city. This last factor is perhaps the most important for distinguishing when the use of public property will require a franchise from when it will not.

Use of Public Property Must Be Nearly Permanent

Where a private party is providing a public service that requires the government's permission to use public property, it nevertheless does not always require a franchise. A degree of permanence in the use of the public's property typically must be present.[36] In *Saathoff v. City of San Diego*, the city contracted with a private paramedic service. Under the contract, American Medical Services used city ambulances and support vehicles, housed some personnel in fire stations, and operated the city's 911 communications center using city equipment. However, the city could terminate the agreement for failure to meet material provisions. The court held that no franchise was required because the agreement "frequently comes up for reconsideration by the government, and does not involve the creation of a substantial infrastructure on public property."[37]

Conclusion

The permanence of a franchise distinguishes it from a mere license to operate on city property, which is typically temporary and revocable at the will of the grantor.[38] A temporary or revocable use of public property should not require a franchise.

Many general service contracts do not rise to the level of a franchise. If a contract does not involve a "public service," no franchise will be required. Even for public service contracts, if the services may be provided by a private party without government permission, then no franchise will be required. If government permission is required only because public property must be used to provide the service, then a franchise will be required only if the use is permanent or nearly permanent.

In fact, most local franchises involve provision of public services requiring the long-term use of public property. A case can be made that more privatization is what is needed to avoid the requirement of granting a franchise. For example, if a city sold a subsurface easement to a private company instead of engaging in a long-term permit or contract to provide cable television service, then arguably no franchise would be required because the private company would own the property being used.[39]

CIVIL SERVICE PROVISIONS

Municipal employees are typically required to be civil servants. Independent contractors, on the other hand, are not. Public employee organizations in California have had some success at interfering with privatization projects using the argument that services that could be performed by civil servants must be performed by civil servants. Fortunately for the future of local privatization, this argument seems to be limited to the eroding beachhead in California and has not been accepted in other jurisdictions.[40]

The nature and origins of the civil service privatization barrier in California suggest that the argument should be taken seriously in all jurisdictions. Article VII of the California Constitution includes in the civil service system "every officer and employee of the state," with some exceptions.[41] This seemingly benign language, a variant of which may appear in any local charter, constitution, or ordinance nationwide,[42] has been interpreted to preclude a private party from performing a public function that public employees are capable of performing. This interpretation has been most heavily litigated at the state level in California, but the interpretation could easily be transplanted to the local level and could spread beyond California's borders.[43]

California's Constitutional Civil Service Provision

Article VII came to the fore when, in the late 1980s, the state of California realized that it did not have enough money to fund the state's growing transportation needs.[44] The legislature therefore enacted a bill permitting the California Department of Transportation (Caltrans) to contract with private firms to construct four toll roads.[45] A labor organization representing state-employed engineers challenged the contracts on state constitutional and statutory grounds.[46] This lawsuit and others like it raise a potentially devastating barrier to contracting out-type privatization at the state level: Are the parties that contract with the state civil servant employees subject to the myriad of civil service regulation, appointment, and testing requirements? Article VII of California's Constitution could be read broadly to suggest that private contractors are "employees."[47] This suggestion has been used in attempts to thwart contracting out at the state level.

Although Article VII was intended to eliminate a political spoils system, public employee organizations have used it to protect their members from private sector competition. Early Supreme Court interpretation of this clause in *State Compensation Insurance Fund v. Riley* applied the "nature of the services" test.[48] Under that test, the state could only contract with a private party if the nature of the services precluded a civil servant from performing them.[49]

In a case following *Riley, California State Employees' Association v. Williams*,[50] the appellate court observed two implications of the nature of the services test. First, the Constitution does not prohibit state agencies from contracting with private parties when civil service personnel cannot satisfactorily perform the service.[51] Second, the Constitution does not prohibit contracting out for new state functions.[52] Recent litigation has focused on what constitutes "satisfactory performance" by civil service personnel and what constitutes a "new state function."

For example, contracting out to save money does not violate the Constitution's civil service provision.[53] In *California State Employees' Association v. State of California*, the court pointed out that "at some point a service which is more costly when performed under civil service than when contracted out may on that account be one which cannot be performed satisfactorily."[54]

Likewise, in *Professional Engineers in California Government v. Department of Transportation*, discussed earlier, the court read the phrase "new function" broadly. The case involved the state's contract with four private companies to finance, design, build, and operate four toll highway projects throughout the state.[55] In finding that these contracts involved new state functions, the court reasoned:

Without question Caltrans engineers could design the roads in question and other civil servants could construct them. Nor are the design and construction of roads, new state functions or activities. But appellants take too literal an approach when they say that the demonstration projects do not translate into a new state function under Williams. As the trial court correctly pointed out, the novelty of the contracts and legislation lies in the privatization of project financing and management. After all, the private sector, not the state, will pay for the services engaged pursuant to the exclusive franchise agreements.[56]

The court suggests that so long as the contract implements a new approach to the basic state functions, and the private sector is paying for the services under the contract, such contracts are considered to be for new state functions.[57]

This bodes well for contracts involving "user fees" where private citizens pay contractors directly for services provided. Under the *Professional Engineers* rationale, private contractors could conceivably manage parks for the state, inspect buildings for the state, and so on. The state ought to be able to contract out such services where it adopts a new approach to the provision of the service, and the contractor will charge the private sector directly. Under *Professional Engineers*, these would be considered "new functions" not covered by the state constitution's civil service clause.

Arguably, then, some state contracting out fails for not going far enough, that is, for not privatizing the financing with the function. In *Department of Transportation v. Chavez*, for example, the Court voided a state contract to have private firms maintain roadside rest areas.[58] In 1963 the legislature had enacted a statute permitting the Department of Transportation to contract with private firms for maintaining rest areas.[59] For 20 years after that enactment, however, the state used civil service employees on nearly all of the rest areas.[60] Then, after a short test period, in 1985 Caltrans contracted out the maintenance of all roadside rest stops.[61]

The issue before the court was whether a state function had to be "new" at the time enabling legislation was enacted or at the time the contracts were executed.[62] The court held that "newness" is determined at the time of contract execution.[63] Because Caltrans executed the contracts after twenty years of using state employees to provide the service, the contracts were void as violative of Article VII of the California Constitution.[64]

If the contracts had specified that the private firms maintaining the rest areas were financed solely out of fees paid by motorists using the rest areas, it could be argued under the *Professional Engineers* analysis that because the private sector would be providing the financing and the function, the contracts would involve "new state functions." On the other hand, perhaps the *Professional Engineers* and Chavez analyses represent irreconcilable differences between districts.[65]

Confining California's Civil Service Argument to California

The best argument against California's civil service barrier to privatization is to point out exactly where California's courts went wrong. In the seminal case, *Riley*, the California Supreme Court incorrectly concluded that the test to determine whether Article VII's restrictions applied was "not whether the person is an `independent contractor' or an `employee.'"[66] This one conclusion sent the state down the path away from privatization. Fortunately, other jurisdictions have not followed California's lead on this issue and have hinged the issue on a party's status as a contractor or employee.[67]

As a policy matter, making a distinction between employees and independent contractors makes good sense. Most localities are subjected to intricate requirements for entering into public contracts, and there is no reason that the civil service requirements should duplicate or overlap this function. Employees should be subject to civil service provisions while independent contractors should be subject only to public contract restrictions. Moreover, methods for distinguishing independent contractors from employees abound. For example, the Internal Revenue Service has long been faced with the contractor/employee problem and has developed a list of factors to determine when someone is an employee.[68] Such a list would include examining who gives instructions to a worker, who trains the workers, and where the work is performed.

Because the employee/contractor test is used more widely than California's "nature of the services" test, municipalities should take care to assure that private contractors cannot be construed to be employees. The more discretion that municipalities give to private contractors as to how to run their operation, the less likely will be a charge that the contractors should be subject to civil service requirements.

CONTRACT IS OUTSIDE THE "SPECIAL SERVICES" SAFE HARBOR

Many jurisdictions that, either by statute or local charter provision, require competitive bidding or other heightened scrutiny for public contracts will forgo that scrutiny if the contract is one for "special" or "personal" services.[69] Often, specific services will be designated in the relevant statutes as falling outside the competitive bidding requirements.[70]   Aside from any specific provisions, however, local efforts to contract out for the provision of services that neglect to include competitive bidding may be inviting litigation by opponents over whether the service to be provided is special.

Determining When a Service is "Special"

Jurisdictions use a variety of tests to determine when a service is special. Typically, "whether services are special requires a consideration of factors such as the nature of the services, the qualifications of the person furnishing them and their availability from public sources."[71]   Making this determination is easy in certain cases.

The nature of the services, whether technical or artistic, is often enough to characterize a service as special. Contracts with artists and computer experts are often saved by this rationale.[72]   Likewise, the services rendered by someone licensed to practice, such as an attorney, insurance broker, or engineer are considered "professional" and as such are rarely subject to competitive bidding requirements.[73]   Services requiring special training, skill, or licensing are typically contrasted with those involving merely clerical tasks or where the service provider's personality plays no role in the service to be performed.[74]

Ability of Public Employees to Perform Task Precludes Service from Being Special

Most competitive bidding challenges are not directed at privatization per se. Such a challenge is most likely to come from a competing service provider who would like the public contract to be let but who wants an opportunity to bid on that contract. However, a competitive bidding challenge could arise in protest to the shift in service provision from public to private sources. Public employees may argue that their ability to provide the services sought from a private provider precludes those services from being characterized as "special," and that, therefore, the services must be put to competitive bidding.

At least one court has found that the inability of current public employees to perform a certain task makes that task "special" for purposes of a competitive bidding requirement.[75]   In 1977, the county of San Mateo, California, sought to contract with National Medical Enterprises, Inc., for the provision of management services at two county health facilities. A taxpayer filed suit, alleging that the contract was not for special services and as such should have been subjected to competitive bidding. The court, in holding against the taxpayer, found that the management services to be provided were in fact special. A major factor in that determination was National Medical's ability to perform "services not otherwise available to the County generally, in that they provided persons with expertise not possessed by County employees, and who could be called upon instantly for specific projects."[76]

The *San Mateo County* case was a direct descendant of another California case, this time from Kern County.[77] In *Jaynes v. Stockton*, a school district in Kern County wanted to contract with a private attorney for legal advice on issues related to a retirement plan. The county counsel claimed it was willing, competent, and qualified to perform the services at issue, and the county superintendent of schools contended that the services to be provided were not special because of county counsel's availability.

The court began its analysis by recognizing that the question of what constitutes a "special" service has been addressed in many jurisdictions across the country. Despite the fact that legal services are almost universally recognized as being "special," the court in *Jaynes* indicated otherwise in this situation. The court reasoned that

the services desired may be special services as far as the school district is concerned because they are in addition to those usually, ordinarily and regularly obtainable through public sources, even though they are the usual, ordinary and regular services rendered by a person in the particular field of endeavor of which the desired services are a part. The architectural services required by a district may be regarded by an architect as ordinary and usual architectural services but, nevertheless, they are the services of a person possessing a particular skill and are unusual and out of the ordinary to the district if not available to it through official channels.[78]

Because the parties had stipulated that the private law firm and the county counsel were equally trained, competent, and experienced to perform the services in question, the court did not have a problem deciding that the services were not special.

Competitive Bidding May Involve a Public Agency

A contract can be derailed for lack of competitive bidding because a public employee is capable of performing a service that is therefore no longer "special." The obvious measure for preventing derailment is to put the contract out to bid in the first place. In *Jaynes*, the court did not discuss the possibility of competitive bidding because, the court asserted, the school district could avail itself of the county counsel's services "free of charge." Under that analysis, a tax-funded service provider would always win a bidding contest. Analysis of local contracting out has become more sophisticated since Jaynes so that it is now generally recognized that merely because a public employee provides a service, that service is not free.

The requirement that a general service contract be put out to bid should not mean that the public entity capable of providing the service necessarily is awarded the contract. Local governments, including New York, Phoenix, Indianapolis, and Coral Springs, Florida, have permitted competition to encompass private providers and public departments.[79] One report states, "In early 1995, New York City's Department of Transportation outbid private competitors for sign repairs, but only after agreeing to increase the number of signs installed or repaired from 35,000 to 54,000 with no increase in personnel. This 55-percent increase in productivity is directly attributable to the threat of competition."[80]

CONCLUSION

Any local government agency contemplating the privatization of one of its functions must keep in mind each of the four potential legal challenges discussed. Local governments are not generally immune from federal antitrust liability, and a lack of competitive bidding raises the issue of whether a municipality or its contractor is engaging in anticompetitive activity. The three remaining potential challenges result from the type of contract at issue: a contract characterized as involving a franchise, civil servants, or general services will often encounter higher procedural hurdles than those contracts that cannot be so characterized.

Underlying each of the challenges discussed is the notion of accountability. Privatization should not be used as a vehicle for displacing competition or giving away public property or monies to political cronies. As the foregoing discussion illustrates, the benefits of privatization can be achieved with accountability.

NOTES

1. This discussion is not intended to an exhaustive survey of all legal challenges to a public/private contract. Instead, the discussion focuses on four challenges that could arise in most local jurisdictions where a service is being privatized, that is, a service previously provided by public employees will be contracted out to a private company. The discussion specifically excludes legal challenges particular to one jurisdiction because of esoteric charter or statutory provisions. Likewise, the discussion excludes common procedural challenges typically brought in contract disputes between two competing private contractors.

2. 746 F.2d 1370 (9th Cir. 1984).

3. Id. at 1372.

4. Id. See Sherman Anti-trust Act (15 U.S.C. §§ 1, et seq.).

5. Id. at 1374-75.

6. See generally, *Parker v. Brown*, 317 U.S. 341 (1943).

7. 435 U.S. 389 (1978).

8. 455 U.S. 40 (1982).

9. 726 F.2d 1430 (9th Cir. 1984).

10. *Id.* at 1433.

11. *Id.*

12. *Id.* at 1434.

13. *Id.*

14. 746 F.2d at 1371-72.

15. *Id.* at 1373. The idiosyncrasies of state law on this point are crucial. For example, while California law permits a city to grant an exclusive franchise for handling solid waste, it does not allow an exclusive franchise for the collection of recylables not discarded by their owners. *Waste Management of the Desert v. Palm Springs Recycling Center* (1994), 7 Cal. 4th 478.

16. 445 U.S. 97 (1980).

17. *Id.* at 99-100.

18. *Id.* at 101.

19. *Id.* at 103.

20. *Id.* at 106.

21. 746 F.2d at 1374.

22. Of course, where the government comes between the service provider and the paying customer, a problem arises with customer satisfaction. In the example of garbage collection, the price may be lower for a particular contractor, but because the city is paying the bills no party will directly complain about cans and trash thrown about or other signs of poor service. However, if the government were to completely relinquish its role as middleman, competitive pressure would keep service quality high. If service dipped, consumers of garbage collection service could change providers as easily as they change milkmen.

23. See 36 Am. Jur. 2d (1968), Franchises, § 1, p. 723 and *Copt-Air v. San Diego* (1971) 15 Cal. App. 3d 984, 987 (franchises pertain to a privilege that only the government can bestow).

24. See, e.g., Charter of the City of San Diego, § 103 (requiring 2/3 of city council members to approve franchise which is then subject to referendum); *Walla Walla v. Walla Walla Water Co.* (1898), 172 U.S. 1 (discussing lack of constitutional protection for franchise granted outside municipality's charter powers).

25. See, e.g., *Community Tele-Communications v. Heather Corp.* (Colo. 1984), 677 P.2d 330, 338 (finding that 10 year permit to lay cable and construct and operate cable television system was a franchise and that city acted unlawfully by not following franchise provisions).

26. *Frost v. Corporation Commission* (1929), 278 U.S. 515, 517.

27. 36 *Am. Jur.* 2d (1968), Franchises, § 3, p. 725.

28. Compare *Copt-Air v. City of San Diego* (1971), 15 Cal. App. 3d 984, 988-989 (discussing services that government is obligated to provide), with *Finney v. Estes* (Colo.

29. *Ponti v. Burastero* (1952), 112 Cal. App. 2d 846, 852.

30. *Copt-Air v. City of San Diego* (1971), 15 Cal. App. 3d 984, 988-89.

31. *Finney v. Estes* (Colo. 1954), 273 P. 2d 638, 640-41.

32. 36 *Am. Jur.* 2d (1968), § 1, p. 723, fn. 10 reads in part as follows: "Where all persons, including corporations, are prohibited from transacting a banking business unless authorized by law, the claim of a banking corporation to exercise the right to do a banking business is a claim to a franchise ... People ex rel. *Atty. Gen. v. Utica Ins. Co.* 15 Johns (NY) 358."

33. 36 *Am. Jur.* 2d (1968), § 3, p. 725.

34. *Frost v. Corporation Commission* (1929), 278 U.S. 515, 519.

35. *Dunmar Invest Co. v. Northern Natural Gas Co.*, 185 Neb. 400, 176 N.W. 2d 4.

36. *Saathoff v. City of San Diego* (1995), 95 Daily Journal D.A.R. 7028.

37. *Id.* at 7031. But see *Ray v. City or Owensboro* (Ky. 1967) 415 S.W. 2d 77, 80 (indicating that franchise could be used for ambulance company to operate exclusively in city for 10 years).

38. *White Top Cab Co. v. Houston* (Tex), 440 S.W. 2d 732, rehearing denied (holding that permits to operate taxicabs are mere licenses to operate on city streets, not franchises).

39. Compare *Community Tele-Communications v. Heather Corp.* (Colo. 1984), 677 P. 2d 330, 337 (requiring franchise for 10 year permit to lay cable and construct and operate cable television system) with *Texas & P.R. Co. v. El Paso*, 126 Tex 86, 85 S.W. 2d 245 (distinguishing between a franchise and an easement).

40. *Westchester County Civil Service Employees Assoc. v. Cimino* (1977), 58 A.D. 2d 869, 396 N.Y.S. 2d 692 (holding that municipalities may contract with private service provider so long as private entity's employees are not controlled and supervised by government officials); *Haga v. Seattle*, 3 Wash. 2d 31, 99 P. 2d 623 (civil service provisions not applicable to an independent contractor where contract entered into in good faith and is not otherwise unlawful); State ex. rel. *Cooper v. Baumann*, 231 Wis. 607, 286 N.W. 76 (civil service provisions applicable where the contractor and governmental body are or should be in the relationship of servant and master).

41. Cal. Const. Art. VII, § 1(a).

42. See, e.g., *City and County of San Francisco v. Boyd*, 17 Cal. 2d 606 (1941); Los Angeles County Charter § 44.7.

43. An opinion of the Office of the County Counsel for Los Angeles County illustrates the chilling effect that the threat of litigation can have based on the civil service theory. In the April 5, 1982, letter, the Attorney for Los Angeles County details the long history regarding the county charter provision mandating a civil service. For decades, the county has been applying to its own charter provision the principles handed down in cases regarding the state constitution's provisions. This resulted in a restriction on what the county would contract out.

44. *Professional Engineers in California Government v. Department of Transportation*, 13 Cal. App. 4th 585, 589 (1993).

45. Cal. Sts. & High. Code § 143, at issue in *Professional Engineers*, was a statute specifically designed to permit the California Department of Transportation to contract out. Gov't Code § 14130, et seq., is a similar provision permitting Caltrans to contract out for various engineering, architectural and environmental services. This paper does not discuss in great detail any particular privatization enabling statute.

46. *Id.*

47. Cal. Const. Art. VII.

48. *State Compensation Insurance Fund v. Riley*, 9 Cal. 2d 126, 135 (1937).

49. *Id.*

50. *California State Employees' Association v. Williams*, 7 Cal. App. 3d 390 (1970).

51. *Id.* at 396.

52. *Id.* at 399.

53. *California State Employees' Association v. State of California*, 199 Cal. App. 3d 840, 851 (1988).

54. *Id.*

55. *Id.* at 590.

56. *Id.* at 593.

57. The court quoted approvingly the trial court's observation: "No case has ever suggested that article 7, section 1 [of the state Constitution] restricts the use of private funds, or prohibits the State from transferring what theretofore had been a state function to private hands if public funds are not used to pay for the project. Such a restriction would be inconsistent with one of the objectives underlying the constitutional provision-- to promote efficiency and economy in state government " Id. at 593 n.4.

58. *Department of Transportation v. Chavez*, 7 Cal. App. 4th 407, 409 (1992).

59. *Id.* at 410.

60. *Id.*

61. *Id.*

62. *Id.* at 415.

63. *Id.* at 416.

64. *Id.*

65. *Department of Transportation v. Chavez*, 7 Cal. App. 4th 407, is a Third District California Court of Appeals opinion, while *Professional Engineers in California Government v. Department of Transportation*, 13 Cal. App. 4th 585, is a First District California Court of Appeals opinion.

66. 9 Cal. 2d at 135.

67. *Westchester County Civil Service Employees Assoc. v. Cimino* (1977), 58 A.D. 2d 869, 396 N.Y.S. 2d 692 (holding that municipalities may contract with private service provider so long as private entity's employees are not controlled and supervised by government officials); *Haga v. Seattle*, 3 Wash. 2d 31, 99 P. 2d 623 (civil service provisions not applicable to an independent contractor where contract entered into in good faith and is not otherwise unlawful); State ex. rel. *Cooper v. Baumann*, 231 Wis. 607, 286 N.W. 76 (civil service provisions applicable where the contractor and governmental body are or should be in the relationship of servant and master).

68. See IRS Revenue Ruling 87-41 (1987), "20 Common Law Factors Indicating Employee Status."

69. See 15 A.L.R. 3d 733, "Contract for Personal Services as Within Requirement of Submission of Bids as Condition of Public Contract" (listing numerous jurisdictions that exclude personal services contracts from bidding requirements).

70. See, e.g., *SCA Services of Georgia, Inc. v. Fulton County*, 238 Ga 154, 231 SE2d 774 (involving statute specifically excluding from competitive bidding contracts for garbage disposal services).

71. *Darley v. Ward* (1982), 136 Cal. App. 3d 614, 627-28.

72. *Autotote, Ltd. v. New Jersey Sports & Exposition Authority* (1981), 85 NJ 363, 4217 A.2d 55 (discussing contract involving sophisticated computer system and services of technical and scientific nature); *Scobie v. Cass* (1910), 13 Ohio CC NS 449, 32 Ohio CC 208, aff'd 84 Ohio St. 443, 95 NE 1157 (discussing contract for interior decoration of county courthouse as artistic in nature).

73. *Neal v. Board of Education* (1935), 40 NM 13, 52 P.2d 614 (ruling that public school board need not let contract to lowest bidder where it required representation by attorney in litigation); *Hazard v. Salyers* (1949), 311 Ky 667, 224 SW2d 420 (no requirement for competitive bidding for engineering contract to expand water works system); *Lynd v. Heffernan* (1955) 286 App. Div. 597, 146 NYS2d 113, rearg. and app. den. 1 App. Div. 2d 793, 149 NYS2d 236 (discussing special nature of contract with insurance company).

74. *Layman's Security Company v. Water Works & Sewer Board* (1989 Ala.), 547 So. 2d 533 (holding that contract between security company and city water works came under state competitive bid law because providing security did not involve individual personality as decisive factor); *Council of New Orleans v. Morial* (1980 La.), 390 So. 2d 1361, cert. den. (La.) 397 So. 2d 804 (contract for administrative services in city's health care plan subject to charter bidding requirement because bulk of work involved odinary clerical services).

75. *Darley v. Ward* (1982), 136 Cal. App. 3d 614, 627-28.

76. *Id.* at 628.

77. *Jaynes v. Stockton* (1961), 193 Cal.App.2d 47.

78. *Id.* at 52.

79. Reason Foundation (1995), *Privatization 1995*, 2.

80. *Id.*

Chapter 15

How Contracting Out City Services Impacts Public Employees

Stephen Moore

The contracting out of traditional government services is a popular form of privatization that is growing at a remarkable pace in cities and counties throughout the United States. Traditionally, contracting out has involved such routine commercial activities as garbage collection, data processing, janitorial services, and street cleaning. City surveys reveal that local jurisdictions are increasingly turning to the private sector to perform a wider range of activities, including fire fighting, ambulance service, air traffic control operations, correctional responsibilities, and even the city management function itself (Touche Ross, 1987). Today there is probably not a single type of municipal service that is not contracted out in some city in the U.S.

Local governments contract out for two primary reasons. The overriding motivation is to cut the cost of providing services to taxpaying residents. The second reason that cities contract out services is to employ specialized skills and resources that may be unavailable within the city government. For example, many cities contract out wastewater treatment plant operations and hospital services for precisely this reason.

The largest current impediment to contracting out is the concern that as private firms begin to perform government functions, public sector workers will lose their jobs or will suffer reduced wages. Public sector unions have vehemently resisted local contracting-out initiatives (AFSCME, 1986). In many cases, their opposition--through such methods as lobbying campaigns, strikes, and lawsuits–has succeeded in blocking proposals to contract out city services. Despite some recent exceptions, contracting out is much more uncommon in large unionized cities than in smaller jurisdictions. A 1987 survey of city managers by the accounting firm Touche-Ross discovered that 47 percent of the respondents felt that "union or employee resistance" was a major impediment to privatization.

CONTRACTING OUT AND PUBLIC EMPLOYMENT: SURVEY RESULTS

How valid are the public sector union complaints against privatization? To answer this question, several of my colleagues at Dudek and Company and I performed a study for the National Commission on Employment Policy (NCEP), a research arm of the U.S. Labor Department (NCEP, 1989). We investigated the impact of privatization on employment in cities and counties throughout the United States.

Our study, "The Long-Term Employment Implications of Privatization," extensively reviewed the employment effects of privatization of thirty-four city and county services privatized within the last ten years. We interviewed eighty-six city and county public officials, affected government workers, and contractor personnel. We also examined financial records and other documents supplied by the city and county governments.

Cities and counties were not chosen randomly. The objective of the study was to examine a wide range of privatized services. As a result, we selected local governments that had privatized unusual types of services, including public housing management, fire protection, ambulance service, and wastewater treatment. Table 15.1 lists the localities and the privatized services. A minimum of ten workers were affected by each of the privatization initiatives studied.

We examined eight employment-related privatization issues: extent of worker layoffs resulting from privatization; amount of unemployment insurance collected by displaced government workers; number of private sector jobs directly resulting from privatization; estimates of the indirect employment gains resulting from increased efficiency and cost savings of privatization; level of job satisfaction of government workers who became employed by contractors;

comparisons of wages and benefits between government agencies and private contractors; source of cost savings for private contractors; and quality of service ratings of private service providers. Our major findings are as follows:

1. *Job Displacement from Privatization Is Minimal.* For the thirty-four services examined, there was a total of 2,213 affected government workers. Directly after the privatization took place, their employment status was as follows:

Table 15.1
List of Privatized Services Studied

City/County	Service/Type	City/County	Service/Type
Arlington, VA	Garbage Collection	New Orleans, LA	Garbage
Arlington, VA	Waste/Energy	Newton, MA	Ambulance
Auburn, AL	Wastewater Treatment	Orange County, CA	Data
Bay County, FL	Prison	Peoria, IL	Data
Chandler, AR	Garbage Collection	Santa Fe, NM	Jail
Charlotte, NC	Custodial Services	St. Charles, MO	Wastewater
Charlotte, NC	Garbage Collection	Sarasota, FL	Golf Course
Columbus, OH	Vacant Lot Cleanup	Scottsdale, AZ	Cultural Arts
Corsicana, TX	Garbage Collection	South Lake Tahoe,	Bus Service
Fort Dodge, IA	Wastewater Treatment	Tucson, AZ	Parks
Gainesville, FL	Fleet Maintenance	Tucson, AZ	Transit/Hand
Hamilton County, TN	Children's Services	Virginia Beach, VA	Lawn
Hamilton County, TN	Penal Farm	Washington, DC	Public
Imperial Beach, CA	Police Services	Wichita, KS	Engineering
Los Angeles County,	Fleet Maintenance	Wichita, KS	Home Health
Los Angeles County,	Hospital Food	Wichita, KS	Landfill
Mt. Vernon, IL	Wastewater Treatment	York County, SC	County Hosp

• 7 percent of the affected government workers were laid off.
• 58 percent of the workers affected by these contracts went to work for the private contractor.
• 24 percent of the workers were placed in other government jobs.
• 7 percent of the workers retired.

These findings correspond closely with other research on the job displacement issue. For instance, several studies of federal contracting out by the U.S. General Accounting Office have concluded that only about 5 percent of affected workers were displaced due to privatization (U.S. General Accounting Office, 1981, 1985).

2. *Government Workers Affected by Privatization Receive Very Little Public Assistance.* Critics of privatization maintain that any anticipated cost savings are subsumed by the "hidden cost" of public assistance to laid-off government

workers. We found this problem to be exaggerated. In seven out of ten of the cases studied, the city of county did not pay out any public assistance benefits. In one out of ten cases the government paid out some unemployment benefits, and in slightly less than two of ten cases the locality paid out some early retirement benefits. These costs do not constitute a significant cost to jurisdictions that privatize services.

3. *Privatization Does Not Just Eliminate Jobs; It Also Creates Jobs.* Local government privatization may cause a reduction in the public sector work force, but private local employment is increased. The number of public sector jobs lost can be expected to surpass the number of private sector jobs created, however. This is because most studies on privatization have found that private contractors, in contrast with government agencies, are generally more capital-intensive (and less labor intensive), experience lower rates of employee absenteeism and have longer work schedules, and have higher rates of employee productivity.

We found that 2,004 jobs were lost due to privatization in the thirty-four local governments but that in the private sector, 1,753 new jobs were created. This led to a direct net job reduction of only 12.5 percent of the number of affected workers.

We found that for traditionally contracted municipal services, such as street cleaning and garbage collection, private firms were more efficient because they were more capital intensive than the government agencies they supplanted. For instance, private trash collectors typically had the newest and most efficient trucks with laborsaving equipment. In the cases of human services, such as hospital care, and public safety services, such as fire protection, the private sector normally hired about the same number of workers as the government agency. In some cases, the private sector hired more workers.

4. *Privatization Generates Indirect Local Employment Growth.* One of the overlooked employment issues related to privatization is the indirect job gain due to monetary savings and efficiency improvements of the private sector. If privatization saves the government money, then public officials can use these cost savings to expand other public services (which creates public sector jobs), or it can roll back taxes or services fees (which puts more money into the hands of consumers, who create jobs with their increased purchases of goods and services). We found that in the first year alone, the thirty-four privatization initiatives saved local governments $17 million.

How were these cost savings used? Table 15.2 shows the results. In over half the cases, the cost savings were used to expand the privatized service or other services.

Based on these findings we concluded that, in most cases, the job loss in the public sector is offset by at least an equal amount of job gain in private industry. Privatization thus does not shrink the employment base but shifts jobs from the public to the private sector.

5. *Labor Turnover Rates Are Not Usually High with Private Service Providers.* A commonly used method of measuring job satisfaction of private sector workers within a particular company or industry is to examine the "quit rate" or the labor turnover rate. If workers are leaving the firm or industry more rapidly

Table 15.2
How Local Governments Use Budget Savings from Privatization*

Lower the Cost of the Service	17%
Expand the service	25%
Expand other services	33%
Reduce Taxes/Avoid Tax Increase	13%
Balance the Budget	13%

*Does not add to 100 percent due to rounding. City administrators were asked to provide single best explanation for use of the savings.

than normal, then this typically means that wages or benefits are too low, or job conditions are unsatisfactory. Conversely, if the quit rate is below average, then this is one signal that workers may be well satisfied with their job and compensation. It is commonly charged by privatization opponents that working conditions with private contractors are inferior to conditions in the government or with those in other private firms not engaged in privatization.

We examined the labor turnover rate with twenty-five private contractors. If workers were not content with their private sector employers, then one would expect higher than normal labor turnover rates. Three to five years after the private contractor took over, years only 38 percent of the workers had left.

How does this compare with worker turnover rates in all industries? According to the U.S. Bureau of Labor Statistics, the mean time that a given worker had been with his or her current employer was 4.2 years. We found that after three to five years, roughly 60 percent of workers (including former government workers and other workers) who took jobs with the private provider were still working for the company. These turnover rates suggest levels of worker satisfaction with contractors that, in fact, were not significantly different from worker satisfaction with the typical private sector employer.

6. *Worker Pay Is Not Lower with Private Contractors, but Fringe Benefits Are Less Generous in the Private Sector Than with Government Agencies.*

A standard criticism of privatization is that private firms save money only by trimming wages of workers (AFSCME, 1986). In only four of twenty-eight cases we examined were wages significantly reduced by private contractors. These tended to be the traditional services, such as garbage collection, where labor costs are the primary cost of the service. On balance, we found no significant pattern of lower wages paid by private firms. In fact, there were more cases where wages rose than cases where wages fell after privatization.

On the other hand, the study did find that fringe benefits are significantly less attractive with private contractors than with the local government. In about half the cases, fringe benefits were rated worse with the private company whereas in only 16 percent were benefits substantially and consistently worse with private employers. A loss of generous fringe benefits thus appears to be the single area where government workers are harmed by privatization. Cities and counties should therefore adopt employment policies when contracting out services that will minimize the loss of promised benefits for affected workers. One way to achieve this is to require the private provider to guarantee that it will match the government worker or to assure affected workers that they will receive another job with the government with comparable pay and benefits.

7. *Contractors Save Money by Improving Service Efficiency, Not Just by Cutting Back Labor Compensation.* In almost 90 percent of the cases we examined, government officials indicated that privatization had saved the locality money. These cost savings normally fell in the range of 15-30 percent. This is consistent with several earlier studies examining the extent of cost savings attributable to privatization.

We also investigated how these cost savings arose. In about half the cases, cost savings were attributable, at least partially, to labor cost reductions (see Table 15.3). Typically, labor costs were cut by hiring fewer workers, increasing worker productivity, cutting compensation, or a combination of these factors. The study also finds that efficiency improvements by contractors led to significant cost savings for local governments. These efficiency improvements included: better management, better equipment, better use of new technology and capital, and lower administrative overhead.

8. *Private Contractors Provided High Quality Service to Local Communities.* Government unions object that private contractors save money by sacrificing the quality of public services. They charge that with contracting out, the public receives less for its money than when provided by dedicated government workers. The American Federation of State, County, and Municipal Employees (AFSCME) has published advertisements in leading magazines that proclaim that contracting out leads to a serious deterioration of service.

We discovered that this criticism was without merit for almost all of the thirty-four service contracts it investigated. As shown in Table 15.4, more than four out of five local officials rated service quality "very favorable" or "slightly favorable" with the contractor. Overall privatization has been very successful for these communities in terms of service quality.

CONCLUSIONS

Many charges have been made by supporters and critics of privatization. This chapter provides some scientific data to validate or dispose of these arguments about the labor market effects of privatization.

Table 15.3
How Thirty-Two Contractors Cut Local Service Costs*

Cost Cutting Factor	Respondents Citing This Factor
Delete Maginal Services	6%
Hire Fewer Workers	20%
Higher Quality Service	20%
Better Equipment	32%
Less Overhead	38%
More Efficient Management	28%
Lower Labor Pay/Benefits	28%
Higher Worker Productivity	32%

*Question was asked of private contractors. Respondents were permitted to list up to three factors. Two contractors failed to respond.

Table 15.4
Rating the Service Quality of Privatized Services
(Based on responses of 39 local government officials from 26 of the cities)

Rating	
Very Favorable	5%
Slightly Favorable	10%
Slightly Unfavorable	13%
Very Unfavorable	72%

Critics of privatization tend to focus only on the immediate and short-term costs to workers who may be displaced because of contracting out or the sale of a government facility or operation. By contrast, we examined the overall impact of contracting out over a five-year time span. Our most important conclusion is that few government workers lose their jobs because of privatization. In the majority of cases, cities and counties have done a commendable job of protecting the jobs of public employees. Most get other jobs with the local government or are offered jobs with the private contractor. In general, their pay is not lower with the private contractor, and in many cases it is higher. Only in the case of fringe benefits do government workers suffer as a result of privatization.

When the local government fails to protect the job security and wages of public employees affected by privatization, community support for the initiative is often eroded. Privatization should never leave behind a trail of embittered employees or the concept will have little political momentum in the future. The most favorable long-term experience will be in those cities and counties that work closely with affected workers and unions and assure them that there will be no worsening of their financial position.

REFERENCES

AFSCME (American Federation of State, County and Municipal Employees) (1986). "When Public Services Go Private: Not Always Better, Not Always Honest, There Must Be a Better Way." Washington, DC.

NCEP (National Center for Employment Policy) (1989). "The Long-Term Employment Implications of Privatization." U.S. Department of Labor, Washington, DC: U.S. Government Printing Office.

Touche-Ross. (1987). *Privatization in America: An Opinion Survey of City and County Governments and Their Use of Privatization.* New York.

U.S. General Accounting Office. (1981). *Civil Servants and Contract Employees: Who Should Do What for the Federal Government?* Washington, DC: U.S. Government Printing Office, June.

U.S. General Accounting Office. (1985). *DOD Functions Contracted Out under OBM Circular A-76: Contract Cost Increases and the Effects on Federal Employees.* Washington, DC: U.S. Government Printing Office, July.

Chapter 16

Competition Between Public Agencies and Private Vendors: Vehicle Maintenance Services in Greeley

Jack Sterling

In the face of rising costs, cities have investigated various management techniques to restrain cost. One of the most effective of these techniques is to open up government services to competitive bidding and to accept bids from private vendors as well as from existing government departments. This public-private competition has proven to be an effective management tool. Faced with outside competition, government agencies have demonstrated that they can match the effectiveness of private vendors.

The city of Greeley, Colorado (population 64,000) has two fleet designations. The Central Fleet includes a total of 254 vehicles and other equipment. The Transit Fleet has a total of twenty transit-related vehicles. In 1991, the city entered into an inter-governmental agreement with Weld County that provided vehicle maintenance services for both fleets through an independent private contractor, utilizing the county shop facilities. Prior to the termination date, the city and the county requested new proposals for its vehicle maintenance services. The requests for proposals for the city were divided into two fleet operations: the Central Fleet and the Transit Fleet. In 1993, Greeley City Council allowed its staff to prepare a formal in-house proposal for both the Central Fleet and the Transit Fleet for the next three years.

PRIVATIZATION VERSUS COMPETITION

All too often when privatization is used to describe an alternative to "in-house" services, the implication is that the in-house method is inefficient, costly, unresponsive to the users, and a drain on a community's limited resources. The general public and some policymakers regard privatization as the only way to curb rising costs. They make general statements such as, "Only the private sector can do it more cheaply and more efficiently." While privatization does work for some situations, given a well-managed operation, the latest in automotive maintenance equipment, and trained staff, a service provided by in-house staff can compete successfully with a private contract operation.

Another alternative that works in Greeley and other municipalities throughout the country is competition. The difference between competition and privatization is that the latter only contracts out work,, while competition gives city workers the ability to compete to keep work done by the city. If in-house staff are allowed to compete fairly on municipal services, they can be as competitive as most outside private contractors. Phoenix and Indianapolis have proven that time and time again; Greeley did in 1994.

One of the main arguments against in-house competition is that the municipality does not fully allocate its costs to any one service. Therefore, the costs given are not comparable to private contract prices. Another argument is that the municipality does not have to actually "compete" on the same level as the private contractor. The city of Greeley was able to demonstrate our ability to answer both questions.

THE CENTRAL FLEET PROPOSAL PROCESS

Using the bid specifications developed in 1991 and revising them based on three years experience with a private contractor, we were able to develop a comprehensive proposal package for both the Central Fleet and the Transit Fleet. Why did the city separate the fleets?

Based on the previous three years, we did not feel the Transit Fleet received the same level of service as the Central Fleet. The Transit Fleet is serviced at a separate, city-owned transit facility and has its own separate budget for vehicle maintenance services. Finally, there were considerably more private firms providing transit vehicle maintenance services as a stand alone operation.

After the city developed the proposal packages, they were mailed to every known private contractor who provided these special services. The staff decided on using a proposal method rather than a bid process to give the city more flexibility in reviewing and accepting the proposals. The staff requested the prospective contractor's candid comments on the specifications and met with a selected number of contractors, after which the documents were revised. The contractors also were informed up front that the city would submit a competitive proposal.

Five proposals for the city's Central Fleet were received in late 1993. Weld County received the same five proposals for its own Central Fleet (it does not have a Transit Fleet) and the combined city and county fleets. Since Greeley had an intergovernmental agreement with the county to utilize its facilities, the contractor chosen for the city's Central Fleet had to be the same contractor as the county selected. This was a major factor in the decision-making process.

Referring to Table 16.1, firm "A" submitted the lowest amount proposed for the combined fleets. Note that while firm "C" was lowest for the city's fleet, it was not the lowest for the county fleet or the combined fleets.

Table 16.2 indicates the summary of the proposals submitted for the city's Central Fleet. As the request for proposals for the city's Central Fleet was to be combined with the county's fleet, and all of the fleet services were to be conducted at the county's facility, the city had to review and compare the total package received from Firm "A" with the city's proposal.

EVALUATION PROCESS

In order to be as unbiased as possible, the city's proposals were treated the same as the other proposals, and all proposals were reviewed by an independent Citizens Budget Advisory Committee. The two major differences were that the city did not have to provide insurance (the city is self-insured), and the city did not have to provide a performance bond. The evaluation form used by the committee is shown as Table 16.3.

As shown in Table 16.3, the city fared well in the technical evaluation but, due to its initial higher price, was rated overall lower. However, since firm "A" was the firm selected by the county, the comparison was reduced to Greeley's proposal and firm A's proposal.

Based on that comparison, the following results were noted:

Provider	Amount		Points
Firm A	$303,173	--------	2.0
Greeley	$317,230	--------	2.5

Table 16.1
Central Fleet: Equipment Maintenance Services
(Summary of Total Proposals)

Firm	City	County	Total	Possible Bonus	Total
Firm "A"*	$303,173	$735,508	$1,038,681	$56,399	$1,095,080
Firm "B"	$312,800	$1,040,873	$1,353,673	$19,840	$1,373,513
Firm "C"	$242,873	$ 927,476	$1,170,349	N/A	$1,170,349
Firm "D"	$311,605	$952,614	$1,264,219	N/A	$1,264,219
Greeley	$317,230	N/P	N/A	N/A	N/A

* Firm selected by the County to provide vehicle maintenance services for their fleet.

If the staff had been awarded both fleet contracts (Central and Transit) and allowed to bring both fleets back in-house, the staff could have reduced administrative charges and deducted an amount of $10,715, reducing our proposal to $306,515. By adding a $12,500 administrative charge the county charged for using the county's facility to firm A, firm A's costs would have increased to $315,673. Table 16.4 indicates these two factors.

As can be seen from Table 16.4, the city's cost was low by $9,158 or 3.0 percent. There was a possibility that the low proposal may have contained some undisclosed discounts to initially obtain the contract. In the vernacular this is known as lowballing or "buying into the business." This is not considered totally negative; in fact, it can be considered a positive in that it may result in a lower cost to the city. It does, however, impact the management concern discussed later. In the discussion earlier with the Budget Committee, the staff had informed the committee that a variance in the range of 10 percent should be a threshold that, if reached, should initiate a change in the method of providing the service. The 10 percent factor is simply an indicator that recognizes a compelling need for change. Applying the same philosophy to the privatization issue led to the conclusion that, with respect to cost alone, privatization of maintenance services should continue. Finally, with respect to cost, the proposals received represent a fixed commitment by the vendors. The same commitment cannot be made by in house staff simply because it is a governmental entity that cannot transfer the risk of cost overruns.

Table 16.2
Greeley: Equipment Maintenance Services
(Summary of Proposals)

COMPONENT	FIRM "A"*	FIRM "B"	FIRM "C"	FIRM "D"	GREELEY
Parts/Supplies	$165,800	$92,000	$71,125	$95,406	$95,000
Labor	90,837	161,568	113,158	193,818	149,869
Sub-let	(inc)	23,000	25,218	(inc)	45,000
Administration	20,715	16,232	9,572	13,304	27,361
Management Fee	25,821	20,000	23,800	9,076	N/A
Subtotal	$303,173	$312,800	$242,873	$311,604	$317,230
Maximum bonus	21,431	3,200	N/A	N/A	N/A
TOTAL	$324,604	$316,000	$242,873	$311,604	$317,230

*Firm selected by the County to provide vehicle maintenance services for their fleet.

Table 16.3
Central Fleet: Equipment Maintenance Services

Evaluation Criteria	Value	A	B	D	C	Greeley
Understanding of Project (1-5) Understanding as communicated by the offeror of the issues and requirements of this project.	10%	3 (0.3)	4 (0.4)	1 (0.1)	2 (0.2)	5 (0.5)
Responsiveness to RFP Requirements (1-5) The degree to which the proposal meets or exceeds the terms of the Request for Proposal.	20%	5 (1.0)	3 (0.6)	2 (0.4)	1 (0.2)	4 (0.8)
Project Management Experience (1-5) Experience dealing with county and municipal governments in projects of similar size, scope, and nature.	10%	2 (0.2)	5 (0.5)	1 (0.1)	3 (0.3)	4 (0.4)
Management Team Experience (1-5) Experience and resumes of key personnel assigned to the project.	10%	2 (0.2)	5 (0.5)	1 (0.1)	3 (0.3)	4 (0.4)
Reporting and Management Information Capabilities (1-5) Includes evaluation of information system for managing this project, and providing documentation and reports for administration and management of the respective fleets.	10%	3 (0.3)	5 (0.5)	1 (0.1)	2 (0.2)	4 (0.4)
Subtotal points		2.0	2.5	0.8	1.2	2.5
Fee Structure (1-5) Based on the services to be provided and measured in terms of the annual target cost budget.	40%	$303,173 4 (1.6)	$312,800 2 (0.8)	$311,605 3 (1.2)	$242,873 5 (2.0)	$317,230 1 (0.4)
TOTAL POINTS		3.6	3.3	2.1	3.2	2.9

Table 16.4
Equipment Maintenance Services: Cost Comparison

| | (Central Fleet) | |
	FIRM "A"	CITY OF GREELEY
Parts and supplies	$ 165,800	$ 95,000
Labor	90,837	149,869
Sub-let	(inc.)	45,000
Administration	20,715	27,361
Management fee	25,821	N/A
Subtotal	$ 303,173	$ 317,230
Deduction for both		
central & transit fleets	0	10,715
Subtotal	$ 303,173	$ 306,515
County shop facility		
usage costs	12,500	N/A
Net cost to city	$ 315,673	$ 306,515
DIFFERENCE	9,158 (3.0%)	

With respect to control, it is realistic to believe that the city staff has less control over a vendor performing maintenance services than it would over its own employees. However, in reviewing the approval rating comments of the previous private vendor, the user acceptability ratings varied from very positive to negative. On the whole, the Citizens Budget Committee felt this concern was not compelling enough to warrant a change of operations.

With respect to management, the question is whether the city has management personnel who are capable of performing the services in a professional and efficient manner, providing for the training of employees, and holding costs in line. It was felt the city does have that quality of management personnel. However, the private contractor's method of performing the work and those proposing for the contract also have management capability. It was believed that when deficiencies do exist, they are more readily visible with a contractor's performing the services and, when noted, are easier to correct than when the deficiencies are within the city itself. The committee concluded, therefore, that the city should use its management abilities in structuring the contract and monitoring the work to achieve the best possible results for the city overall.

Finally, with respect to local economic impact, the committee was concerned that the funds expended in the performance of the contract should be spent locally as opposed to using out-of-city suppliers. The labor portion of the contract is obviously provided by local personnel, and the present contractor was obtaining most parts and material locally.

Therefore, the contract was awarded to firm A. After the city entered into negotiations, the county passed its savings of $27,595 (the difference between the county's combining with the city and the county's going alone) on to the city, further reducing the city's first-year costs, using firm A, to $288,078 as shown in Table 16.5. While the in-house staff did not get the opportunity to bring the services back in-house, the staff did feel it was competitive in its approach. It felt confident to submit a competitive proposal on the Transit Fleet.

Firm	County Costs Without City	County Costs Jointly With City	Difference
Firm "A"	$763,103	$735,508	$27,595 *

* County was willing to pass this savings on to the City if City joined in contract.

Table 16.5
Net City Costs

(Equipment Maintenance Services)

Firm "A"	City Costs Jointly With County	Savings From County	Net Cost To City
	$315,673	($27,595)	$288,078

THE TRANSIT FLEET PROPOSAL PROCESS

Based on the experience gained during the Central Fleet proposal process, staff was ready to submit proposals on the Transit Fleet vehicle maintenance services. This proposal was easier as it was not complicated by the following:

1. Not tied to the county by an intergovernmental agreement
2. No extra charges to utilize the county facilities (separate city facility)
3. No incentive bonuses by private contractors
4. No savings if both city and county fleets were combined

Again, after a review by prospective contractors, the proposal was revised, and a date was set for receiving proposals. Table 16.6 indicates the summary of the proposals received. As can be seen, Greeley's was the lowest proposal received by some $49,041. The Citizens Budget Advisory Committee met twice to review all Transit Fleet proposals.

Table 16.7 indicates the results of the evaluation process. The city received an overall rating of 3.5, and the estimated savings were greater than 10 percent; therefore, the committee recommended to City Council that the staff be allowed to provide the vehicle maintenance services for the Transit Fleet.

Table 16.6
Transit Fleet Maintenance: Proposal Summary Comparison

Item	A	B	C	Greeley
Parts / Supplies	$111,598.78	$ 99,395.00	$ 91,395.00	$102,000.00
Labor	150,536.85	149,406.00	168,428.00	106,668.00
Administration	13,276.30	34,576.00	11,952.00	21,841.00
Management Fee	35,792.54	24,053.00	7,795.00	N/A
Target	$311,204.74	$307,035.00	$279,570.00	$230,529.00

CITY COSTS

How did the city develop its costs to provide vehicle maintenance services? Attempting to compare the costs of in-house and contract services delivery is difficult. One major national study suggests that the cost of in-house service delivery is frequently underestimated by as much as 30 percent (Savas, 1987). Case study evidence also suggests that the cost of contract service delivery is often underestimated as well, due to a failure to properly account for such costs as contract administration and monitoring (Kelley, 1984; Martin, 1992; U.S. General Accounting Office, 1980).

Part of the difficulty is inherent in the nature of the task. As Jonathan Richmond of the Massachusetts Institute of Technology Center for Transportation studies has observed: "Cost analysis is an art, not a science. In complex organizations, a number of assumptions must be made about how costs are to be allocated to various parts of the organization. Many costs are shared by a number of services; therefore, often there is no one apparent way of assigning them to their sources" (Richmond, 1992). The failure of governments to compile accurately the costs of in-house and contract service delivery is also related to the absence of a consistent methodology that ensures that all relevant costs are calculated (Reason Foundation, 1993). In a survey of the contracting-out practices of 120 cities, counties, and special district governments nationwide, 50 percent of the respondents reported having no formal methodology for conducting cost comparisons (*Findings of a National Survey*, 1987).

In any event, the process must be kept simple, must be understandable, and must be accepted by managers, policy makers, and competitive contractors. There are two basic methods of determining the true cost of an in-house service: fully allocated costs and avoidable costs.

Table 16.7
Transit: Equipment Maintenance Services Evaluation

EVALUATION CRITERIA	VALUE	A	B	C	GREELEY
Understanding of Project (1-4)	10%	3	2	1	4
Understanding as communicated by the offeror of the issues and requirements of this project.		(0.3)	(0.2)	(0.1)	(0.4)
Responsiveness to RFP Requirements (1-4)	20%	4	1	2	3
The degree to which the proposal meets or exceeds the terms of the Request for Proposal.		(0.8)	(0.2)	(0.4)	(0.6)
Project Management Experience (1-4)	10%	4	2	1	3
Experience dealing with municipal governments in projects of similar size, scope, and nature.		(0.4)	(0.2)	(0.1)	(0.3)
Management Team Experience (1-4)	10%	4	2	1	3
Experience and resumes of key personnel assigned to the project.		(0.4)	(0.2)	(0.1)	(0.3)
Reporting and Management Information Capabilities (1-4)	10%	4	2	1	3
Includes evaluation of information system for managing this project, and providing documentation and reports for administration and management of the respective fleets.		(0.4)	(0.2)	(0.1)	(0.3)
Subtotal points		2.3	1.0	0.8	1.9
Fee Structure (1-4)	40%	$311,204	$307,035	$279,570	$230,529
Based on the services to be provided and measured in terms of the annual target cost budget.		1 (0.4)	2 (0.8)	3 (1.2)	4 (1.6)
TOTAL POINTS		2.7	1.8	2.0	3.5

Table 16.8
Cost of Service: Transit Vehicle Maintenance

TYPES OF COSTS:	FULL	AVOIDABLE
DIRECT COSTS:		
Service provision		
Salaries/Wages	$88,886	$88,886
Employee benefits	17,802	17,802
Services/Supplies	57,746	10,959
Parts/Sublet	102,000	102,000
Operational Subtotal	$266,434	$219,647
Equipment costs		
Buildings	490	490
Equipment	2,126	2,126
Equip Cost Subtotal	$2,616	$2,616
TOTAL DIRECT COSTS	$269,050	$222,263
INDIRECT COSTS: Division Costs		
Salaries/Wages	$26,588	$4,485
Employee benefits	16,829	3,581
Services/Supplies	1,584	0
Division Subtotal	$45,001	$8,066
City/Department Overhead		
Salaries/Benefits	$25,999	$200
TOTAL INDIRECT COSTS	$71,000	$8,266
TOTAL COST	$337,434	$230,529

Fully allocated costs are the sum of the direct and overhead costs. Using the fully allocated costs method is useful in determining if the in-house cost of providing a particular service is comparable with private sector market prices.

The use of the fully allocated costs method is generally inappropriate in estimating the savings to be realized by contracting out a target service that is currently being conducted in-house (Reason Foundation, 1993). In other words, the amount of money that is likely to be saved is not simply the difference between fully allocated in-house costs and the total contracting costs. Contracting out does not generally result in a dollar-for-dollar reduction in governmental overhead costs. For example, the contracting out of a particular service or a portion thereof may result in decreasing the workload of support departments such as personnel, finance, and facilities management. However, the workload reductions may be insufficient to have any significant effect on the costs of maintaining these support departments when attempting to determine the potential cost savings associated with the contracting out of a particular service. The more appropriate method of computing in-house costs to use in the comparisons is the avoidable costs method.

Avoidable costs are those in-house costs that will not be incurred if a particular service or portion thereof is contracted out (Dobler, Burt and Lee, 1990). Still not a simple task, but one that Greeley has used previously with acceptance. Therefore, the city developed its proposal based on avoidable costs.

The avoidable costs method is the amount used for the city's proposals and the amount that was used to compare all other proposals. Table 16.8 details those costs for the Transit Fleet.

While the total fully allocated costs are $337,434, only $230,529 was designated as avoidable costs. The city still maintained a facility, still had to administer the fleet maintenance contract, and still had to administer the fleet maintenance operations. There were not enough significant savings for the other support services to move over to the avoidable cost column.

how can the city do the same? Obviously, staff can't, because the risk of cost overruns cannot be transferred.

Very simply put, pride and a commitment to keep the cost down are the staff's "guarantee." As the operation will be reviewed on an annual basis, with the possibility of having to again submit the services for outside consideration, the staff has the incentive to keep the costs down.

PERFORMANCE OF THE CITY'S STAFF

At the end of the first nine months, the staff completed an evaluation of the transit vehicle maintenance operations. The comparison of costs to the budget is as follows:

TARGET: (1) Costs   = $180,230 = 78%
                     Budget = $230,529
                     (As compared to 75% anticipated at the end of 9 months)

NONTARGET: (2) Costs = $11,562 = 35%
                         Budget = $32,834
                    (As compared to 75% anticipated at the end of 9 months)
TOTAL PROGRAM: Costs = $191,792 = 73%
                    Budget = $263,363
                    (Overall as compared to 75% anticipated at the end of 9 months)
(1) TARGET: The controllable portion of the budget and the in-house proposal amount.
(2) NONTARGET: The uncontrollable portion (accidents, vandalism, major engine replacements, etc.) of the budget. This item is over and above the proposal.

As can be seen, the costs are below the budget for the first nine months by 3 percent or $5,730.

How does staff's performance compare with the previous private contractor's performance? While it is somewhat difficult to make direct comparisons, Table 16.9 gives a basic analysis: Overall, the staff feels that it is meeting its pledge to the council and, more importantly, meeting the needs of the users.

Table 16.9
In-House Versus Private Contract Services
   (no change in fleet size or makeup)

	Private Contractor 1/1/93-9/30/93	In-House Staff 1/1/94-9/30/94
Target Costs	$ 208,973	$ 180,230
Non-Target Costs	12,842	11,562
Total Costs	$ 221,815	$ 191,792
Work Orders	1,556	1,699
Average Cost / Work Order	$ 143	$ 113
Percent down time	36.7	4.4
Mechanic productivity (%)	79.4	91.7

SUMMARY

An alternative to either traditional in-house services or private contracted services is competition. The key to competition is being able to identify the avoidable costs associated with this service. While the city staff was not successful in winning the Central Fleet vehicle maintenance services, it was competitive and was successful with the Transit Fleet services proposal. The staff was competitive in both cases.

While privatization may be an answer in many situations and should be investigated, competition is viable in all cases. However, your organization must be well managed, must be current on technology, and must have adequate equipment and pride in what you are doing. You must have an acceptable method of determining the costs of the service. You must be customer oriented. If you have all of these, you will be able to provide any service in a competitive manner.

As a sidelight, the staff analyzed what the "total" cost to the city could have been if the city had not been tied with the county through an intergovernmental agreement. The analysis shown in Table 16.10 shows that, overall, the city was very competitive for both services.

Table 16.10
Comparison of Vehicle Maintenance Services

Item	Lowest Private Firm	City Staff
Central Fleet	$242,873	$317,230
Transit Fleet	279,570	230,529
Subtotal	$522,443	$547,759
Deduction if both contracts were awarded to one firm	0	(18,501)
County shop facility usage fee	12,500	0
Total Cost	$534,943	$529,258

REFERENCES

Dobler, David W., David N. Burt, and Lamar Lee. (1990). *Purchasing and Materials Management*. New York: McGraw-Hill, p. 156.

Findings of a National Survey of Local Government Service Contracting Practices. (1987). Atlanta, GA: Mercer/Slavin, vol. 2, pp. 13-14.

Kelley, Joseph T. (1984). *Costing Government Services: A Guide for Decision Making.* Washington, DC: Government Finance Officers Association, p. 103.

Martin, Lawrence L. (1992). "A Proposed Methodology for Comparing the Costs of Government Versus Contract Service Delivery." in *Municipal Yearbook 1992.* Washington, DC: International City/County Management Association, pp. 12-15.

Reason Foundation. (1993). *How to Compare Costs between In-house and Contracted Services, How to Guide # 4.* Los Angeles, March.

Richmond, Jonathan. (1992). "The Costs of Contracted Service: An Assessment of Assessments." MIT Center for Transportation Studies, July 20.

Savas, E. S. (1987). *Privatization—The Key to Better Government.* Catham, NJ: Chatham House, p. 259.

U.S. General Accounting Office. (1980). *Synopsis of GAO Reports Involving Contracting Out under OMB Circular A-76.* Washington, DC, p. 5.

Chapter 17

The Mechanics of Contracting Out

Paul Seidenstat

This chapter examines the process of contracting out services by government agencies. The mechanics of purchasing of goods or capital assets will not be considered here. We shall follow the contacting process from the determination of what to outsource to the post contract evaluation.

CONTRACTING OUT OPTIONS

The contracting arrangement can take a variety of forms. Table 17.1 lists several possible purchasing options. The government buyer may engage a single provider or may choose to use multiple providers, each supplying a portion of the service. Multiple suppliers may divide the market geographically, as in the case of trash collection routes in a city, or by vertical steps in the production process; for example, one provider collects trash and delivers it to another provider who disposes of it.

Table 17.1
Options

Number of Providers:
   One   More Than One
Percent of Service Purchased:
   100   Less Than 100:
                 Ancillary Service Only
                 Support Service Only
                 Management Only:
                 Core Service Only
                 Support Service Only
                 Ancillary Service Only
Facilities:
   Owned   Leased

The public agency buyer may also choose between having one or more providers supply the entire service or only a portion of it. An example of this choice can be seen in contracting out for correctional services. Instead of hiring a private firm to operate a correctional institution with its own employees supplying guarding as well as all ancillary services such as food service and medical care or support services such as counseling or accounting, only certain aspects of the complete service package may be contracted out. Some or all of the ancillary/support services may be entrusted to private providers.

Another option would be to contract out for the management of the service with government employees. The hired management may be confined to various ancillary or support services such as counseling or training of prisoners or may be utilized for the operation of the basic functions of the correctional institution.

An additional option available to a public contracting agency is to lease the required assets for operation from a private provider rather than own them itself. For example, the state corrections department may lease the prison facilities on a straight lease or may lease with a provision to purchase after a stated time period. Rather than leasing major facilities, the government may lease specific assets such as computers or hospital equipment.

ASSESSING POTENTIAL CANDIDATES

Given the possible options available to the government decision-maker to involve the private sector in the rendering of government services, a decision process would kick in to make the determination to contract out a service. Several steps would be taken in arriving at the decision. Pinpointing possible service candidates would involve:

      examining the experience of other governments
      a careful review of existing performance data
      ascertaining the potential degree of provider competition
      identifying desirable features of the service for bidding and contract monitoring

Government Experience

A cursory survey of government experience around the U.S. would reveal a wide application of privatization via contracting out. A vast array of public services is being entrusted to private contractors. The government can pick and choose from among a long list of ancillary, support, or even core services that have been subjected to private production. In fact, the only core services that most governments would exclude from any target list of promising services for outsourcing would be those pure public services that operate in sensitive legal, political, or regulatory areas, such as direct police services, licenses and inspection, and environmental protection.

The pattern of contracting out typically is to start with ancillary administrative and support functions. These activities are less controversial as compared to core services since they impact relatively few jobs, the output is used by public agencies rather than by the public directly, and the contracts are easier to monitor and control.

The services to investigate for contracting out often are those that offer significant potential for cost savings or improvements in service quality. Historically, the prospect of cost savings has appeared to be the major motivating force for contracting out services. Choosing the services to be rendered by the private sector usually involves a case-by-case, piecemeal decision for a limited, discrete, single service function.

Once an extended, preliminary list of privatization candidates is formulated, posing a number of specific questions can allow the decisionmaker to pare the list to the most promising candidates. The questions for each candidate service might include the following:

1. Do costs appear to be high compared to other governmental units or to private suppliers?
2. Have costs been rising rapidly relative to the overall cost of government or to the general level of prices?
3. Is the quality of the service generally well regarded or is it often criticized in the community?
4. Has service quality been declining?
5. Has there been a reduction in service levels in order to reduce costs?

For those services that appear to have high costs or poor quality levels or face fiscal pressures that have resulted or can result in declining quality, further consideration of turning to the private sector for help might be pursued.

Political Mechanism

Since the government is a political entity, any decision about contracting to the private sector has political elements. The traditional way of making a decision is to follow the chain of command in government. The idea to privatize may be initiated by the executive branch or by the legislative branch of government where there are separate branches, as is the case in most governments, or where a hired manager, although reporting to the elected body, may have a reasonable degree of discretion or political power.

Within the executive branch, the decision may be initiated by a particular agency or department or by the executive's central office, sometimes with the aid of a separate division or office that works with agencies by educating them about options or prodding them to move ahead in the effort. In either case, the chief executive would normally have to approve implementing the idea. In some cases, explicit legislative approval may be required. In all cases, support by the legislative body is an important ingredient for success. The legislative branch may even take the lead in proposing change but the administrative arm of government must support the move if it is to deliver the desired result.

However, if there is potentially strong opposition to the use of the private sector in rendering services, especially direct or core services, a commission or committee technique may be employed to soften opposition or relieve the political pressure from individual agencies or elected officials. These groups, members of which are typically appointed by the executive or legislative branch, are often named Privatization Commissions or Reinventing-type Review Committees. Examples of these committees abound at the state level. For example, Arizona and Illinois have a Private Enterprise Review and Advisory Board, Maryland established a Governor's Advisory Council on Privatization, and Virginia has a Blue Ribbon Strike Force Commission of Government Reform.

These advisory groups usually have politically astute members and have the ear of the chief executive. The usual composition of the group includes members of the executive and legislative branches of government as well as representatives of private business interests, nonprofit providers, and government employees and/or public sector unions. An outside "expert" is often added to the mix to assist the professional staff of the committee. The key function often is to analyze contracting out opportunities and target the most promising candidates. Also, benefits and costs of privatization proposals are weighed and information on existing contracting initiatives is assessed.

The commission can not only systematically assess promising candidates for contracting out but also identify barriers to privatization in the form of legal or constitutional constraints. With the wide range of interests on the commission, a consensus of the members gives political cover to elected officials and often will blunt the opposition to the hiring of private sector suppliers. At the same time, the diverse interests on the commission may weaken the effort to contract out and result in only a narrow range of politically safe initiatives being pursued.

Potential Competition among Contractors

One major reason that contracting out may improve performance is that competition among contractors can spur reduced costs or improved service since the government agency supplier does not face the threat of other producers' taking business away from it. Moreover, the consumer has no choice. In most cases the obligation to fund the service through taxes removes even the threat to the government supplier of nonpurchase by buyers.

Competition can take two major forms: private-private or public-private. Traditionally, a government agency would solicit bids or proposals from various private contractors. One or more contractors would then be hired based on the ability to perform the service at a minimum price. On the other hand, existing government agency producers would be allowed to submit bids along with private producers. All or part of the contract could then be awarded to the government agency if its bid was competitive. Phoenix was one of the first cities to introduce competitive contracting. Indianapolis and Philadelphia also become active in utilizing this technique.

In general, the benefits of competition are clear-cut. With a reasonable number of competitors, the price will be driven down to minimum average cost. The ever-present threat of entry as the contract expires creates a strong incentive for contract compliance and acceptable performance. The inability of the contractor to fulfill contract requirements or the withdrawal of the contractor before the completion of the contract will be only a minor irritant if other contractors waiting in the wings can jump into the breach and complete the task.

In the absence of competition in the private market the bidding may not be spirited, preventing the cost of service from being driven down to the minimum average cost level. Without the threat of entry, contract performance may be less than satisfactory, and withdrawal of the contractor may create a major disruption in service.

The public-private version of competition may effect better performance in another dimension. The pressure to compete with private contractors can force improvements in efficiency within the government sector. Examples include the elimination of excessive staffing levels and less resistance to the introduction of new laborsaving technology. Additionally, the threat of losing the contract to an outside contractor may restrain demands for higher pay and benefits. Thus, the benefits of privatization can be obtained without actually privatizing. Further, if there is a splitting of the work with private contractors, the void created by the nonperformance or withdrawal of an outside contractor could easily be filled by the government producer.

Characteristics of the Service

In choosing services for contracting out, government decisionmakers also should look to the characteristics of the service that would render it effective for outsourcing. Desirable characteristics involve the measurability of both the quantity and quality of output, the noncoercive nature of the service, and the absence of legal or constitutional threats against contracting. In trash collection, for example, the number of pickups can be measured. In addition, measures of quality can be used such as a cleanliness index or number of consumer complaints.

By contrast, contracting out basic services such as police patrol raises serious questions about the measurement of quality of service. What are the dimensions of quality, and how do you assess them? Do you judge on the basis of police behavior as compared to the results of policing, such as arrests and convictions? Can you write a contract with a private policing firm that includes all the relevant factors that citizens expect from their police force?

Using a private police force raises the problem of the sensitivity or even the danger of trusting to a private operator the right to use coercion against private citizens. To a lesser extent, even the use of private prison guards who can use deadly force is a sensitive issue. The employment of private armies in a democracy might be rejected on these grounds. However, only a limited number of government services might be affected by this consideration of the wisdom of employing private force.

The potential use of force can invoke a legal challenge to contracting out police powers. In outsourcing social services, contractors may have a religious affiliation and, so too, could provoke legal action on constitutional grounds. To the extent that existing law or custom has to be changed, contracting out a particular service may not be feasible.

THE MAKE OR BUY DECISION

Having identified promising candidates for contracting out, the decision maker now can analyze whether a particular service ought to be outsourced. The framework to be used for this analysis is that of benefit-cost analysis. The benefits of going outside include cost savings, improvement in the quality of service, and longer-term quality enhancement via more rapid advances in technology, greater investment in new capital, and more specialization in management. The costs of contracting out include the costs of designing, monitoring, and enforcing contracts. Contracting is recommended if the sum of the benefits, in present value terms, exceeds the costs.

The first step in ascertaining the feasibility of contracting out a service is to determine the in-house cost of producing that service. Finding out the costs would appear to be obvious since government expenses typically are carefully documented and verified. However, various elements of an operating department's costs may be excluded and included in the costs of other departments. Generally, these are cost items in the budget of support departments or items maintained centrally for convenience.

The total costs of providing a service, thus, consist of two elements: direct costs and indirect or overhead costs. Direct costs are those costs that can be associated fully with the rendering of the service. These costs include those that are used exclusively in the production of the service, such as salaries and fringe benefits as well as supplies, materials, and travel.

Additionally, the debt service on capital items purchased for the exclusive use of the service-producing department often is a major cost item. Debt service comprises interest on the bond issue or, if the assets are leased, the interest portion of the lease. The balance of the debt repayment is for principle. When no debt service is involved; for example, the capital item is purchased on a cash basis, some type of depreciation or use account should be employed.

The other element of total cost involves expenditures that are not exclusively or fully related to the service activity. These cost elements traditionally are referred to as "overhead."

An example of this cost distribution is the case of a public works department that collects and disposes of trash. Direct costs of labor and materials and supplies are recorded in the public works department's accounts. The debt service on the trucks also would be included in the accounts as an indirect cost.

Other departments provide other services: computer services, payroll administration, accounting, and many others. The public works department's share of these costs would have to be allocated to it.

The primary cost accounting task is to allocate the overhead expenses to particular services of the operating department. Various methods are used to allocate overhead. The methods roughly can be classified as simple cost allocation or activity-based costing.

Simple Cost Allocation

Simple cost allocation takes the overhead costs and allocates them to service production based on one or more of the following:

1. *Personnel Costs*. The proportion of the total salaries or salaries plus fringe benefits of the entire government entity that the operating department's personnel costs represent is the allocating factor. The allocating factor multiplied by the total government's overhead cost yields the operating department's indirect (overhead) costs for the year. The assumption is that   overhead costs are proportional to the department's share of personnel costs. Thus, if the personnel costs of a department are 5 percent of the government's personnel costs, then 5 percent of the total overhead is assigned to the operating department.

2. *Total Direct Costs*. This method typically compares the operating department's budget to the total government's budget. The resultant ratio becomes the allocating factor to be applied to total overhead.

3. *Other Cost Drivers*. A variety of other cost allocator could be employed, such as number of employees or square footage of building space.

These cost allocators are conceptually simple and easy to use. Once the total overhead costs for the government are determined, then an operating department's overhead cost allocation is easy to determine. Overhead costs added to direct costs then gives the total cost of rendering a targeted service. This cost figure is often referred to as "in-house fully allocated cost." Dividing the total costs by units of service rendered yields per unit cost.

Using one simple cost driver to allocate overhead costs may yield imprecise cost results, however. Allocating both the costs of computer services and the costs of building maintenance using one cost driver likely will overallocate costs for one support service and underallocate them for another support activity. Injecting more accurate cost allocations can be done using activity-based costing (ABC).

Activity-Based Costing

ABC looks at the rendering of overhead services as coming from a pool of services. Each support service's cost now can be allocated to its in-house customers (direct service providers) using its own particular cost driver that is applicable for that service. For a general view of applying ABC to service industries, see Rotch (1990: 8).

For example, the public works department's trash collection/disposal production unit uses the central purchasing office to buy its supplies and also benefits from the administrative services department that maintains and cleans the building used by public works. Central purchasing may charge its costs based on the number of purchase orders handled. Administrative services can charge on the basis of square footage of building space. Clearly, a more precise allocation of overhead likely will flow from this multistep, multicost driver allocation procedure.

There are several benefits to using an ABC allocation system. A more accurate picture of in-house costs is the major benefit, especially in making the "make or buy" decision. Also, ABC changes a manager's perception of many overhead costs that were thought to be indirect but now may be identified with particular outputs. Further, more accurate costing leads to better cost control.

The downside of ABC is the more stringent requirement for activity identification and data collection. The manager has to have a good handle on the flow of support and auxiliary services and be able to determine the most meaningful cost drivers to use. Collecting workload data from the support agencies such as number of purchase orders, number of copies of documents, or hours of legal services can be time consuming and costly for the organization.

Once direct costs for a service are tracked and overhead costs are allocated, a fully allocated cost for the service is now available to use in further analysis of the "make or buy" decision. The next step is to compare the costs of contracting out with the relevant in-house costs.

The Costs of Contracting Out

The total cost of contract service delivery is the sum of contractor costs, contract administration costs, and conversion costs. Any offsetting revenues can reduce these costs.

1. *Contractor Costs*. These costs are simply the proposed or bid price to perform the service.

2. *Contract Administration Costs*. These costs include any resource expenditures from the time the decision is made to solicit the services of an outside contractor until the contract is completed. Contract administration can include the preparation of a request for proposal (RFP), the advertising of the RFP, selection of contractor, negotiations with

contractor, award of contract, resolution of disputes and changes in the contract during its life, processing of invoices, monitoring of contract, and performance evaluation.

Various studies have estimated that the contracting cost range up to 25% of the contractor costs (Colorado Association of Commerce and Industry, 1994: 27). If the government agency uses existing personnel to perform the contracting work in addition to their other duties, then contracting costs will be minimal. On the other hand, if additional staff is required to perform the contracting function, and/or additional staffing is required to handle the increased workload in administrative departments such as finance and purchasing, contracting costs will be more significant. Based on its review of government experience, the Colorado Municipal League suggests using 10 percent to 20 percent of contractor cost as the cost of contract administration.

Another approach to estimating the cost of contract administration is used by the federal Office of Management and Budget (OMB). The OMB has developed a formula that relates the number of staff required to provide a service (based on government in-house employees who would be required) to the number of contract administrators. For increments of twenty to thirty in-house staff people, an additional contract administrator would be required. Above 800 employees, contract administration requirements would be 2 percent of the number of staff (U.S. Office of Management and Budget, 1985: IV 37).

The federal contract administration levels no doubt would be higher than those of nonfederal governments since the federal procurement laws and regulations are very complex. A less demanding set of standards would be applicable at the state and local levels. Table 17.2 sets forth the contract administration staffing requirements for nonfederal governments according to the Texas State Auditor's Office.

Table 17.2
State of Texas Contract Administrative Requirements

In-house Staff Requirements	Contract Administrative Staff
Less than 20	1
21-42	2
43-65	3
66-91	4
92-119	5
120-150	6
> 150	2% to 4%

Source: Office of Texas State Auditor, 1984: 32.

The in-house staff requirement is then translated into contract administration costs by determining the direct and indirect costs of the administrative staffing level. For example, if an outsourced service required 100 workers, and if the average employee compensation plus indirect costs for contract administration staff were $40,000 per year, then the contract administration cost would be assessed at $200,000 per year ($40,000 X 5).

3. *Conversion Costs.* There may be costs involved in the transition from in-house to an outsider contractor. These transitional costs may be personnel related or involve other financial obligations. Examples include payments to workers who are displaced by the contract or the costs of terminating existing contracts with suppliers or consultants.

4. *Revenue Offsets.* As a consequence of outsourcing, buildings or equipment used in providing the service may become redundant. For example, if trash collection is contracted out, some or all of the compactor trucks previously used by the government agency now are surplus. Any revenue from the disposal of these assets can be used to offset the costs of contracting.

Identifying Relevant Costs

In making the cost comparison between the in-house and outsourcing alternatives, the government analyst should compare relevant costs. Some in-house costs can be dispensed with if contracting out occurs while other in-house costs remain. The former costs are relevant costs, while the latter costs are irrelevant. In the comparison of in-house costs with contract costs, only relevant costs should be considered.

Some indirect costs are usually irrelevant since many overhead costs assigned to the service being contracted out remain. For example, the total costs of billing, information services, and other support and administrative services are invariant with respect to the dispensing of the contracted service.

At the same time, some overhead costs can be reduced as services are outsourced. For example, there can be reductions in expenditures for janitorial services for a building not to be used or for personnel now excessive as support levels for such things as training are downsized. The overhead costs that can be reduced are relevant costs.

The Decision: Comparing Alternatives

Once the relevant costs are identified, the next step is to compare systematically the costs of in-house service with the costs of outsourcing. Both the level and quality of service must be specified for a fair comparison.

Having accomplished the in-house cost analysis and the costs of contract administration and conversion, the analyst would have to determine the contract price. Short of actually requesting formal bids from contractors, the government analyst could use previous contract prices from its own files or data from comparable governments in the area. Having determined the contract price and estimated the other costs of contracting out, the analyst then can compare relevant costs.

In most cases calculating the present value of each can compare the stream of in-house and contracting out costs. Conversion to present value is advisable even if the annual costs of the alternatives do not differ significantly from year to year during the term of the contract since one time conversion costs or revenue from sale of assets may be involved. Table 17.3 illustrates the decision framework.

The cost comparison between continuing in-house or contracting out a government service helps shape the outsourcing decision. Still, other considerations may be relevant especially uncertainty about achieving the contemplated quality of service and the complexity of contract monitoring and supervision. Given these other factors and the chance of underestimating the costs of contracting out, a rule of thumb may be to not outsource unless the anticipated cost savings reach a certain threshold level; for example, a 10 to 15% savings level is often used.

THE MECHANICS OF CONTRACTING

Once the decision to seek an outside contractor is made, a series of actions are now required to source, to actualize, and to oversee the contractor's compliance with the contract.

Table 17.3
Comparing Relevant In-House Costs with Outsourcing Costs
(present value in dollars)

In-house
    Direct Costs:
        Salaries and Wages, Other Compensation, Overtime Pay, Fringe Benefits
        Supplies and Materials, Rent/Lease, Equipment, Buildings
        Repairs and Maintenance: Equipment, Building
        Telecommunications, Utilities Depreciation, Other Direct Costs
    Indirect Costs
        Relevant Overhead, Other Indirect Costs
    Total Costs (Direct plus Indirect Costs)

Outsourcing Costs:
    Contract Price, Contract Administration, Conversion Costs, Offsetting Revenue (-)

Total Contracting Costs
Source: Office of the Texas State Auditor, 1994: 28.

The Acquisition Process

1. *Request for Proposal (RFP)*. The first step in the actual contracting out phase is to find potential contractors and to provide the data that will be the basis for bidding. Various sources can be pursued to gather a list of potential contractors. The yellow pages of the phone book, chamber of commerce lists, industry trade association databases, and trade publications all can yield a list of potential contractors.

The next step is to prepare the Request for Proposal. The RFP should include a Statement of Work, provisions for penalties and incentives, and the qualifications required of the contractor.

The Statement of Work is a key part of the RFP for it states the precise services to be rendered by the contractor. Ideally, there should be both quantitative and qualitative elements to the service requirement expressed in specific and tangible measures of performance. For example, for contracting out trash collection, the statement of work would provide for the following:

1. pick up trash from residential building once per week
2. special pickups via phone request, once a month
3. three special leaf collections between October 1 and November 30
4. quarterly visual inspections of condition of area after pickup
5. customer complaints to city should not exceed a number equal to 2 percent of the residential units per year
6. the following reports are required on a quarterly basis: tonnage, customer   complaints, and cost analysis

A section on penalties or bonuses would indicate the conditions upon which these assessments would be made. For example, if customer complaints exceed the threshold level, a schedule of penalties would dictate a deduction from the quarterly contract fee paid by the city. On the other hand, a bonus could be given if performance was better than required. For example, if two successive visual inspections show exemplary performance, a 5 percent bonus would be added to the next quarterly payment by the city.

Finally, the potential contractor must be informed as to the length of the contract and the procedure for renewal. A three-year contract, for example, may be automatically renewed for an additional two years for good performance.

2. *Evaluating Proposals.* In response to the RFP, there may be several proposals from private contractors, and a variety of factors can be considered in choosing the winner. These factors include the quality of response to the RFP, the capabilities of the contractor, the cost figures, and the willingness to accommodate the contracting agency.

Some weight often is given to the candor and the willingness of the contractor to meet all requirements of the contract. Heavier weight is placed on contractor capabilities, including the quality of the staff, financial strength, equipment, and facilities to do the work. Additionally, the experience and reputation of the contractor in the marketplace are very important.

Given an acceptable score on the preceding factors, the determining factor in choosing a contractor often is the cost portion of the proposal. Cost usually means total contracting outlay as well as cost per unit. Per unit cost is relevant if the contracting agency cannot provide a precise figure for the quantity of output required so that the total cost could vary. For example, if a social service contract would provide a counseling program for all drivers under the influence of alcohol, the number of enrollees might be subject to a variety of factors such as the intensity of police traffic enforcement, the severity of judicial sentencing, and demographic factors that could affect drunk driving rates. In this situation, a cost per enrollee estimate would be a more useful guide than the total contract course.

The weighting of these elements in the decision matrix might vary. Contracting government agencies might desire to place more emphasis on one or more factors than on other factors. This rating is often based on the type of government service. Some services are more politically sensitive if service quality is subpar, such as trash collection or the operation of a hospital emergency room. In the case of these services, more stress would be placed on reputation and experience than on cost alone. Other services are more complex, such as operating a wastewater plant so that quality of contractor personnel and contractor experience might bear the heaviest weight. The willingness of the contractor to hire displaced government employees could also bear some weight.

3. *Administering the Contract.* Once the contractor is chosen, and the contract signed, the difficult task of monitoring the contract would begin. Often a pre-start-up meeting with the contractor to detail the monitoring process would be useful. The public contracting agency would assign one or more employees to accomplish the monitoring.

The monitoring agents perform several tasks. They have the responsibility of checking the reports furnished by the contractor and in conducting inspections or spot checks on the operation of the contractor. Hearing complaints from service recipients might also be required.

At appropriate times in accordance with the contract, a decision about extension or renewal would be required. At this point, a review of all the data relative to performance would be assembled and assessed. A recommendation of the staff monitoring would be sent to the agency top management for final decision.

POTENTIAL PROBLEMS OR PITFALLS OF CONTRACTING OUT

Although contracting out government services promises major net benefits, including lower costs and better-quality service, still there can be important negative elements that have to be recognized. These negative elements can include lack of viable private competition, the difficulty of contract monitoring, the costs of transition, the losses associated with failure, and the chance of corruption in the contracting process.

The basic premise of involving the private sector in producing services is that competition among potential contractors will drive down the cost of production and ensure that the service will be of high quality. However, if competition among contractors is weak, or if monopoly elements are present, then the benefits of contracting out may be illusory. Of course, if only one firm in the area is capable of providing the service, contracting may not be a good idea. However, if there is a handful of potential suppliers who collude in bidding, then the disadvantages of monopoly behavior will not disappear. Contracting agencies must be vigilant in guarding against collusive behavior of contractors in oligopolistic supplying industries.

In the absence of effective contract monitoring, contracting out may not work well, as contractors may deviate from the provisions of the contract or cheat on the quality of service. Transitional costs may prove to be a problem as well. Turbulence caused by labor problems as government layoffs occur can interfere with performance. Start up problems of the private contractors can also be disruptive. Great care must be exercised in dealing with labor problems and other aspects of the shift to the private vendor.

Another set of potential problems arises if the private contractor fails to deliver in accordance with the contract. Several things can happen to disrupt service: the contractor can have labor problems or be plagued with poor management; bankruptcy can close the contractor down; and there may be litigation involving contractor performance or liability issues in case of breakdowns or accidents.

Finally, there can be a dark side to contracting if government officials collude with private contractors to elevate the costs or dilute the quality of service. Some of the extra profits earned in this way then can be kicked back to government officials in the form of direct bribes or indirect benefits such as campaign contributions or free services. Over the years, there have been a number of these bribery cases exposed in various governments.

In fairness it should be mentioned that there is a long history of corruption within various government operations at all levels. Hiring practices, use of resources, collusion between management and labor as to levels of pay or levels of effort, and other internal operational decisions may not be open and above board, may be unfair, or generally may be contrary to the taxpayers' interest.

CONCLUSION

Contracting out offers an important technique to improve the rendering of government services. Using private contractors injects competition into the system of production. However, even if a service is not totally produced by a private firm, as in the case of contracting out only some areas of the city for trash collection, the competition between the private operators and the government producer will stimulate better performance by the public sector, as cost and quality of service comparisons easily can be made.

Once the decision is made as to services to contract out, a carefully designed and diligently executed plan for contracting is necessary if maximum benefits are to be obtained. The RFP and the resultant contract must be explicit in the scope and quality of services to be produced. Choosing the lowest cost responsible bidder is what is sought. Carefully monitoring the contract for adherence to all its provisions is necessary to avoid the problems and pitfalls that could develop.

Our nation's governments have been contracting with the private sector for goods and services since the founding of the republic. It is an effective way to produce public services and the potential for its extension into most of the service areas of government is great. A well thought out and administered contracting system will allow the contracting out system to achieve its maximum potential.

REFERENCES

Colorado Association of Commerce and Industry and Colorado Municipal League (1994). *Public Private Cooperation*. Denver, January.

Office of the Texas State Auditor (1984). *Guide to Implement the Competitive Cost Review Program.* Austin, TX.

Rotch, W. (1990). "Activity-Based Costing in Service Industries." *Journal of Cost Management* 4, no. 2, Summer: pp 1-15.

U.S. Office of Management and Budget (1985). *Supplement to OMH Circular NO. A-76 (Revised). Performance of Commercial Activities.* Washington, DC: U.S. Government Printing Office.

Index

About the Editor and Contributors

PAUL SEIDENSTAT is co-editor of *Privatizing the United States Justice System, Privatizing Correctional Institutions, Privatizing Education and Educational Choice*, and *Privatizing Transportation Systems*. Currently he is Associate Professor of Economics at Temple University and formerly was director of the graduate program. He has been principal investigator for several research projects for federal government agencies and has served in local governments as financial director and financial advisor. His recent research has been in the area of state and local government finance and management. He has published five books and several articles in this topical area.

DOUGLAS K. ADIE is professor of economics at Ohio University in Athens, Ohio.

SARAH ARMSTRONG is assistant director of the Institute for Law and Policy Planning, Berkeley, CA.

WILLIAM E. BOTKIN is director of planning for Rebound, a private provider of juvenile correctional services.

FRANK W. DAVIS, JR. is a professor in the department of logistics and transportation at the University of Tennessee.

RUTH HOOGLAND DEHOOG is associate professor of political science and director of the Master of Public Affairs program at University of North Carolina-Greensboro.

LARKIN S. DUDLEY is an associate professor in the Center for Public Administration and Policy at Virginia Tech.

VAN R. JOHNSTON is a professor of management, business and public policy at the University of Denver.

RAYMOND J. KEATING is an economist and writer focusing on fiscal issues. He serves as chief economist of the Small Business Survival Committee and Foundation and is a partner in the consulting firm of Carolan and Keating.

ROBERT T. KLEIMAN is an associate professor of finance at Oakland University, Rochester, MI.

JACK W. LILLYWHITE is manager of project development for Bechtel Infrastructure.

JAMES C. MCDAVID is Dean of the Faculty of Human and Social Development at the University of Victoria in British Columbia, Canada.

STEPHEN MOORE is director of fiscal policy studies at the CATO Institute.

NICHOLAS MORGAN is an attorney in Los Angeles, practicing with Christensen, White, et al. His practice includes litigation involving public entity liability. He serves as a member of the Charter School Law and Policy Task Force.

DAVID MOULTON is senior analyst of the Institute for Law and Policy Planning, Berkeley, CA.

ALLAN C. RUSTEN headed a consulting firm specializing in local government management.

ANANDI P. SAHU is chairman and associate professor of economics at Oakland University, Rochester, MI.

LANA STEIN is associate professor of political science and director of graduate studies at the University of Missouri-St. Louis.

JACK STERLING is director of public works of the City of Greeley, CO.

SHELDON X. ZHANG is assistant professor of sociology at California State University San Marcos and previously worked as a research analyst for the Los Angeles County Probation Department.

ISBN 0-275-96542-2

EAN

9 780275 965426

HARDCOVER BAR CODE